MARION

For my mum and dad,
who taught me to love and
to dream the big dreams.

And for Tim, who makes
my dreams come true.

MARION

Recipes and Stories from a Hungry Cook

MARION GRASBY

CONTENTS

- IX   HELLO
- 1   MORNINGS
- 21   BOWL FOOD
- 43   SMALL PLATES
- 75   BIG PLATES
- 145   ON THE SIDE
- 165   SWEETNESS
- 191   THINGS IN JARS
- 205   MENUS THAT MAKE ME HAPPY
- 215   THANKS
- 216   INDEX

My mum's village, Nakhon Chum, west of Bangkok in Thailand. Mum and I are cooking lunch for my grandma and aunties.

HELLO

I don't know when it was that I 'fell in love' with food. It's like asking when you knew that you loved your mum or your sister or your grandfather. You don't know. All you know is that you do and you always have done.

What I love about food is that it is such a beautiful and telling language. Every one of us must eat, and within this most basic act of survival we tell a story about the places we've been and the people we love. It's not just *what* we eat, but the way we gather our ingredients, the way we cook and the way we eat that says something deeply personal about who we are. Food is the most fascinating language we have.

In the process of making this book I had to talk to a great many people about 'my food'. It was the first time I'd ever needed to explain and categorise what it is that I cook.

'Well…' I would say. 'I guess it's a little bit Thai, a little bit Australian and sometimes it's neither of those things at all.'

I got many a blank stare in return, but it made perfect sense to me. The way I cook comes from who I am. My mother is from Thailand, so I am a little bit Thai. My dad is from country Victoria, so I am a bit Australian. And the rest comes from living and travelling in a great many different places – the Northern Territory, Papua New Guinea, Queensland, South Australia and New South Wales. And so I guess an introduction to my food inevitably needs a little story about me – about the places I've been and the people I love. It all began in Darwin…

HOT LAKSAS, SWEET MANGOES

I was born in Darwin into long, hot days, hot laksas, spicy pawpaw salads and sweet mangoes. My family and I were only there for the first four years of my life but I can still smell the sweet perfume of over-ripe mangoes splattered across the ground from our backyard tree.

I remember holding on to Mum's hand as we sweated our way through the Rapid Creek Markets past the stacks of coriander, Thai basil, mint, mangoes and pawpaw. I remember tasting my first pawpaw salad and screwing up my nose at the intense chilli as it burned my tongue and made me cry. I loved the market – the fun of grabbing hold of fruits to smell, feeling the texture of Asian vegetables between my fingers, the smell of fragrant herbs and the sizzle of hot oil as spring rolls crisped and browned in an oversized wok.

I travelled back to Darwin many times as a teenager and again when I started writing this book. It's a city whose food culture feels incredibly Asian and yet still retains its own Darwin identity. When I went back to do the photography for this book, we drove out to visit mango farms at Humpty Doo, about 40 kilometres south-east of Darwin. We passed a roadside stall plonked down on the red earth in front of a backdrop of gum trees. Makeshift signs read: mud crab, barramundi and camel steaks. Sitting next to a fridge packed with camel T-bones were shelves laden with Asian herbs, pawpaw and mangoes. Sometimes I think I'm more like Darwin than I realise – a little bit Asian and a little bit Australian.

It's uncanny how many of the moments in my life are remembered through food. I can't remember much of the house we lived in or what our street looked like, but I can recall with vivid lucidity the peanut butter sandwich I was eating the day we drove to a storm shelter as Cyclone Gretel threatened to hit the city. I would have been about three years old. It seems if I'm not eating, I'm not remembering.

X HELLO

MUMUS AND PITPITS

My mum, dad and I moved to Papua New Guinea when I was four and we lived there for about 12 years. My dad was a construction project manager and his job took him all around the world – to Thailand, where he met my mum, to Darwin and then to Papua New Guinea. It was his sense of adventure and desire to not only travel but to really see the world around him that meant we were never a stay-at-home kind of family. My dad took us travelling all over Papua New Guinea. We visited beautiful coastal towns including Alotau on the very southern tip of the country. We sailed down the Sepik River in the north and my father's friends would take us to stay in their village homes near Port Moresby.

My mother would take me shopping to the local open-air markets where we'd buy sweet potato, yams and my favourite vegetable pitpit, which I remember as being a bit like oversized baby sweetcorn. On special occasions we'd buy a live chicken that would peck around in our garden until mid-afternoon when preparations for dinner would begin. I loved the ritual of a local feast called a 'mumu'. Chicken, pork and vegetables were carefully wrapped in large banana-leaf parcels and slow-cooked in a big pit dug out of the ground and filled with rocks that had been heated in a fierce fire.

But Papua New Guinea gave me much more than an experience of eating. It instilled in me a sense of humbleness and gratefulness. It was a poor country and we saw much of the poverty and desperation that came with it during our travels. Living so close to people who must work so terribly hard and on the brink of hopelessness just to put food on their table made me realise that I had much to be thankful for. I think it's for this reason that I've always felt I have an obligation to do what I love in my life because there are many people in the world who just don't have that opportunity.

CHEESE AND ONION SANDWICHES

Boarding school in Brisbane put my culinary adventures on hold. My very first boarding school lunch was a soggy cheese and onion sandwich. I thought someone in the kitchen must really have it in for me. Starved of anything edible during the semester, I would return home to my mum with an enormous craving for my favourite foods. She would call me weeks before the last day of school to ask about what I wanted to eat. I would list off a crazy number of dishes and then count the days. Lucky for me, not only is my mum Thai but she's also a trained chef, which meant spring rolls and chocolate éclairs had equal billing on my list of coming-home treats.

The food of my childhood was dominated by the Thai flavours that came from my mother's heritage. We had wok-fried noodles when others had spaghetti Bolognese. Thai laab salad, fried omelettes with onion and tomato and spicy tom yum soups were our mid-week dinners. Because my mum was also a chef and shared my curiosity and affection for all things food, the kitchen became our playroom. I relished my school holiday lessons in making crème caramel, fruit cake and roast lamb as much as I loved learning how to make Thai green curry and *pad siew*.

WINE AND CHEESE

After five years at university in Brisbane getting a law and journalism degree, I was picked up by the ABC and sent to South Australia as a radio and television journalist. It was an incredible start to my journalism career, but little did I know it was really the start of my food career. I spent nearly three years working in Adelaide and a country town called Renmark, four hours' drive north-east of Adelaide. I wasn't bad at my job. I loved the adrenalin of the newsroom and the art of storytelling. But something was missing.

South Australia has such a remarkable food and wine culture made up of incredibly passionate producers, winemakers and people who simply have an innate appreciation for what they eat and drink. It was here that I met my partner Tim. He was from Queensland too and had also started out his adult life with a law degree as well as a business degree. But instead of following the path of least resistance, he'd packed up his things and driven to South Australia in the hope of working in a field that he truly loved: wine.

The very first dinner he cooked for me was a six-course dégustation of sorts. Mussels steamed with chilli and garlic. There was beef carpaccio and then pan-fried fish with a crab sauce that he'd reduced to a creamy lusciousness over four hours. Each course had its own matching wine. I fell in love. (Just as an aside, I would like to point out that he hasn't cooked anything of the sort since and in a court of law I'm sure I could sue for false advertising... but never mind.)

Through Tim I met so many winemakers, restaurateurs and producer friends who were all doing what they loved. I realised that if they could do it, so could I. It was time I did what I loved. So I quit my job as an ABC journalist and took up a Master of Gastronomy, which is basically a study of history, culture, politics, anthropology, sociology and theology but through the lens of a food and wine lover. I loved the studying but it was tough. I had to pay the bills somehow, so I took a job as a phone girl and general office runabout at a gourmet food and wine company, Bottega Rotolo.

By this stage my friends at school were taking jobs with banks, advertising companies and law firms. I was answering phones. But sometimes you have to take a few steps back in order to get ahead.

That's what I was hoping for, anyway. So the Rotolos took me in. I had no idea about European cheeses, wines, cured meats or any of the products sitting in shiny jars on the shelves. It was my job to take food and wine orders from chefs over the phone, but I didn't even know what on earth *Fromager d'Affinois* was, let alone how to spell it.

What could I do but eat my way through just about every product we sold at Bottega Rotolo. I tried everything, from *jamón Ibérico de bellota* (which I discovered was the most delicious cured ham in the world) to white Alba truffles from Piedmont. Rosalie Rotolo taught me anything I cared to learn about cheese, couverture chocolate, artisan pasta and so much more. Rosalie's family was Italian, which meant the business had a distinctly Italian flavour. Rosalie's mother, Connie, taught me how to make pasta and, Fonz, her father, invited me to their home to gather vegetable cuttings for my own garden.

Not only did I find myself in a new job but I also found myself in a new home. Tim and I had moved to Sellicks Beach, just on the outskirts of the McLaren Vale wine region. I had always thought of myself as a city girl and this new semi-rural life caught me off guard. It was quiet. But it was a quiet that I grew to love. The region changed with each season. Lush green vineyards turned to stark bare vines in winter, then came the madness of vintage when the grapes were harvested, before mellowing into a rhythm of tending vineyards through the rest of the year.

On my days off we'd go fishing for Australian salmon off the beach or squid off the Noarlunga jetty. And every Saturday morning, I would wander through the Willunga Farmers' Market, buying, watching, listening and talking my way through the stalls. It was a ritual that taught me so much about the seasons and to have the confidence

to treat the fruits and vegetables of those seasons with respect. I never went to the market with a recipe. I went to be inspired by the golden beetroot, bulging fennel bulbs and lush, ripe figs. And I was.

For more than two years I worked hard at studying for my Master's degree while stuffing my face with gourmet cheeses, learning everything I could about every single food product and bottle of wine I sold and discovering the joys of a local farmers' market. It was hard at times but it was heaven most of the time. And then came a little show called *MasterChef*.

TV DINNERS

It was my 27th birthday the day I went for my audition. I was so scared I nearly dropped the giant snapper head I'd brought to cook as I lifted it out of my esky. It was over in a flash. Gary and George had tasted my favourite childhood dish *khao tom* (a Thai rice soup that I flavoured with prawns and meat from the snapper head; see my recipe on page 18). Gary gave me a high five and that was it. I was off to Sydney.

If quitting my job as a journalist was a turning point in my life of food, then *MasterChef* was a giant catapult. I wasn't sure how it was going to turn out but I knew I wanted the experience. I wanted to meet chefs that I had no hope of otherwise meeting. I wanted to cook in commercial kitchens, I wanted to learn and I wanted a chance.

My time on the show was amazing. I spent six months thinking about nothing but food. We weren't allowed to have much contact with the outside world while living in the *MasterChef* house. One phone call a week was generally all the contact we had. No mobile phones. No TV. No newspapers. No radio ... only a library of cookbooks and a bunch of foodies for company. At the time I felt a little bit like a caged animal, but when I look back I feel that it was the most free I have felt my entire life. I was free to do what I loved to do and nothing else … to cook.

I'm a firm believer that it's the people you meet that give true meaning to an experience. I feel incredibly grateful to have met and cooked with people such as Heston Blumenthal, Maggie Beer, Tony Bilson, Damien Pignolet, Rick Stein and so many others. I feel humbled to have had mentors including Gary Mehigan, George Calombaris and Matt Preston. And most of all, I feel so thankful to have been loved by the 24 friends I lived with in the *MasterChef* house. Some of my most treasured memories come from those times away from the cameras – making tarts with Callum, laughing with Skye, preparing a massive Mexican feast with Aaron and sharing an Asian breakfast with Alvin and Adam. Each of us shared our lives and our food.

PINCHING MYSELF

And so here I am, pinching myself as I write the introduction to my own cookbook. *MasterChef* gave me the chance I needed to make all the little dreams I had come true. This book is one of them.

In making this book, I did a bit of exploring. I went back to where it all started. I travelled to Darwin and went back to the markets that I love. I sat down at the Parap Market and slurped up a bowlful of laksa. I watched as ladies pounded and packed my spicy pawpaw salad. I smelled the sweet perfume of blushing, ripe mangoes. And I remembered the food I was born into. I travelled to Thailand with my mum and we ate our way through the streets of Bangkok. My mum and I walked for hours finding the carts and street vendors who sold the dishes I'd eaten as a child on our many trips back to my mother's home. And we went back to my mother's village, Nakhon Chum, two hours' drive west of Bangkok.

IN THE VILLAGE

It had been 24 years since my grandmother had laid eyes on my mum and me. I wasn't sure if she would know who we were at first. She's in her eighties and village life had been hard, I'm sure. But then she smiled a toothy smile and wiped away a couple of rogue tears with her weathered hand. I couldn't understand what she was saying because I can't speak her dialect but I could certainly feel what she was saying. She had missed her daughter.

I wasn't sure what to expect from the village because I was four the last time we were there. We had pulled into a dirt road and parked the car next to an old wooden house. It was so peaceful. We walked out past the house and into a cluster of wooden homes surrounded by banana trees. My Aunty Niew, who had picked us up from Bangkok, said some of the

HELLO XV

houses were more than a hundred years old. They were beautiful – made from heavy, dark wooden panels, some intricately carved and some incredibly weathered.

Our dinner was cooked over two little outdoor clay stoves. Everything here seemed broken down into its most basic elements. We cooked over the fire. We slept on the floor and we sat down to eat on a woven mat spread with little bowls of curry, vegetables and dried fish. We spent the night sleeping on the floor of a wooden house – myself and the photographer stretched out beneath our mosquito net. In the morning we shared a breakfast of *khao tom* and warm soy milk before my uncle took us to the village temple. We knelt before my mum's childhood friend who was now the head monk at the temple. His serenity seemed to blanket the room in peacefulness. I felt privileged to have been there and to have learned the life of my mother's people. I felt humbled to have come from here.

RECIPES AND DREAMINGS

The recipes in this book are not simply recipes that I've plucked out of thin air. Each recipe tells a little story about me, where I've been and the people I love. It's not a cheffy, fancy food sort of book. Mainly because I'm not a cheffy, fancy food sort of person. I'm a home cook and incredibly proud of it.

You won't find an entrée or main course menu like you would in a restaurant, instead I've grouped my recipes into chapters that reflect the way we eat at home: small plates or big plates, depending on your mood, and things in jars because, quite simply, that chapter includes recipes for things in jars.

Ouch! I just thought I'd pinch myself one last time as I finish off this introduction. I had always hoped but never actually thought these pages would be mine and now they are. If there's one life lesson I've learned so far, it's that if you have a little dream, if you take a little chance and you work a lot hard, you might just get what you want.

Happy dreaming and happy eating!

MORNINGS

WE ARE WHAT WE EAT FOR BREAKFAST

Morning. What's for breakfast? Well, that depends on where you are and who you are. What we choose to eat as that first crucial meal of the day is so culturally specific and so telling of where we come from and where we've been.

I love Bangkok's buffet breakfasts. Morning light breaks over a sea of skyscrapers and for just a moment the city seems at peace. It's the calm before the Bangkok storm – the chaos of cars, motorbikes and tuk-tuks are held at bay while this enormous city wakes and stirs. I turn down a street and walk into a steaming sideshow alley of trolley carts and makeshift street kitchens. Wafts of simmering spice and charry wok-fried smoke permeate the air and cling to my clothes and hair. What should I eat for breakfast? *Khao Tom* (rice soup; see page 18) or *khanom jeen nam ya* (a spicy fishy noodle dish) or *khai dao* (fried egg) with fish sauce and rice. Now that's my kind of breakfast buffet.

A Saturday breakfast back at home is a little less spicy but no less joyful. It's my local farmers' market that provides the entertainment here. First on the menu is coffee. Two lattes will do the trick. What should I eat for breakfast? Fresh free-range eggs are a must. A loaf of sourdough bread makes it into my wicker basket along with little bunches of fragrant herbs. Here my breakfast heroes are decided by what the producer has picked that morning and what's in season; peaches, figs and strawberries make delightful appearances from time to time. And if all else fails, a good hunk of goat's cheese will sort things out. Now that's my kind of breakfast basket.

I know as well as the next person that breakfast is such a luxury when the train, the bus and the working day just won't wait. But the delicious ritual of breaking the night's fast is surely something to be cherished whenever possible.

my grandma taew's house in the village is about 100 years old.

Some of the best food in Thailand comes from the street cart vendors that line Bangkok's busy streets.

SUGAR-GLAZED PEACHES WITH ROSEWATER & HONEY YOGHURT

I love playing with fire and sugar. I'm mesmerised as the tiny white sugar crystals burn and melt into little pools of amber liquid before seizing up into a burnished sheet of sugar glass. You're basically creating a crème brûlée top for the peach cheeks. A small kitchen blowtorch is the best thing to use for caramelising sugar because you can control the flame and its affect on the sugar. This yummy breakfast moonlights as a light dessert option at my house.

2 cups good-quality thick natural yoghurt
2 tablespoons honey, or to taste
¼ teaspoon rosewater
4 large peaches
1 cup caster sugar
½ cup shelled pistachios, roughly chopped

Fold together the yoghurt, honey and rosewater in a bowl. Use more or less honey, depending on how sweet you like your yoghurt.

Cut the peaches in half and scoop out the stone with the help of a teaspoon.

Using a fine sieve, dust the cut-side of each peach cheek evenly with the sugar. Grab hold of a kitchen blowtorch and run the flame over the sugar so that it scorches and caramelises.

Serve the glazed peach cheeks with a generous dollop of the yoghurt and a sprinkling of pistachios on top.

SERVES 4

TOASTED BRIOCHE WITH GINGER RICOTTA, STRAWBERRIES & HONEY

Fresh ricotta is such a thick, creamy joy to behold. It looks quite firm but will soften into creamy cottage-cheese-like curds at the slightest provocation. You should find it sitting in a large tub at the deli section of a supermarket or at a good cheese providore. Brioche is a French bread that's made with loads of butter and eggs. It's beautifully rich but expensive to make, which means it can be difficult to get a hold of. If you can't find brioche, use any other type of good-quality bread.

4 thick slices brioche
300 g firm ricotta
¼ cup glacé ginger, finely chopped
finely grated zest of 1 lemon
250 g strawberries, hulled and quartered
⅓ cup honey

Toast the brioche – be careful as brioche tends to burn easily.

While the bread is toasting, combine the ricotta, ginger and lemon zest in a bowl and mix well.

Spread a thick layer of the ricotta mixture on each slice of brioche. Top with the strawberries and drizzle with the honey.

SERVES 4

RICOTTA PANCAKES WITH FIGS & HONEY BUTTER

I never met a fresh fig until I was 23. We lived in Darwin and Papua New Guinea for the first 16 years of my life and for all that time it seemed only natural to make friends with the seemingly bottomless fruit bowls of mangoes, bananas, pineapples and pawpaw. I remember craving our very infrequent trips to Victoria to visit my grandpop, so I could devour bowlfuls of sweet strawberries slathered in thick cream; there was not a strawberry to be met in Papua New Guinea. Not to mention figs. I never knew what I was missing until I moved to South Australia and met a humble little fig at a market stall. We fell in love.

1 cup plain flour
1 teaspoon baking powder
2 tablespoons caster sugar
¼ teaspoon table salt
250 g firm ricotta
½ cup milk
2 eggs, separated
1 teaspoon natural vanilla extract
butter, for cooking
4 large figs, quartered
ice cream or double (thick) cream, to serve (optional)

HONEY BUTTER
50 g unsalted butter
¼ cup honey

For the honey butter, place the butter and honey in a small saucepan over low heat and cook until melted and combined. Set aside and gently reheat just before serving.

For the pancakes, combine the flour, baking powder, sugar and salt in a large bowl. Place the ricotta, milk, egg yolks and vanilla extract in a separate bowl and mix until combined. Add to the flour mixture and mix well with a wooden spoon.

Place the eggwhite in a small bowl and beat, using electric beaters, until stiff peaks form. Fold half of the eggwhite into the ricotta mixture to lighten, then fold through the remaining eggwhite.

Melt about 1 teaspoon of the butter in a large non-stick frying pan over medium heat. Add ¼-cup amounts of batter to the pan, cooking 2–3 pancakes at a time. The batter will be thick, so you may need to spread it out with the back of a spoon. Cook for 2 minutes, or until bubbles appear on the surface, then flip over and cook for another 2 minutes, or until golden. Remove from the pan and cover with aluminium foil to keep warm. Wipe out the pan with paper towel or cloth and repeat the process with the remaining butter and batter.

Serve the pancakes topped with the figs and drizzled with the honey butter. If you want to be a little naughty, enjoy with ice cream or cream as well.

MAKES ABOUT 8/SERVES 4

POACHED EGGS WITH SMOKED TROUT & HERBS

Things that make me smile: cupcakes frosted with pink icing, the shattering crack of sugar as my spoon hits the top of a crème brûlée and perfectly poached eggs. Little fluffy white puffs all innocent and delicate until their molten yolks explode at the push of a fork and rich little rivers of sunlight-yellow pool on the plate. Bliss.

To poach the perfect egg, add vinegar to the poaching water to help set the eggwhite. Use fresh eggs with the longest use-by date because if they're old, the eggwhite will separate from the yolk. And finally... practise.

100 g hot-smoked trout, skin and bones removed, flesh flaked
1 tablespoon finely chopped dill
1 tablespoon finely chopped basil leaves
1 tablespoon finely chopped flat-leaf parsley
½ cup extra-virgin olive oil
juice of ½ lemon
¼ teaspoon sea salt
2 tablespoons white vinegar
4 eggs, at room temperature
4 thick slices toasted sourdough bread, to serve
freshly ground black pepper

Place the trout, dill, basil, parsley, olive oil, lemon juice and salt in a bowl and give everything a quick mash with a fork. Set aside until ready to serve.

Now let's poach some eggs. Fill a large deep frying pan with water, add the vinegar and place over medium heat. Heat until little bubbles start to form and rise from the base of the pan. You want the water to be hot but not simmering rapidly otherwise the egg may break up. Crack each egg into a cup or small bowl, then slide them into the water. Poach for about 4 minutes, or until the eggwhite is just set but the yolk is still wobbly like soft-set jelly. Scoop out each egg with a slotted spoon, allowing as much water as possible to drain away. Slide onto a plate while you get the toast ready.

Spread each piece of toast with a spoonful of the trout mixture. Top with a poached egg and spoon over more of the trout mixture. Finish with generous grindings of pepper.

SERVES 2

MORNINGS 15

MUSHROOM & TALEGGIO TOASTIES

I love a stinky cheese and Taleggio is one of my favourites. It's a washed-rind cheese from Italy with a mottled orange rind and a soft, creamy centre. If strong and stinky isn't your thing, use slices of cheddar or a mild swiss cheese instead.

50 g butter
3 tablespoons extra-virgin olive oil
3 garlic cloves, sliced
1 sprig rosemary, leaves picked and finely chopped
500 g mixed mushrooms, such as Swiss brown, field and oyster, cleaned and thickly sliced
1 teaspoon sea salt
freshly ground black pepper
4 thick slices sourdough bread
100 g Taleggio, thinly sliced

Preheat the oven grill to high.

Heat the butter and olive oil in a large frying pan over medium heat until the butter starts to foam. Add the garlic and rosemary and cook for a few seconds, or until you can just start to smell the frying garlic. Throw in the mushrooms but don't flip them around just yet. Leave them to brown for about 30 seconds, then gently flip and toss the mushrooms as they cook for about 2 minutes, or until they're lightly golden but still a little firm. If you cook them for too long, you'll get soft, sloppy mushrooms. Season with the salt and generous grindings of pepper.

Meanwhile, toast the bread. Pile the mushrooms onto the toast, top with the slices of Taleggio and grill for about 1 minute, or until the cheese is melted and bubbling. Serve piping hot.

SERVES 4

GOAT'S CHEESE & CHORIZO SCRAMBLE

Make this scramble for breakfast, lunch or a lazy dinner. Goat's cheese and chorizo is my favourite combination but you could also use smoked trout with a sprinkling of dill or roasted tomatoes with fresh basil. If you don't want to add chorizo, simply fold through the other ingredients just as the eggs start to set in the pan.

10 eggs
¼ cup milk
3 teaspoons butter
1 tablespoon extra-virgin olive oil, plus extra for drizzling
2 dried chorizo sausages, thickly sliced — *I like to use a dried chorizo from a good deli, but you could also use fresh chorizo from the sausage section of your supermarket.*
100 g goat's cheese
¼ cup grated parmesan
2 tablespoons finely chopped chives
sea salt and freshly ground black pepper
4 thick slices toasted bread, buttered, to serve

Preheat the oven grill to high.

Lightly whisk the eggs and milk together in a large bowl. Heat the butter and olive oil in a large deep ovenproof frying pan over high heat. Cook the chorizo for about 3 minutes, turning and browning each side as you go. You want the chorizo to start oozing its lovely amber-coloured oil.

Pour in the eggs and let them set slightly while you scatter over clumps of the goat's cheese. Give everything a quick scramble with a spatula, then sprinkle over the parmesan and grill for 3 minutes, or until the egg is just set and the parmesan has melted. (If your pan doesn't happen to fit under your grill, leave it on the stove to finish cooking. Reduce the heat to low, fold through the parmesan and cook for about 3 minutes, or until the eggs are just set. You won't get a golden crust on the top but it will still be just as delicious.)

Sprinkle with the chives, season to taste with the salt and pepper and drizzle over a generous glug of olive oil. Dig out big spoonfuls and serve on toast.

SERVES 4

KHAO TOM
[THAI BREAKFAST SOUP]

A long time ago, in a little village in Thailand, my 'yai' (grandmother) makes breakfast for her daughter, my mum. A steaming pot of rice soup simmers on the stove just as it did when my yai was a little girl. Decades later, in a little kitchen in Australia, my mum makes breakfast for her daughter, me. A steaming pot of rice soup simmers on the stove, just as it did when my yai was a little girl.

1 cup long-grain rice, unrinsed
4-cm piece of fresh ginger, peeled and finely chopped
300 g prawns, chicken or fish ← [see notes]
4 tablespoons fish sauce, plus extra to serve
1 teaspoon white sugar
1 teaspoon soy sauce
1 egg, lightly beaten
½ cup roughly chopped coriander leaves and stems
⅓ cup thinly sliced spring onion

GARLIC OIL
½ cup vegetable oil
6 garlic cloves, roughly chopped

CHILLI VINEGAR
1 fresh long red chilli, thinly sliced
⅓ cup white vinegar

I like to make the condiments first so they're ready to go when the soup is cooked. For the garlic oil, heat the vegetable oil in a small frying pan over medium heat, add the garlic and gently fry for 3 minutes, or until just starting to brown. Pour into a small heatproof bowl and set aside.

For the chilli vinegar, combine the chilli and vinegar in a small bowl and set aside.

For the soup, place the rice and ginger in a large saucepan and top with 1.25 litres of water. Bring to the boil over high heat, then reduce the heat to low and gently simmer for 5 minutes, or until the rice is just tender, stirring every so often. Add the prawns (or chicken or fish), fish sauce, sugar and soy sauce. Simmer for a further 8 minutes, or until the rice is very soft.

Stir through another cup of water to loosen the soup to a thick porridge consistency. Bring the soup back to a gentle bubbling boil (it needs to be hot when you add the egg). Slowly pour in the egg, while gently stirring the soup with a fork. Remove from the heat and ladle into bowls.

For the final flourish of flavour, top with the coriander, spring onion, a good 2 teaspoons of garlic oil, 1 teaspoon of chilli vinegar (more, if you like it spicy) and a little splash of fish sauce. Enjoy hot.

SERVES 6

NOTES: You will need 300 g of shelled, deveined prawns, so if you're buying them whole and unpeeled, you'll need to get 600 g. For chicken, use thigh fillets, sliced into thin slivers. For fish, cut the fillet into chunks and let it flake into the soup during cooking.

If you want to reheat any leftover soup or if you've made it a couple of hours before you want to eat it, then you'll need to add 1–2 cups of water as you warm it up because it will thicken when it gets cold.

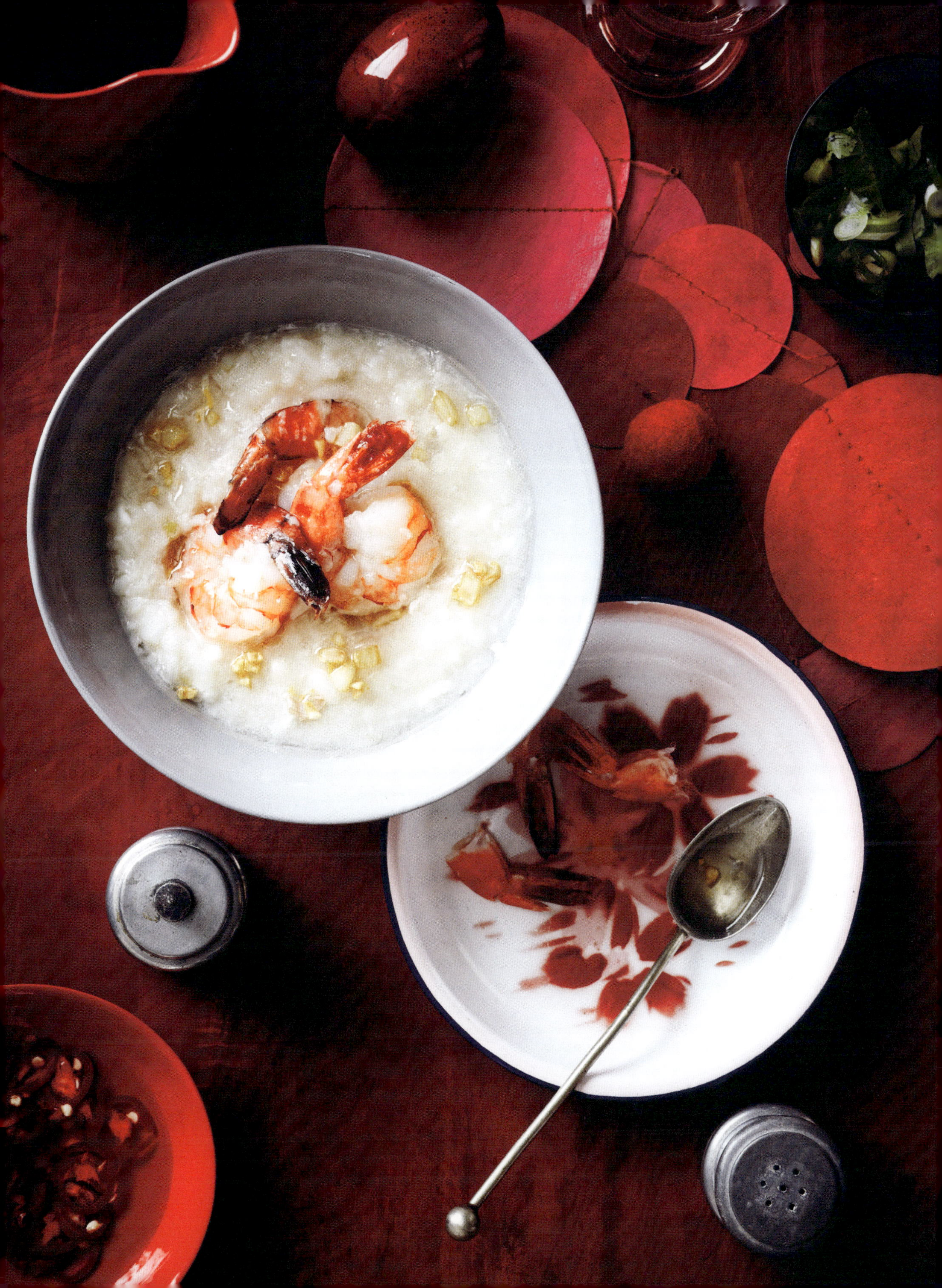

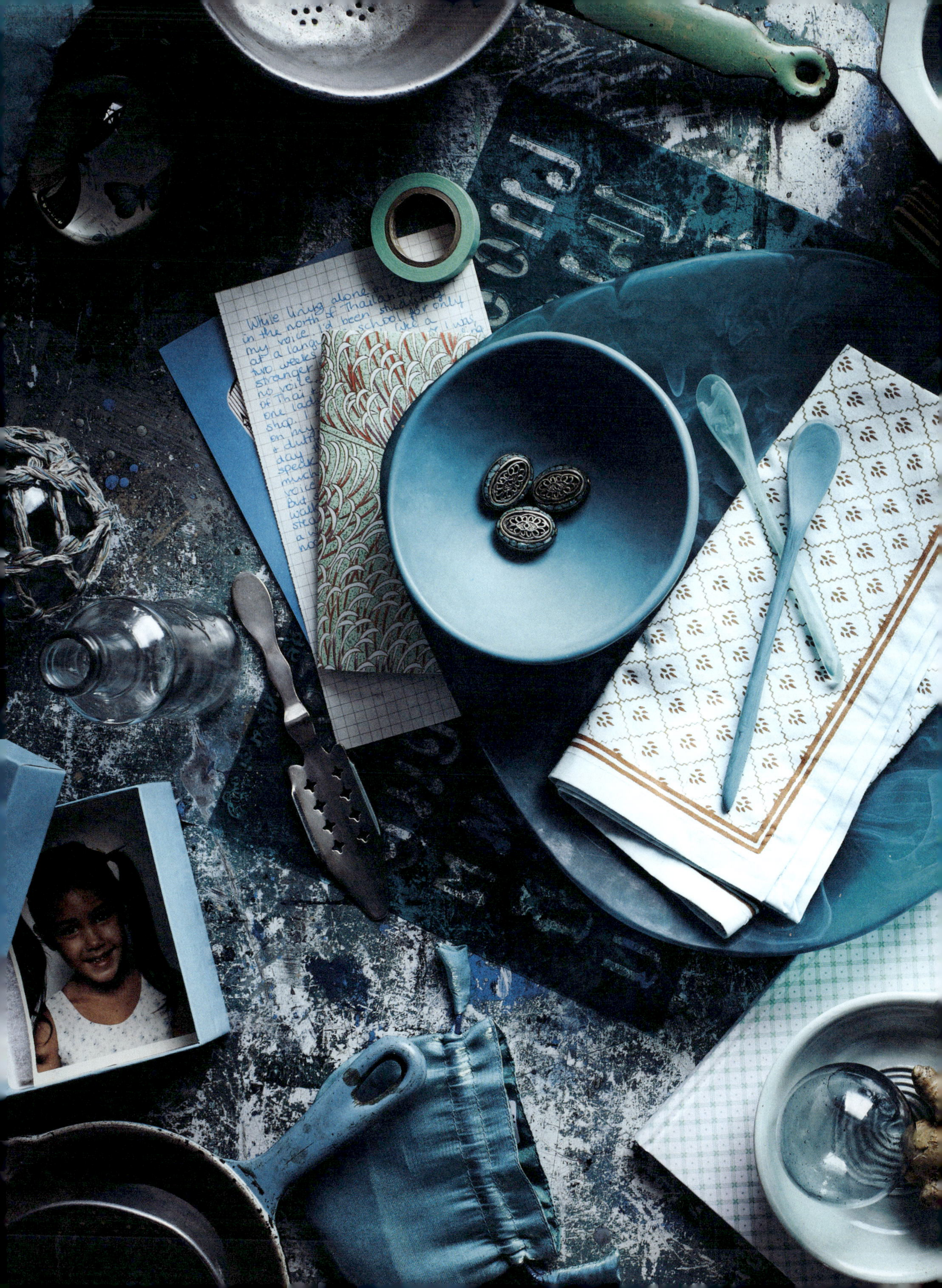

BOWL FOOD

IN THE VILLAGE

Aunty Niew sits in the shade of a tree as she fans the charcoal embers burning under a pot of rice. This is her kitchen. There are no blenders, no gas burners, no fancy electronic steam oven. In fact, there's no oven at all. Her kitchen consists of a large tree, two little clay stands that hold the burning charcoal and a wok or pot that sits on top of the stands. I have to admit that at this point I'm humbled and more than just a little embarrassed about my kitchen at home, the wealth of gadgets and the ease of cooking at the flick of a switch – all of those things that I take for granted.

Nothing is taken for granted in my mother's village in Thailand. Instead of flicking a switch to turn on the stove, Aunty Niew must collect, chop and store enough wood to cook the evening's meal. Each precious piece of wood is used to within an inch of its life and snuffed out and stored in a metal box if it can still be used for the next meal. Nothing is wasted, particularly when you have to work so hard to get it in the first place.

Kaffir lime leaves are picked from the garden. Chillies are ground in a mortar with a pestle along with shrimp paste, garlic and a few shallots. Rice simmers in a pot over one clay stove and a wok heats over the other. Aunty Niew's mother sits next to her under the tree and slices vegetables into a bowl sitting in her lap. Her gentle serenity is so beautiful; her worn and creased hands work expertly and calmly.

A woven mat is laid down on the floor of a wooden house that has stood for more than a hundred years. Aunty Niew lays out bowls of curry, vegetables, dried fish and rice. We kneel down on the mat and we eat: my mother, my mother's mother, Aunty Oi, Aunty Niew and her mother, and me. I'm here with the women of my mother's village. I cannot converse with them because we do not speak the same language… And yet we do: the passing of plates, the serving of rice, the joy of eating together after more than two decades. I am grateful for this. I am grateful for the language of food we share.

I think these century-old houses in my mother's village are beautiful.

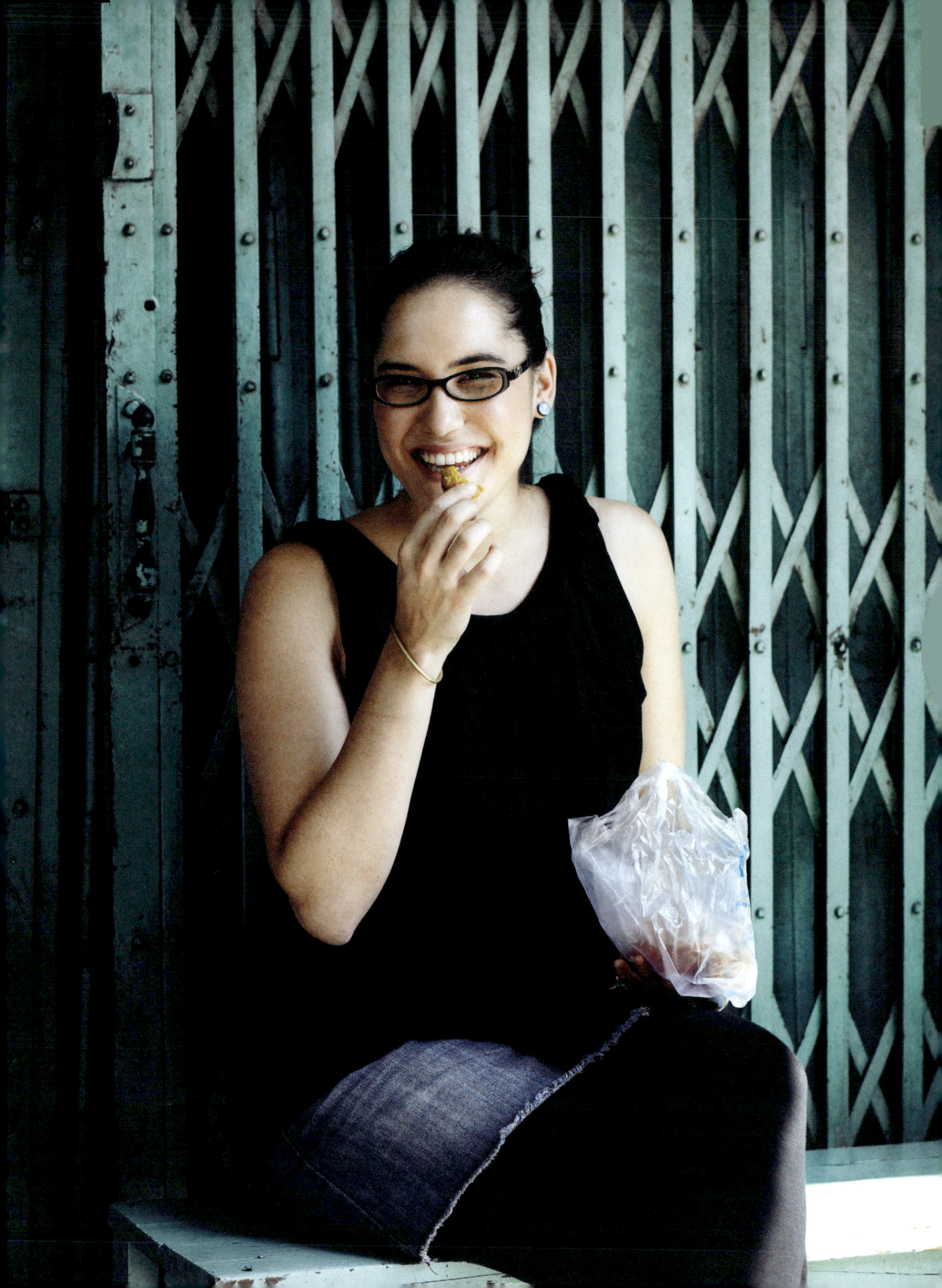

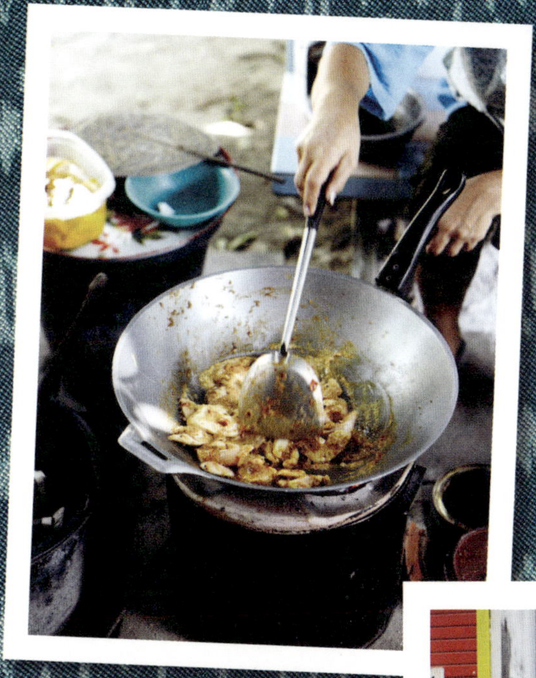
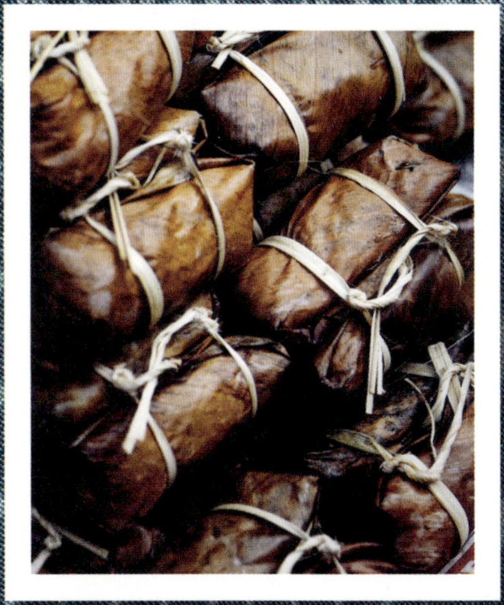
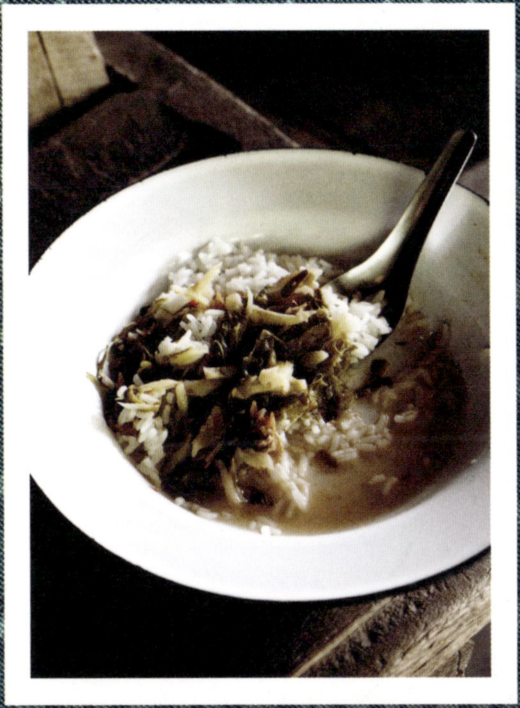
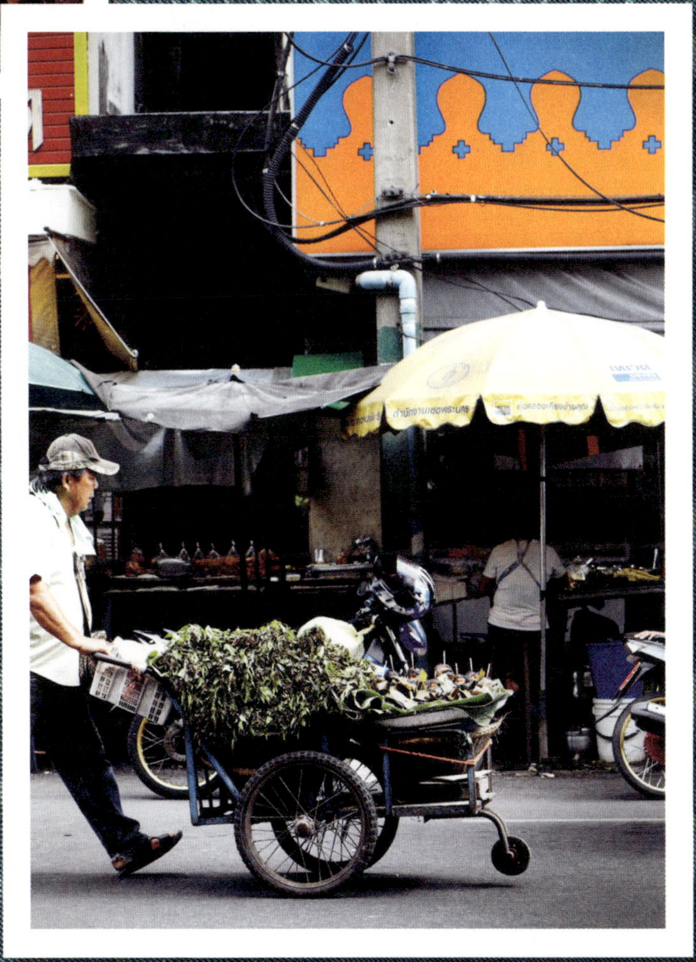

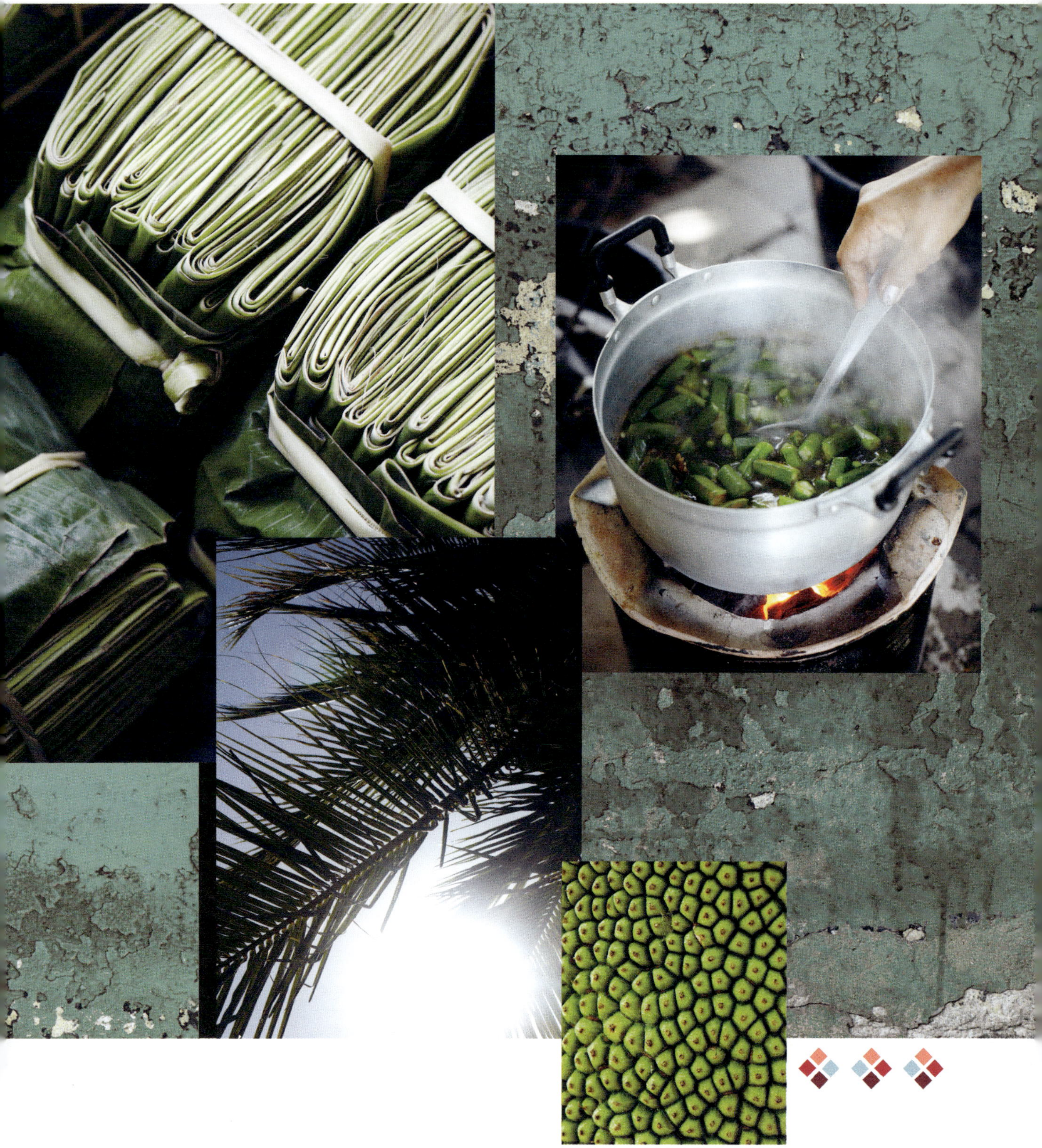

10 บาท

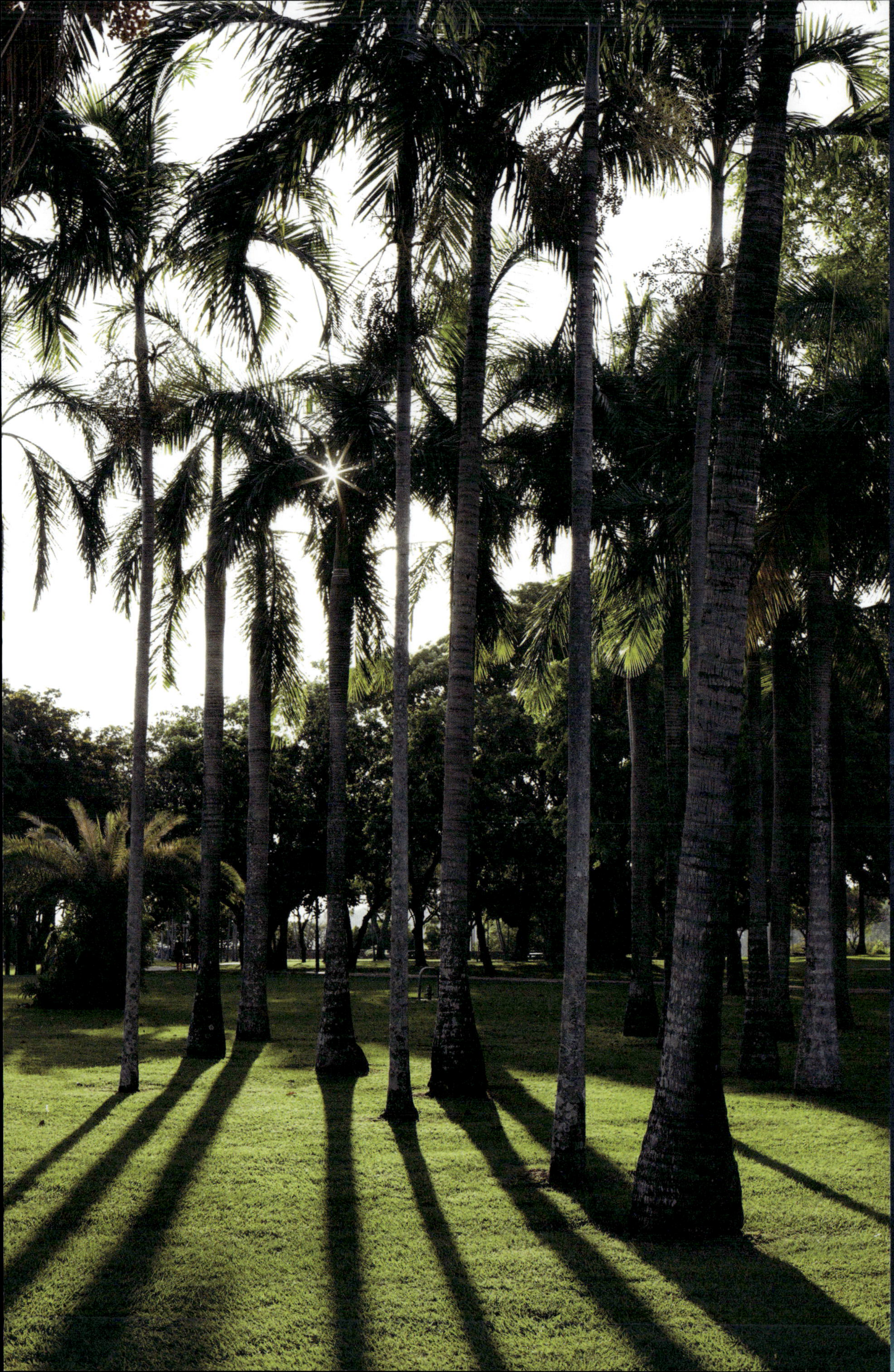

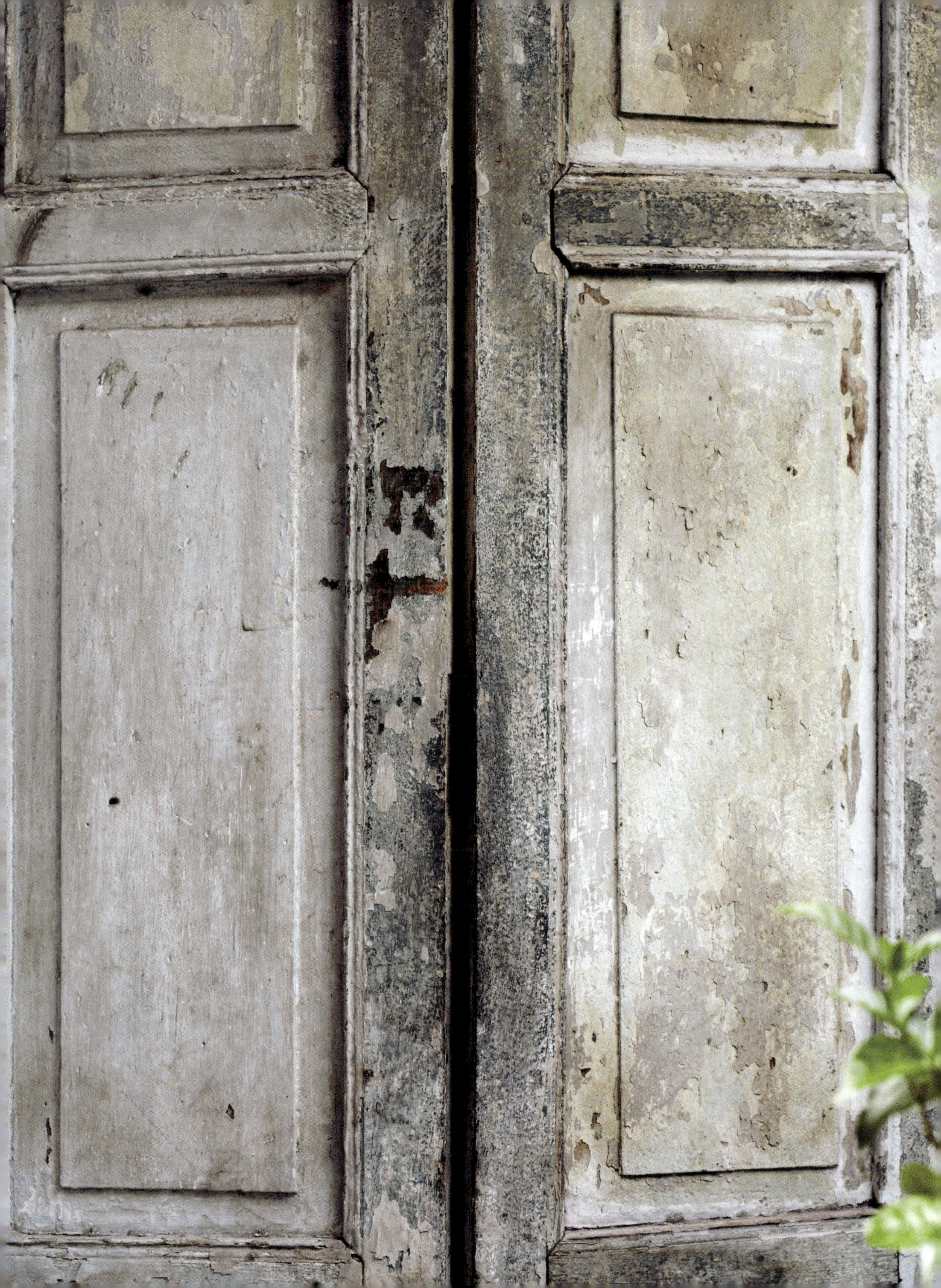

SATURDAY AFTERNOON CHICKEN STOCK

It's Saturday afternoon. I've just returned from my weekly trawl through the Farmers' market and it's time to get my chicken stock on. I use a combination of wings and necks for the best flavour. I like to fish out the wings and eat them warm with some of mum's Red Ginger Jam (see page 200) and Steamed Rice (see page 157), so my Saturday afternoon chicken stock becomes an easy Saturday night dinner.

1 kg chicken wings
1 kg chicken necks
2 carrots, roughly chopped
2 celery stalks, roughly chopped
2 fresh or dried bay leaves
4 sprigs flat-leaf parsley
1 teaspoon black peppercorns
1 teaspoon sea salt

Throw all the ingredients into a large (at least 10-litre capacity) stockpot and top up with 6 litres of water. Place over high heat and bring to a gentle simmer. Reduce the heat to medium and let it gently bubble away for 3 hours. You'll find some grey foamy-like matter rising to the surface, which you'll need to skim off every 30 or so minutes.

Strain the stock through a sieve lined with clean muslin (or a Chux will do). Ladle into airtight plastic containers and freeze for up to 6 months.

MAKES ABOUT 3 LITRES

EGG & CHIVE SOUP

This is the soup I crave when I'm feeling sick and sorry for myself. Silky chunks of omelette and batons of soft garlic chives come together in a salty, peppery broth. Garlic chives look like long, dark blades of grass. They have a mild, garlicky flavour and soften into silky strands in the soup. You can find them at Asian grocers.

2 tablespoons vegetable oil
3 eggs, lightly beaten
3 cups Saturday afternoon chicken stock (see previous page) or water
2 tablespoons fish sauce
1 teaspoon white sugar
¼ teaspoon freshly ground white pepper
1 bunch garlic chives, chopped into 3–4-cm batons

GARLIC OIL
½ cup vegetable oil
6 garlic cloves, roughly chopped

For the garlic oil, heat the vegetable oil in a small frying pan over medium heat, add the garlic and gently fry for 3 minutes, or until the garlic is just starting to brown. Pour into a small heatproof bowl and set aside.

For the soup, heat the vegetable oil in a wok over high heat. Pour in the eggs and let them set for a few seconds, then use a spatula to gently flip and agitate the eggs for about 30 seconds, but you don't want scrambled eggs – you want the eggs to just start to set and form a loose omelette. Add the stock and, using the spatula, break the omelette into large chunks. Add the fish sauce, sugar and pepper and taste. Add more fish sauce, if you like it saltier. Stir through the garlic chives. Remove from the heat and ladle into bowls. Spoon over the garlic oil and some of the crisp garlic bits.

SERVES 4

KHAO SOI
[CHIANG MAI NOODLE SOUP]

While living alone in Chiang Mai in the north of Thailand, I lost my voice. I'd been studying at a language school for only two weeks and still felt like a stranger in the small city. There I was, no voice, a limited understanding of Thai and no friends, except for one lady at a tiny little noodle shop. I discovered her noodles on my first day in Chiang Mai and dutifully went back every day thereafter. She didn't speak English, I didn't speak much Thai and, when I lost my voice, I couldn't speak at all. But she smiled every time I walked in and handed over a steaming bowl of 'khao soi' without a word. Thank you, lovely noodle lady.

200 g fresh thin egg noodles ← [see note]
2 tablespoons vegetable oil
3 tablespoons Thai Red Curry Paste (see page 110)
¼ teaspoon ground turmeric
½ teaspoon ground cardamom
4 cups coconut milk
2 tablespoons fish sauce
1 teaspoon white sugar
300 g chicken thigh fillets, thinly sliced

NOODLE CONDIMENTS
150 g deep-fried egg noodles, gently broken into large chunks
3 red shallots, thinly sliced ← [see note]
100 g pickled mustard greens, drained, rinsed and thinly sliced
1 cup roughly chopped coriander leaves
1 lime, cut into wedges

Cook the fresh noodles in boiling salted water for 2–3 minutes, or until just cooked. Drain, refresh under cold running water. Drain again well and set aside.

Heat the vegetable oil in a heavy-based saucepan over medium heat. Add the curry paste, turmeric and cardamom and cook for about 1 minute or until fragrant and steaming. Add 1 cup of the coconut milk and simmer for 2 minutes to let the flavours infuse. Add the remaining coconut milk, the fish sauce, sugar and 2 cups of water. Toss in the chicken and simmer for about 5 minutes, or until cooked through.

Arrange small handfuls of the cooked fresh noodles in serving bowls and ladle over the soup. Place a chunk of the deep-fried egg noodles on top. Scatter over a couple of slices of shallots, a pinch of sliced mustard greens and a small handful of coriander leaves. Finish with a squeeze of lime.

SERVES 6

NOTE: Wander the aisles of an Asian grocer to find fresh thin egg noodles, deep-fried egg noodles (which come in ready-made packets) and pickled mustard greens. You'll find red shallots in the fresh fruit and veg section. If you can't find them, you could substitute golden (French) shallots or even half a small, very thinly sliced red onion.

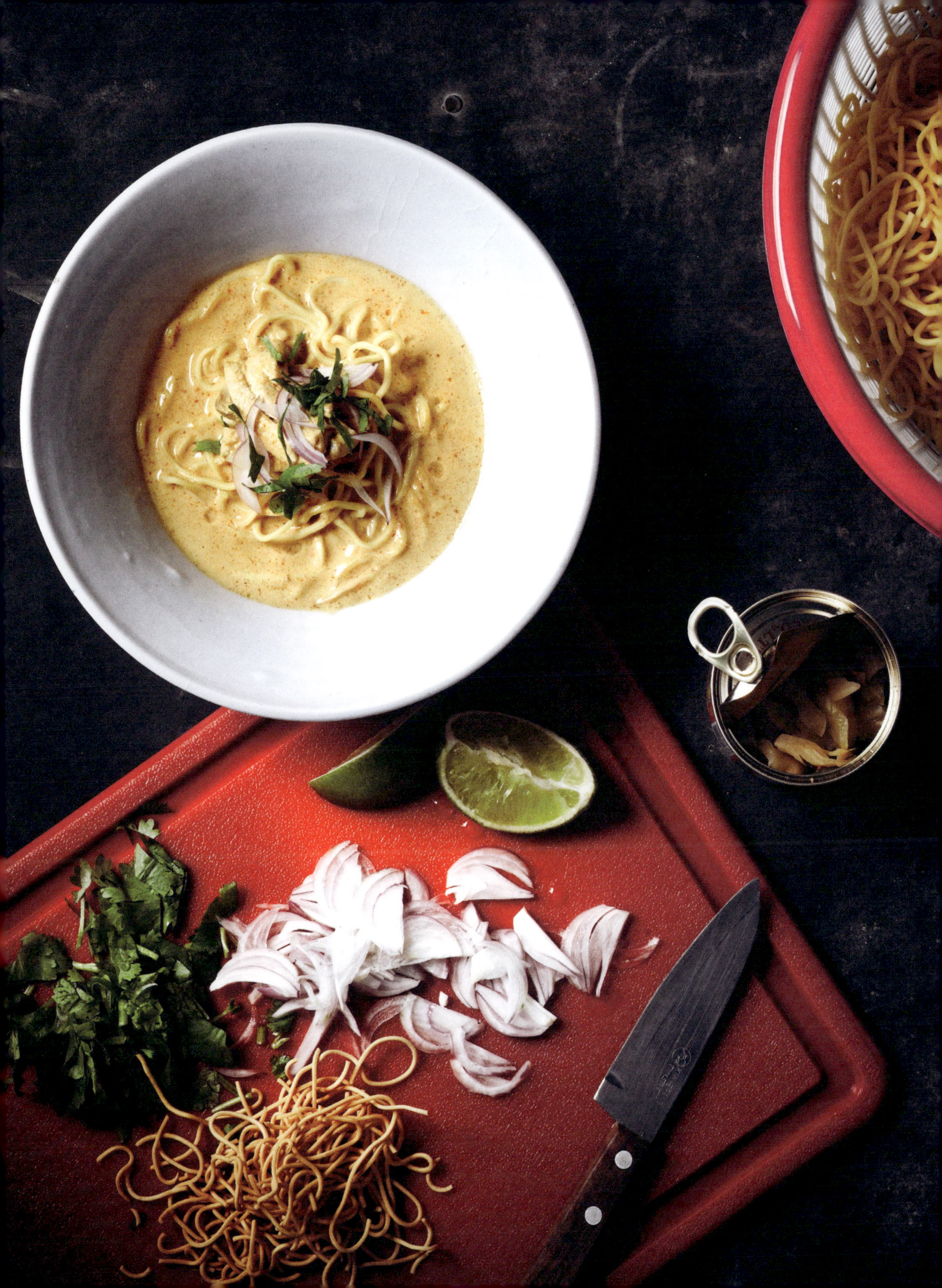

PORK BALL NOODLE SOUP

'This is the way we do it,' says my mum. 'So we don't need to make a stock?' I ask skeptically, wondering how a bit of water, some garlic and a spoonful of peppercorns will produce a tasty broth. 'We make it like this in the willage,' she replies in a very serious tone of voice. 'You mean village,' I say, with a chuckle. My mother's English is peppered with a thick Thai accent even after more than 25 years in Australia. It never fails to make me giggle ever so slightly (and ever so lovingly). 'Yes it's how we do it in the willage,' she says. How can you argue with that?

100 g vermicelli noodles
4 garlic cloves, peeled
2 teaspoons white peppercorns
¼ cup fish sauce
2 tablespoons soy sauce
2 teaspoons white sugar
500 g minced pork
½ cup finely chopped coriander leaves and stems, plus extra leaves to serve
4 spring onions, cut into 4-cm batons
2 cups sliced wombok (Chinese cabbage)

SOY AND CHILLI SAUCE
¼ cup soy sauce
½ fresh long red chilli, thinly sliced

For the soy and chilli sauce, combine the ingredients in a small bowl and set aside.

For the soup, place the noodles in a large bowl, cover with warm water and allow to soak for 10 minutes to soften. Drain and set aside.

Place the garlic and peppercorns in a mortar and pound to a rough paste. Place half of the paste in a large saucepan with 2 tablespoons of the fish sauce, 1 tablespoon of the soy sauce, 1 teaspoon of the sugar and 1.25 litres of water and bring to the boil, then reduce the heat and simmer while you prepare the pork balls.

Place the minced pork, the remaining garlic paste, fish sauce, soy sauce and sugar and all of the coriander in a large bowl and use your hands to squelch the mixture together until well combined.

Using your hands, pinch the pork mixture into rough walnut-sized balls (don't be too fussy about getting them perfectly round), dropping each ball into the simmering liquid. Simmer for about 3 minutes, or until the pork balls are cooked. Add the noodles and spring onion and simmer for 1 minute, then remove from the heat.

To serve, place small handfuls of wombok in bowls, spoon over the soup making sure each bowl has some pork, noodles and spring onion, and top with the extra coriander leaves. Serve with the soy and chilli sauce on the side so that everyone can add their own spoonfuls of spice.

SERVES 4

PEA SOUP WITH CRISP PANCETTA

This is a vibrant, grassy green pool of soup dotted with flecks of salty pancetta. The colour has me mesmerised. I like to serve it at an elegant dinner party or you could pour it into shot glasses for a warm canapé at a springtime cocktail party.

4 thin slices pancetta
40 g butter
2 garlic cloves, sliced
2 fresh or dried bay leaves
500 g frozen baby green peas
2 cups Saturday Afternoon Chicken Stock (see page 30)
sea salt
2 tablespoons finely chopped chives
extra-virgin olive oil, for drizzling

Preheat the oven grill to high. Lay the pancetta on a baking tray lined with aluminium foil and grill for 4 minutes each side, or until crisp. Drain on paper towel and set aside to cool. Break up into little shards and set aside until ready to serve.

Melt the butter in a saucepan over medium heat. Add the garlic and bay leaves and cook for about 2 minutes, or until fragrant. Add the peas and stock, bring to the boil, then immediately remove from the heat. You don't want to overcook the peas or they'll loose their vibrant colour and flavour.

Remove and discard the bay leaves. Pour the pea mixture into a blender and process until smooth. Do this in batches if you need to. Check the seasoning and add salt to taste. Blend again for a couple of seconds. Pour into bowls, sprinkle with the pancetta bits and chives and drizzle with the olive oil.

SERVES 8 AS AN ENTRÉE

SIMPLE SEAFOOD & CHORIZO SOUP

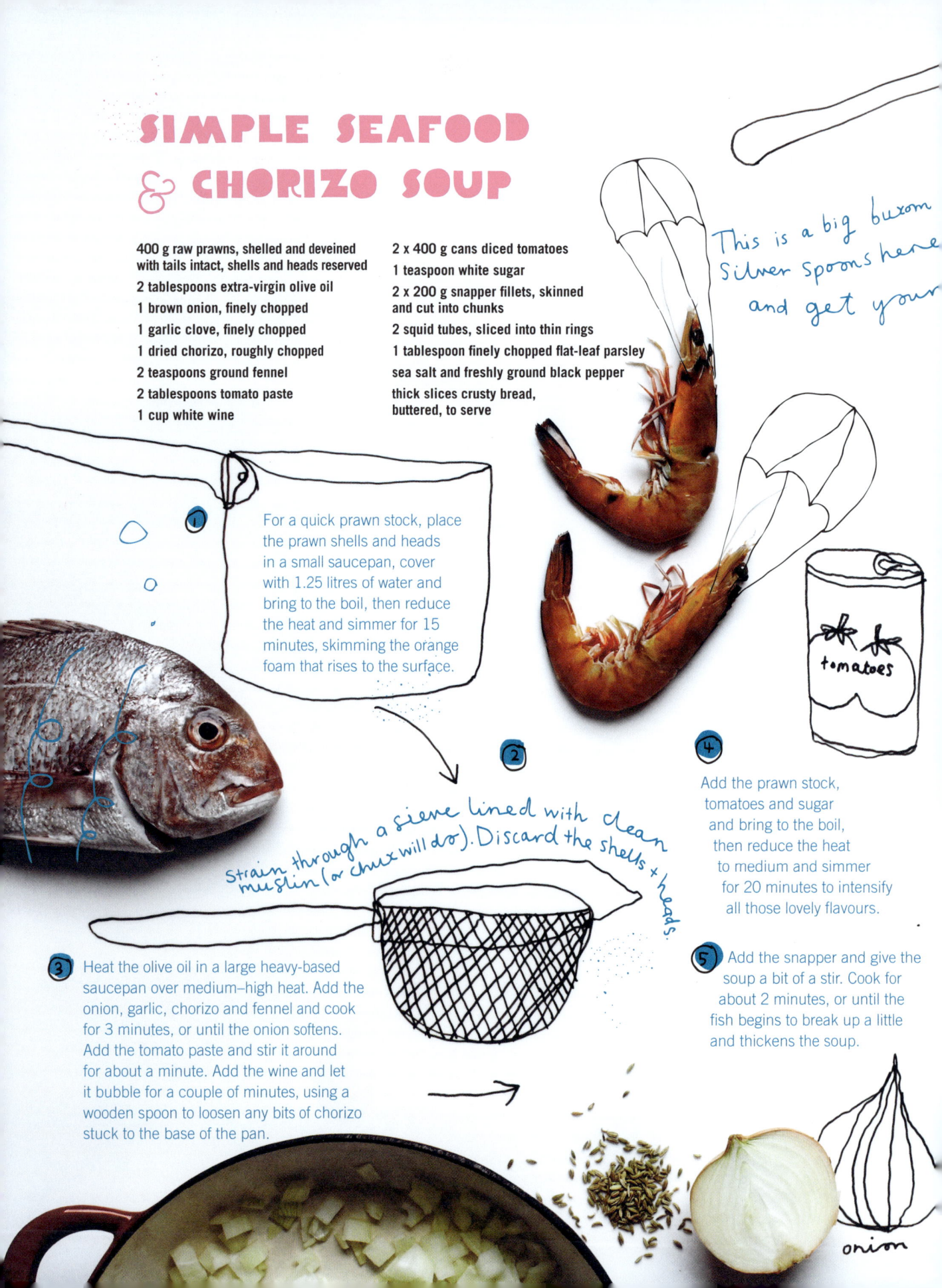

400 g raw prawns, shelled and deveined with tails intact, shells and heads reserved
2 tablespoons extra-virgin olive oil
1 brown onion, finely chopped
1 garlic clove, finely chopped
1 dried chorizo, roughly chopped
2 teaspoons ground fennel
2 tablespoons tomato paste
1 cup white wine

2 x 400 g cans diced tomatoes
1 teaspoon white sugar
2 x 200 g snapper fillets, skinned and cut into chunks
2 squid tubes, sliced into thin rings
1 tablespoon finely chopped flat-leaf parsley
sea salt and freshly ground black pepper
thick slices crusty bread, buttered, to serve

This is a big buxom Silver spoons here and get your

1 For a quick prawn stock, place the prawn shells and heads in a small saucepan, cover with 1.25 litres of water and bring to the boil, then reduce the heat and simmer for 15 minutes, skimming the orange foam that rises to the surface.

2 *Strain through a sieve lined with clean muslin (or chux will do). Discard the shells + heads.*

3 Heat the olive oil in a large heavy-based saucepan over medium–high heat. Add the onion, garlic, chorizo and fennel and cook for 3 minutes, or until the onion softens. Add the tomato paste and stir it around for about a minute. Add the wine and let it bubble for a couple of minutes, using a wooden spoon to loosen any bits of chorizo stuck to the base of the pan.

4 Add the prawn stock, tomatoes and sugar and bring to the boil, then reduce the heat to medium and simmer for 20 minutes to intensify all those lovely flavours.

5 Add the snapper and give the soup a bit of a stir. Cook for about 2 minutes, or until the fish begins to break up a little and thickens the soup.

onion

main course sort of soup. No elegant
Use big chunks of buttered bread as a spoon
fingers sticky peeling off the prawn tails

6 Add the squid and prawns and cook for 3–4 minutes or until the prawns are just cooked through.

1 teaspoon sugar

7 Stir through the parsley + season to taste with salt + pepper

8 Ladle into bowls + serve with the crusty bread.

SERVES 6

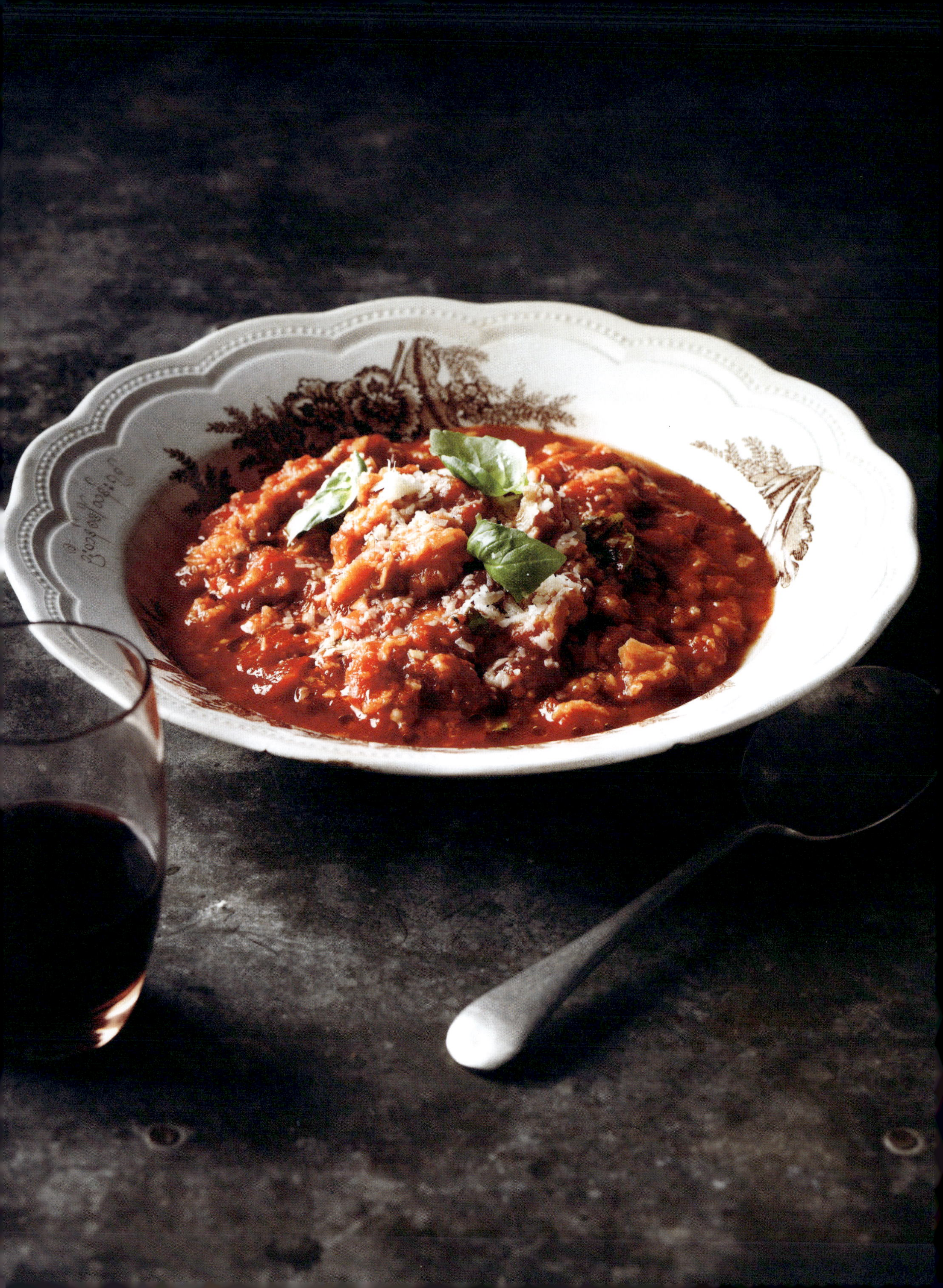

PAPPA AL POMODORO
[TOMATO & BREAD SOUP]

This soup is my go-to-girl when my fridge is looking bare. I've always got some canned tomatoes in the cupboard and there's usually half a loaf of stale bread sitting in my bread basket. From those simple things come a glorious little soup that warms my heart on the coldest of winter evenings.

¼ cup extra-virgin olive oil, plus extra for drizzling

3 garlic cloves, finely chopped

2 x 400 g cans good-quality diced tomatoes

2 fresh or dried bay leaves

2 teaspoons white sugar

2 teaspoons sea salt

1 cup torn-up bits of stale bread (about 2 thick slices)

1 cup basil leaves, roughly torn, plus extra for garnishing

1 tablespoon grated parmesan

Heat the olive oil in a large saucepan over medium heat. Add the garlic and cook for 1 minute, or until fragrant and soft but not coloured. Add the tomato, bay leaves and 3 cups of water and simmer for 30 minutes to thicken and let the flavours intensify.

Check the seasoning and add the sugar and salt to taste. Use the quantities as a guide because every can of tomatoes is different and you may need to add more sugar or less salt depending on their quality and flavour.

Add the bread and stir to break up to achieve a thick porridge-like consistency. This is supposed to be a chunky, hearty sort of soup, but if it's too thick for your taste, simply stir in another cup or so of water. Stir through the basil.

Ladle the soup into bowls, sprinkle with a smattering of parmesan, splash generously with olive oil and garnish with a few extra basil leaves.

SERVES 8

CAVOLO NERO, POTATO & BACON SOUP

Cavolo nero (also known as kale) is the black sheep of the cabbage family. It looks nothing like its savoy or sugarloaf cabbage brothers. It has no heart to speak of, just long palm-frond-type leaves with an intricate crinkly texture and an inky blue-black colour. You'll get some tough love from cavolo nero unless you blanch or simmer it until soft.

500 g cavolo nero (about 1 large bunch) ← *you could use spinach or silverbeet if you can't find cavolo nero*
2 tablespoons extra-virgin olive oil, plus extra for drizzling
1 brown onion, finely diced
2 garlic cloves, finely chopped
4 rashers bacon, finely diced
1 kg potatoes (about 4 large), unpeeled, washed and cut into small chunks
1.25 litres Saturday Afternoon Chicken Stock (see page 30)
½ cup grated parmesan
sea salt and freshly ground black pepper
sourdough bread, to serve

Strip the leaves from the cavolo nero and discard the thick part of the stem. Gather together the leaves and slice thinly.

Heat the olive oil in a large saucepan over medium heat. Add the onion, garlic and bacon and cook for 3 minutes, or until the bacon starts to brown and crisp up. Add the cavolo nero, potato and stock, cover and simmer for 30 minutes, or until the potato is tender and the cavolo nero has softened.

Just before serving, stir through the parmesan. Check the seasoning and add some salt and pepper to taste. Ladle into bowls, drizzle with olive oil and serve with big chunks of the sourdough bread for dipping.

SERVES 4

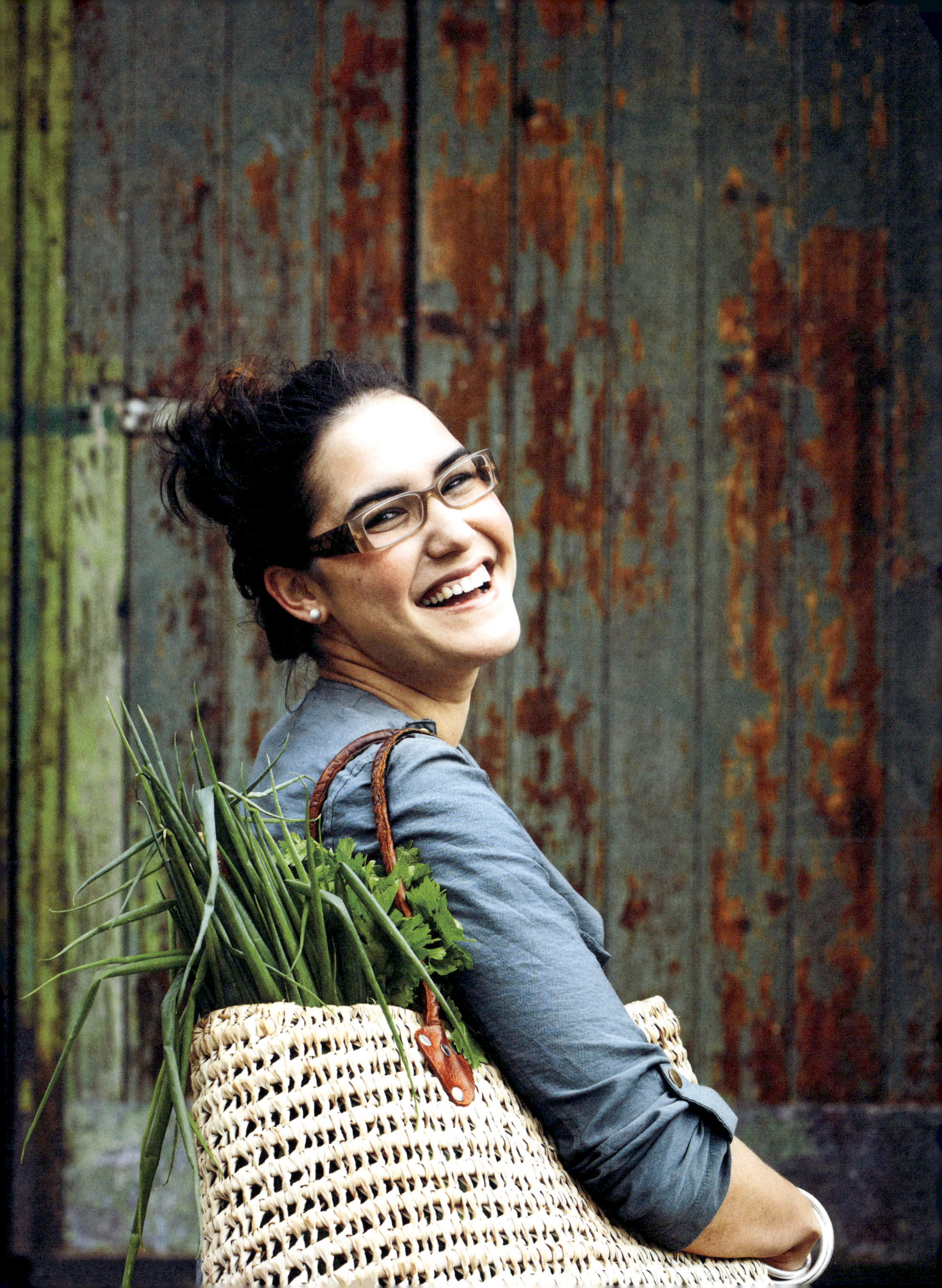

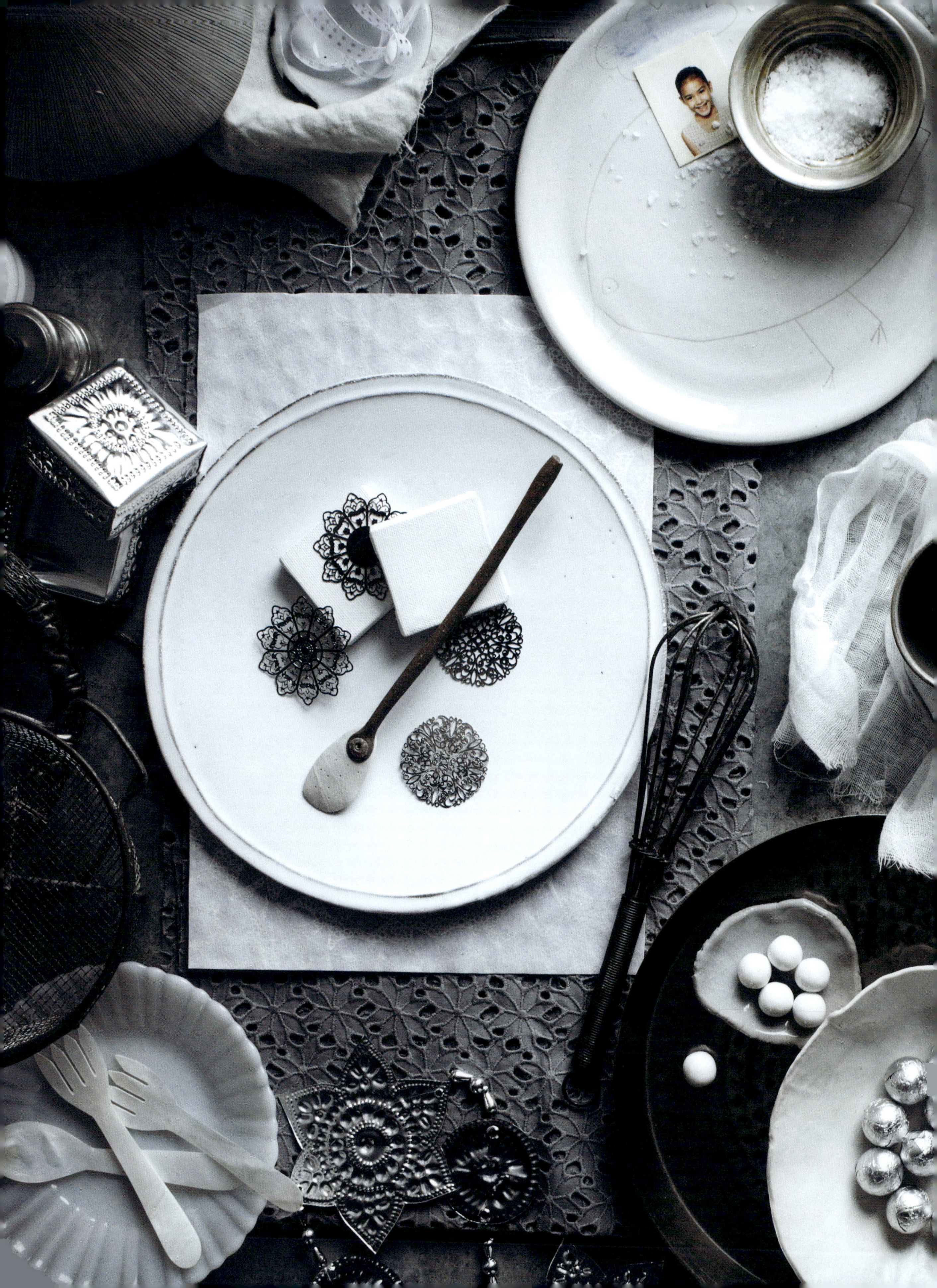

SMALL PLATES

THE LIFE & TIMES OF A TOASTED CHEESE SANDWICH

The toasted cheese sandwich came into my life in a substantial way when I first went to boarding school when I was 11 years old. The most devastating part about leaving my family to live in a strange place with strange people was the food. I had no idea food could be this bad. I can still remember the taste of something called a 'sea shanty'. It was crumbed and fried, but I have no idea what it was that was crumbed and fried. I don't think its mushy filling had ever seen the sea let alone swum in it. I missed my mother's food. I missed the fiery chilli in her curries, I missed the heat of her *laab* salad and I missed her. But, as we all must do in life, I adapted. And I found the toasted cheese sandwich. The melted, gooey, buttery tang of tasty cheese and the crunch of toasted white bread became my comfort food in a sea of mushy shanties.

My addiction to cheese and bread continued through my university years. My little toasties were a much better option than two-minute noodles. But I knew there was something more out there, something more than the tasty cheese and anaemic white bread I had been using. It was time to go professional with my toasted cheese sandwich.

After three years as an ABC journalist, I quit to study the history and culture of all things food. I took a job answering phones at a food-and-wine wholesaler and retailer in Adelaide. And never once did I regret what some would see as a massive step down. How could there be regret when it was my job to taste, cut and sell more than a hundred varieties of Australian and European cheeses. I'd found heaven in a cheese room.

It was exactly what I was looking for to elevate my cheese toastie to the next level. Every day for the next two years I made a toasted cheese sandwich for lunch. That's 730 cheese toasties with which I honed my craft. I'd gone from elastic-ky tasty cheese and uniform white bread to thick, rough-cut slabs of sourdough and the melted ooze of artisan cheeses, such as Comté, Abondance, Gruyère, Beaufort and so many more. I loved them all. Sometimes I spread my bread with thick smooshes of French butter. Sometimes it was an Italian mustard fruit that complemented my cheese melt. It was a lifetime of cheese experience in two years. I'm excited about where my toasted cheese sandwich adventures will take me next.

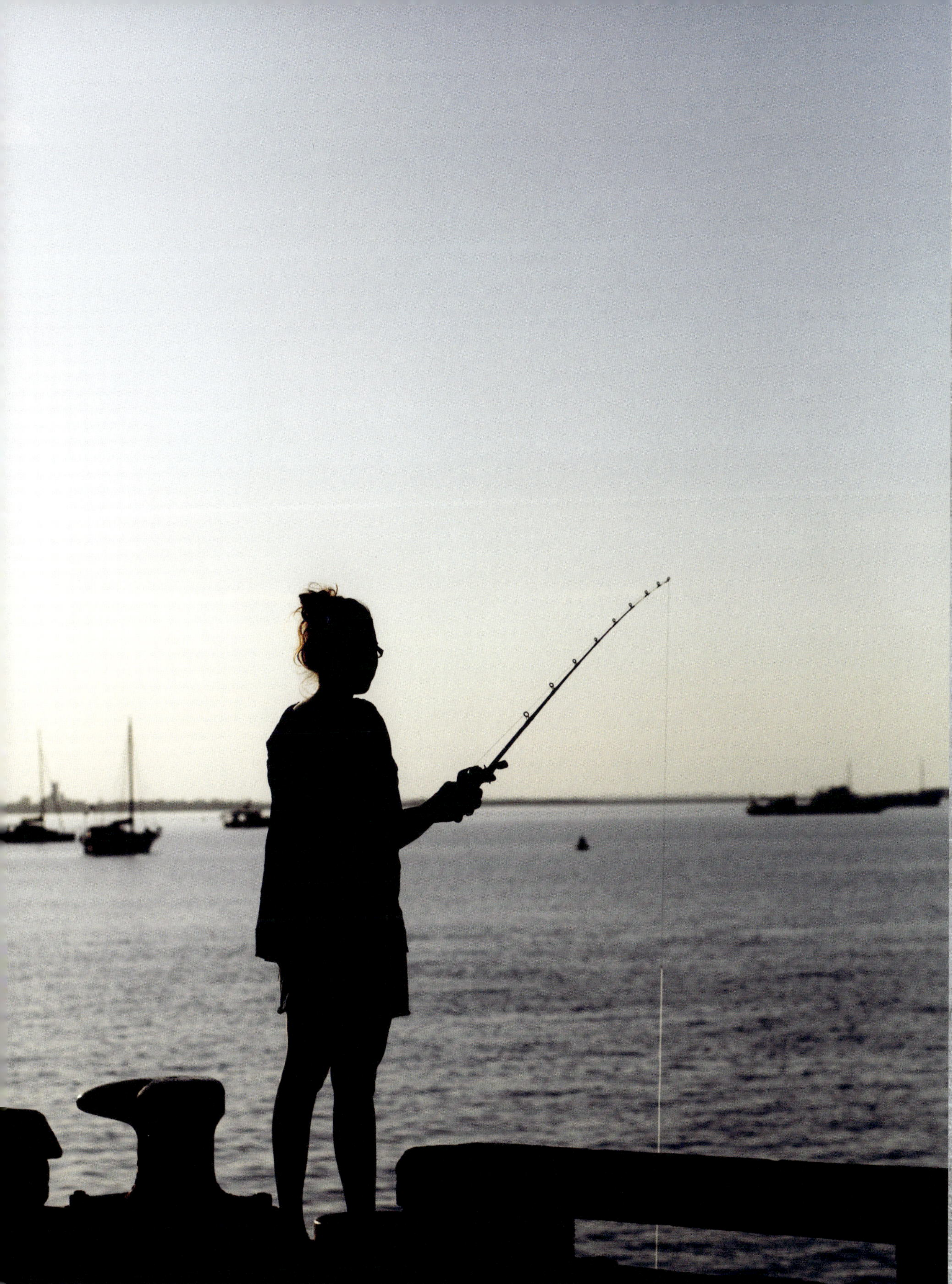

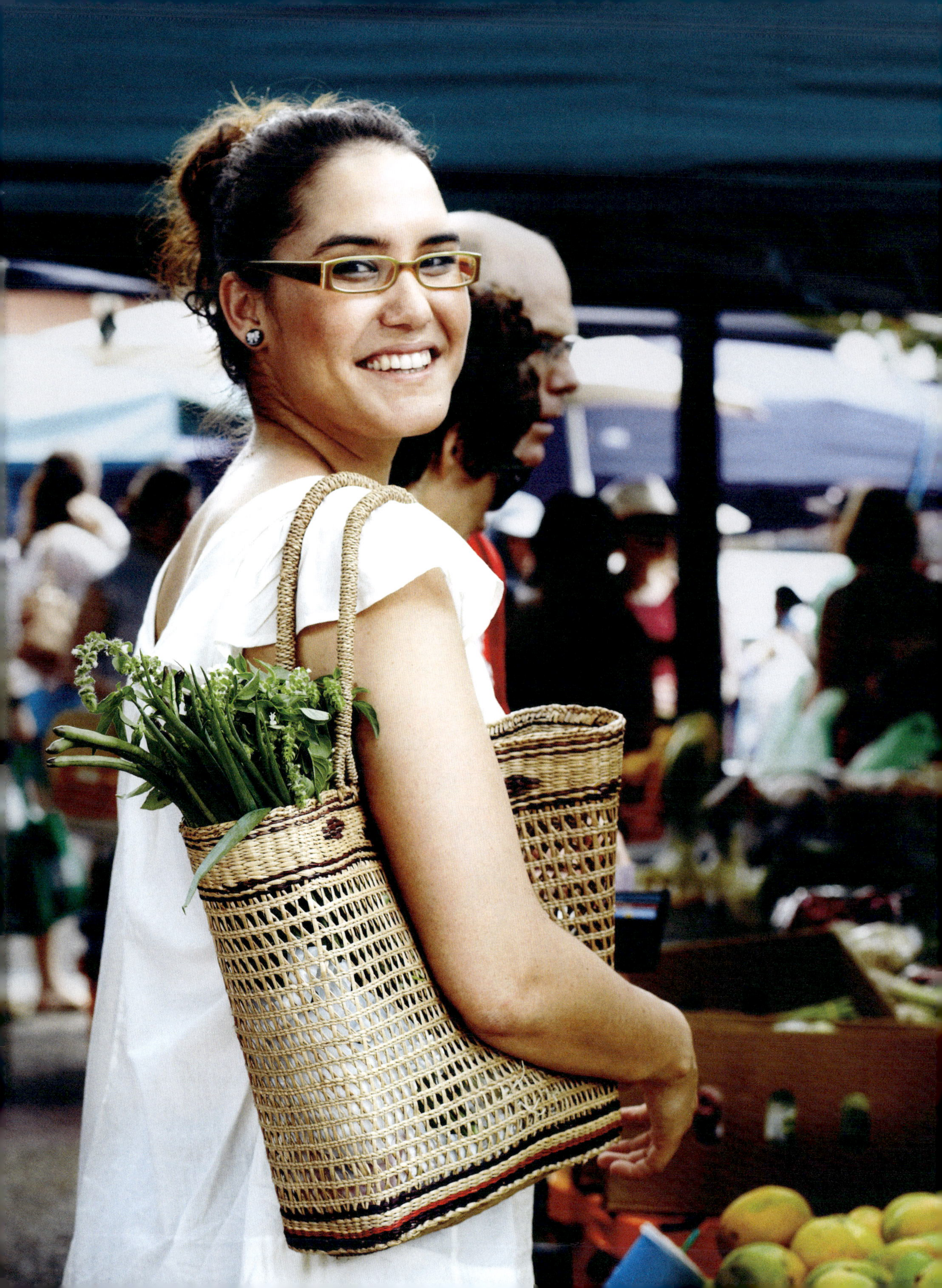

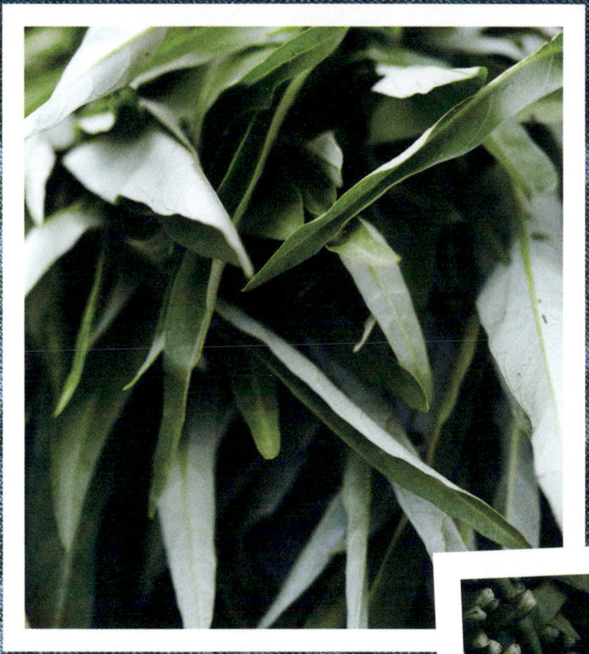

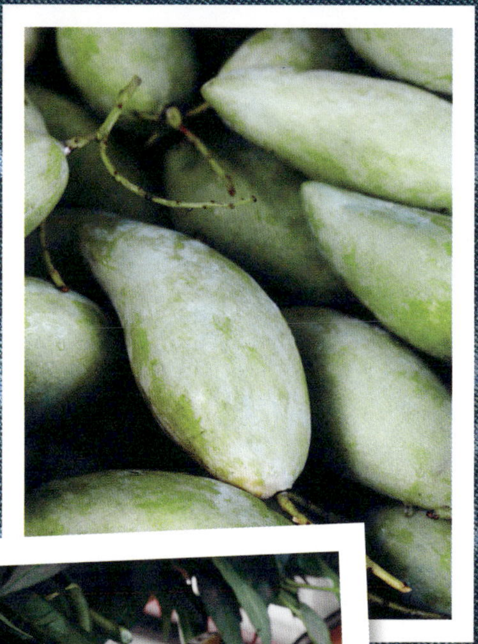

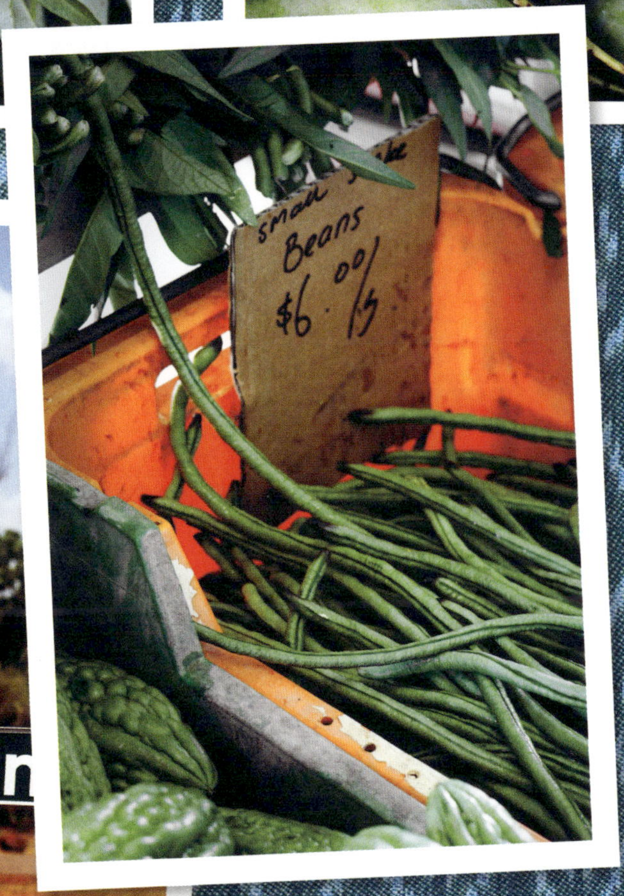

small
Beans
$6.00

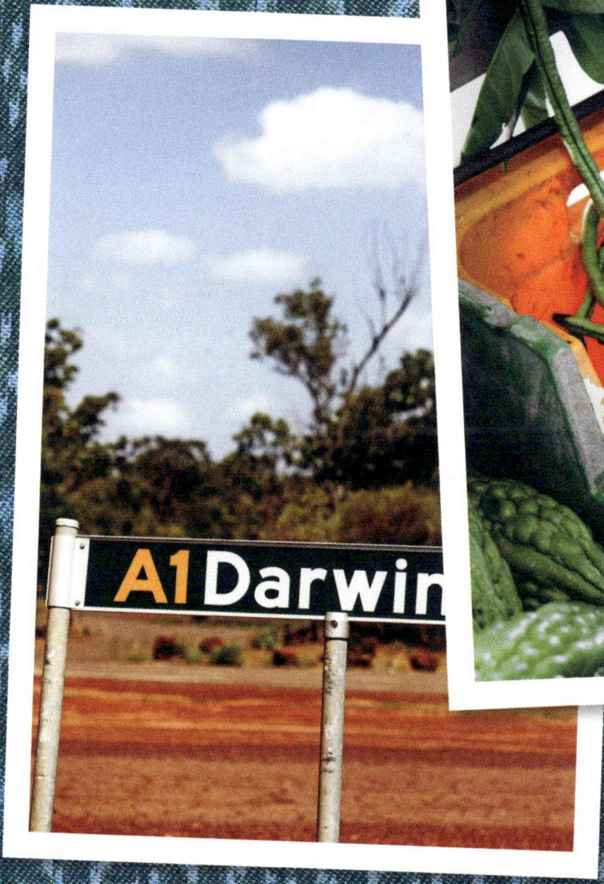

A1 Darwin

oooh I love these spicy laksas
from Darwin's Parap market.

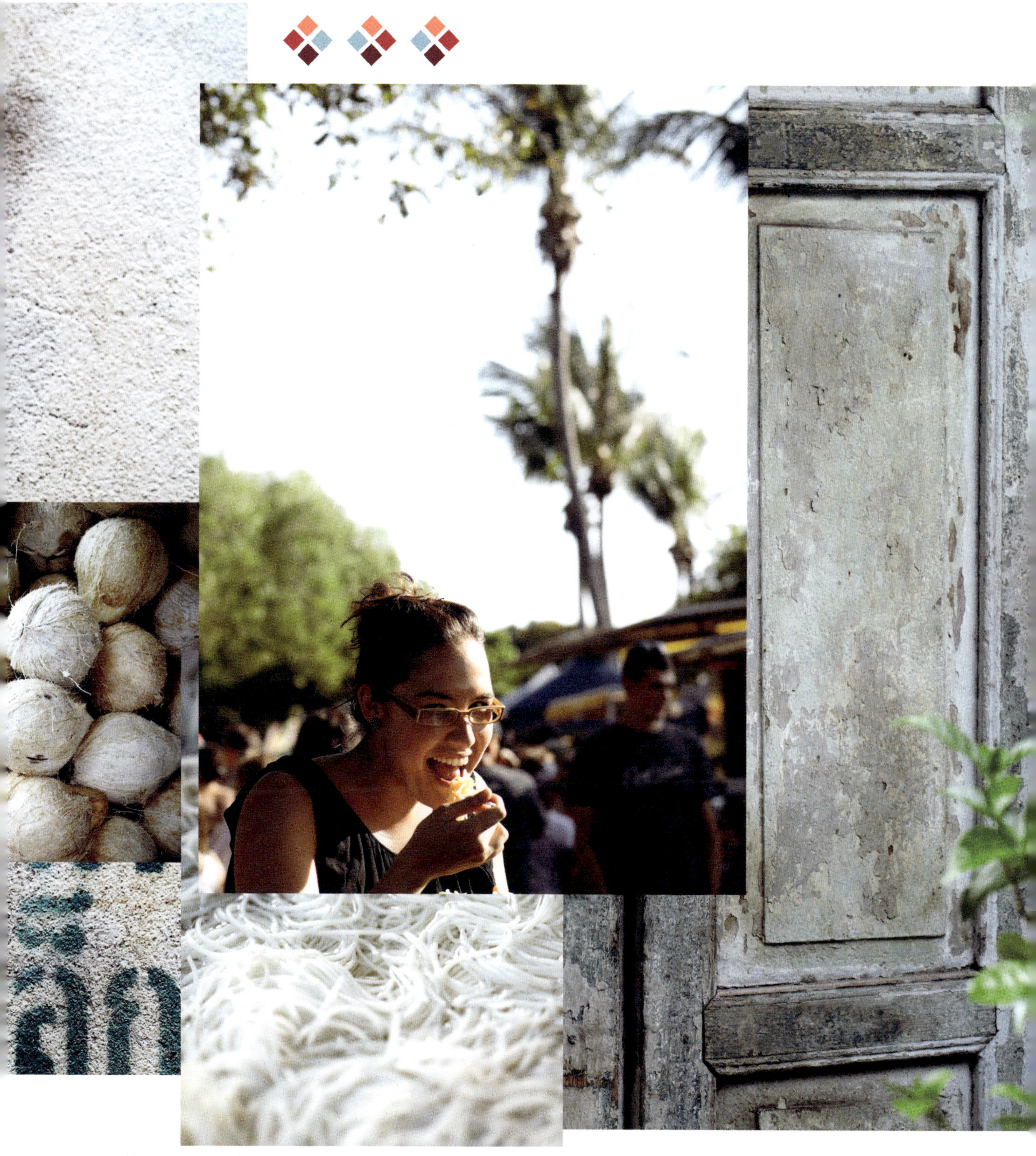

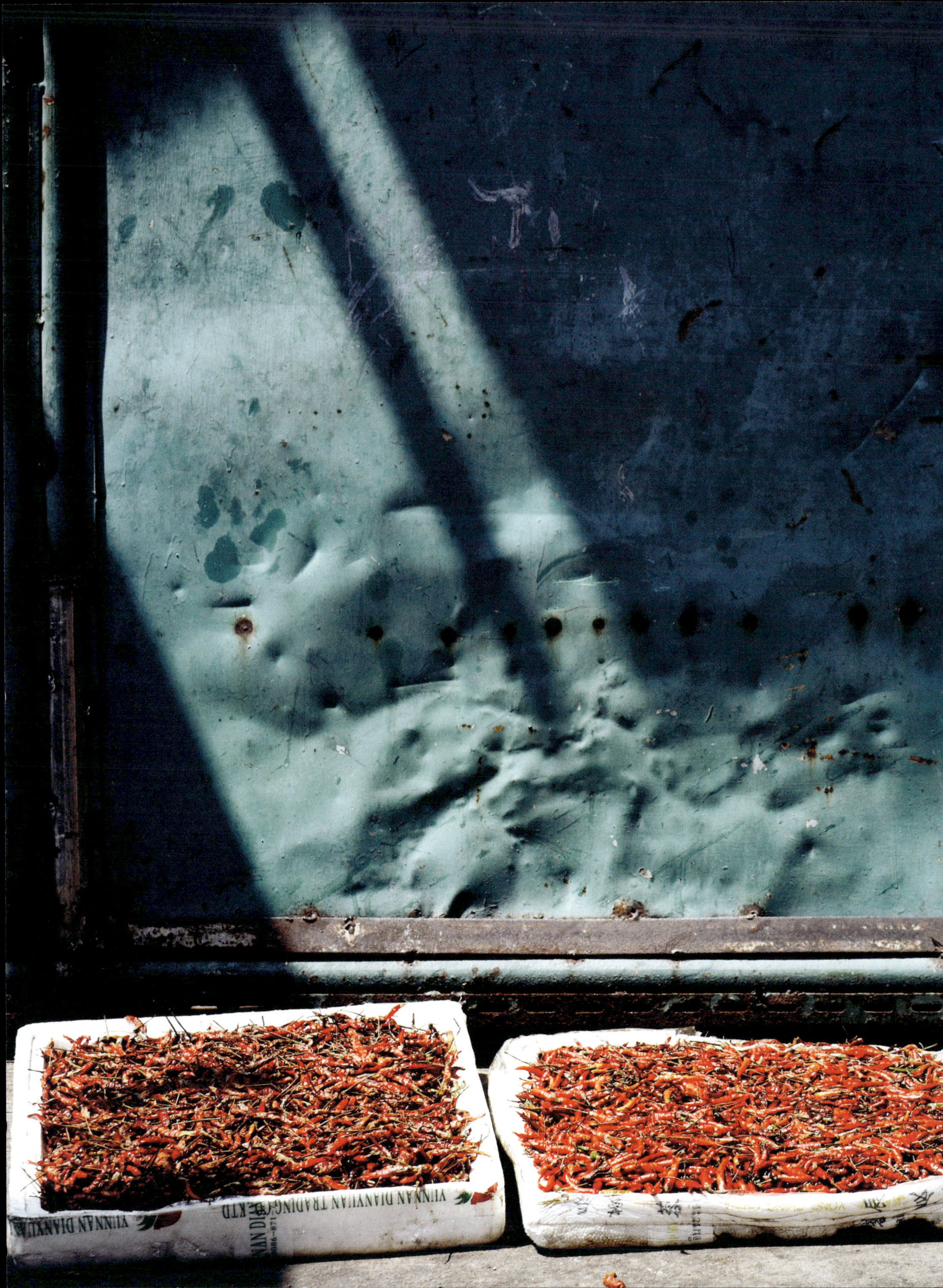

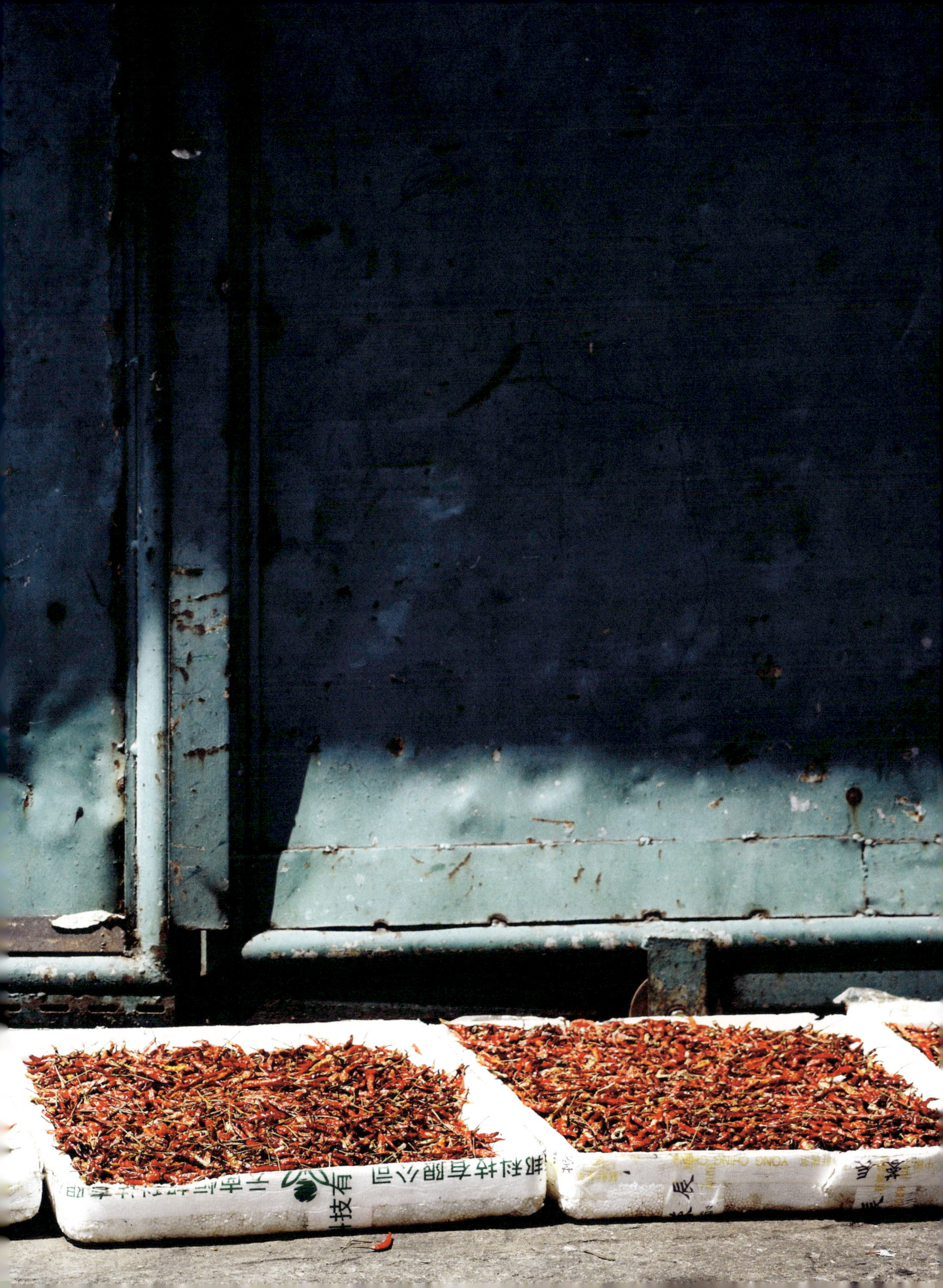

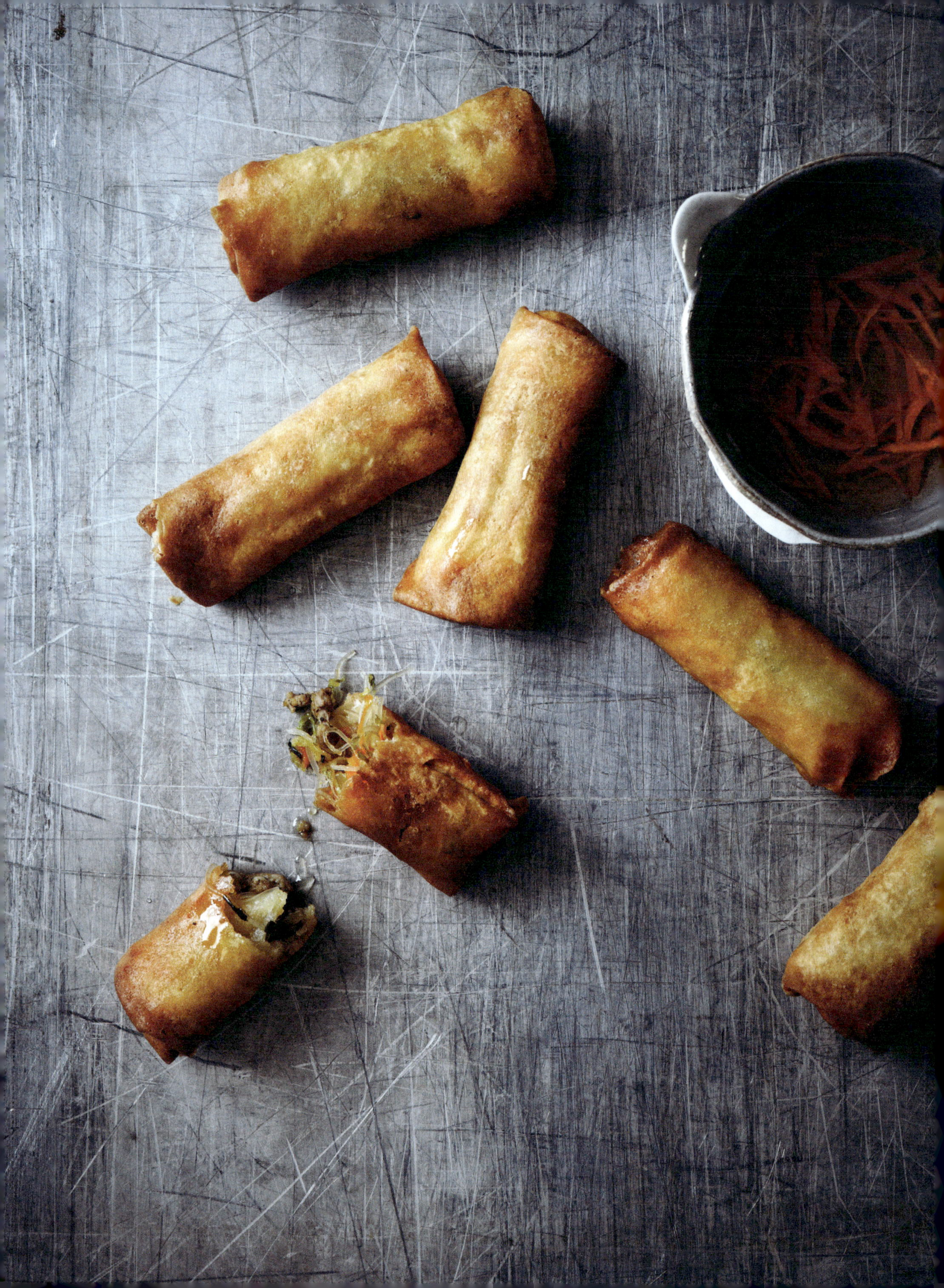

PORK SPRING ROLLS WITH SWEET CARROT DIPPING SAUCE

I'm sitting with a little bowl of spring roll filling all to myself. My mum's not watching. She's busy chatting away in Thai with her friends as they roll and stack hundreds of spring rolls. Neat, uniform little pastry soldiers lined up in neat, uniform little rows. I'm supposed to be rolling too. I'm supposed to be learning the art of building an army of spring roll soldiers. But I don't have any filling left. I've eaten it all.

PORK FILLING
100 g vermicelli noodles
3 garlic cloves, peeled
1 teaspoon black peppercorns
½ teaspoon sea salt
1 tablespoon vegetable oil
200 g minced pork
2 carrots, grated
3 cups finely shredded cabbage
2 tablespoons fish sauce
1 tablespoon white sugar
2 tablespoons finely chopped coriander leaves

SWEET CARROT DIPPING SAUCE
½ cup white sugar
⅓ cup white vinegar
1 tablespoon fish sauce

SPRING ROLL WRAPPERS ← [see note, page 55]
1½ cups plain flour, plus 1 tablespoon for spring roll 'glue'
1½ cups self-raising flour
1 teaspoon sea salt
vegetable oil, for deep-frying

For the pork filling, soak the noodles in warm water for 5 minutes to soften. Drain, then use scissors or a knife to roughly cut the noodles into 5-cm lengths. Pound the garlic, peppercorns and salt to a rough paste using a mortar and pestle. Heat the vegetable oil in a wok or large frying pan over medium heat. Add the garlic paste and cook for about 1 minute. Add the pork and cook until just cooked through, using a fork to break it up as it cooks. Reserve 1 tablespoon of the grated carrot and add the remainder to the pork with the noodles, cabbage, fish sauce and sugar and cook for 3–4 minutes, or until the vegetables have softened. Remove from the heat and stir through the coriander. Set aside to cool completely.

Meanwhile, make the sweet carrot dipping sauce. Place all of the ingredients and 2 tablespoons of water in a small saucepan. Bring to a simmer and cook gently for 3 minutes, or until the sugar has dissolved. Stir in the reserved grated carrot and set aside until ready to serve.

To make the spring roll wrappers, combine both flours, salt and 1¾ cups of water in a bowl and mix until you get a thick paste. Add more water if your mixture looks more like a dough than a paste. Set aside for 30 minutes to rest.

Heat a small, non-stick frying pan over low heat until it's warm to the touch – we're going to use our fingers here, so make sure it's not too hot. Dip your fingers into the flour paste, scoop up about 2 tablespoons and spread it over the base of the pan with your fingers, using fast circular movements. You want to make a thin circle of paste about 15 cm in diameter. Use your fingers to scrape away any excess paste.

[continued overleaf] →

SMALL PLATES

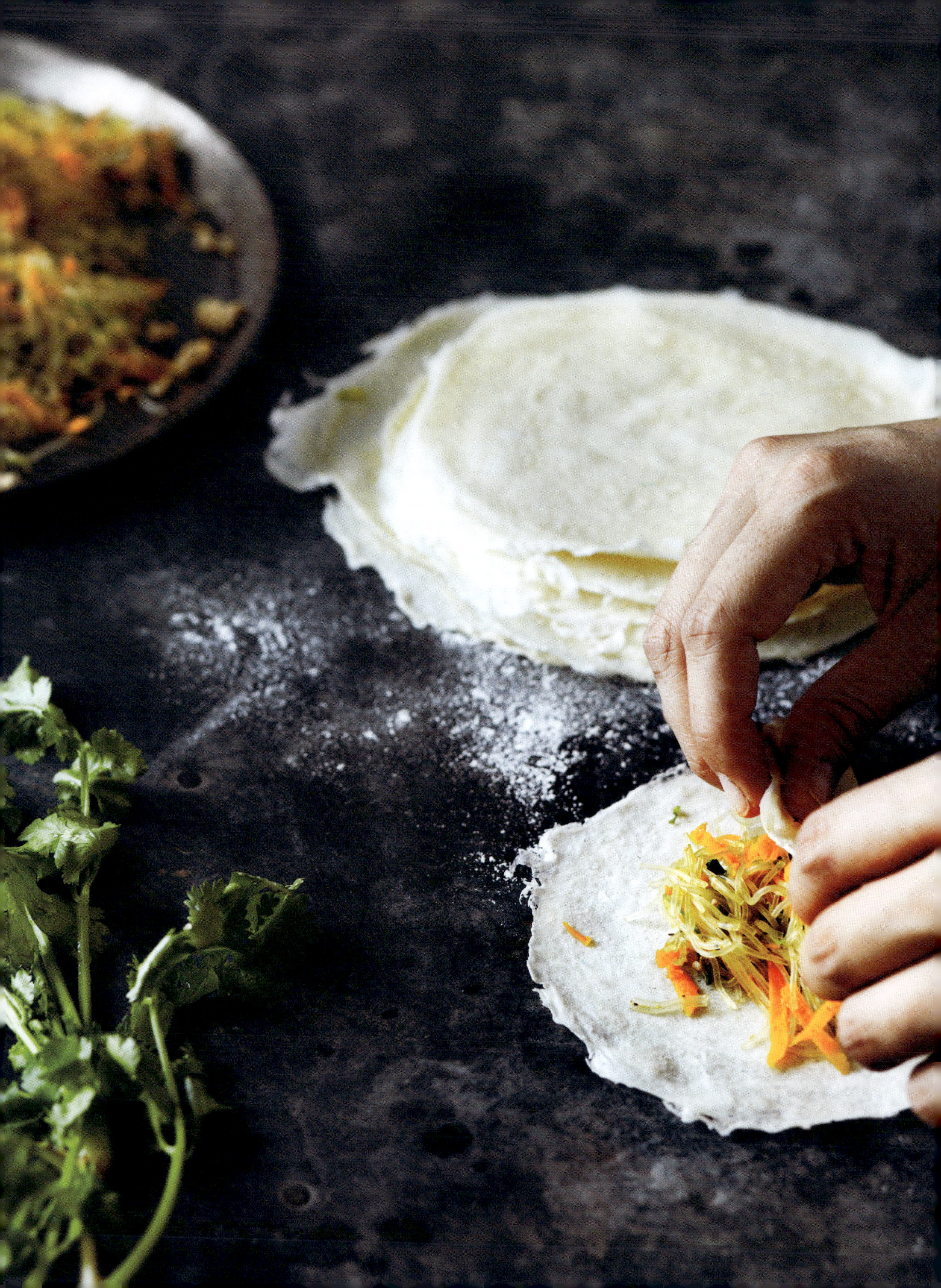

CONTINUED...

Cook for about 30 seconds, or until the wrapper has just set, not browned. You only need to cook one side. You should be able to peel the wrapper off the pan. Place on a plate and repeat with the remaining flour paste. Keep lifting the pan on and off the heat as needed to make sure the pan doesn't get too hot and you don't burn yourself. Cover the wrappers with a tea towel until you're ready to roll. (They should be left at room temperature and used as soon as you've made them as they will dry out and crack if left too long).

Now for the rolling. You will need to make a spring roll 'glue' to seal the spring rolls. Mix the extra 1 tablespoon of flour and 1 tablespooon of water together until you have a thick paste. Place a wrapper, smooth-side down, on a bench. Place 1 heaped tablespoon of filling just off-centre of the wrapper. Fold the wrapper over the filling, then fold in the sides (sort of like an envelope). Now roll up firmly into a cigar. Leave a bit of the wrapper free so you can brush it with the spring roll glue, then seal it up. Place on a tray lined with plastic wrap and repeat with the remaining wrappers and filling.

Heat 10 cm of the vegetable oil in a wok or large heavy-based saucepan to 180°C. You can tell if the oil is hot enough by dipping a wooden spoon into it – if furious little bubbles form around the spoon, then the oil's ready to go. Gently slide the spring rolls, in batches, into the oil and cook for about 3 minutes, or until golden all over. Remove with tongs and drain on paper towel. Serve hot with the sweet carrot dipping sauce.

MAKES ABOUT 25

NOTE: If you don't want to make your own spring roll wrappers, you can use store-bought fresh or frozen ones, thawed first. Store-bought wrappers are usually square instead of round like these homemade ones. If using a square wrapper, to roll them up, place a wrapper on a bench with one corner pointing towards you and roll up like above. While you're assembling the spring rolls, cover the store-bought wrappers with a damp tea towel to stop them drying out.

SMALL PLATES

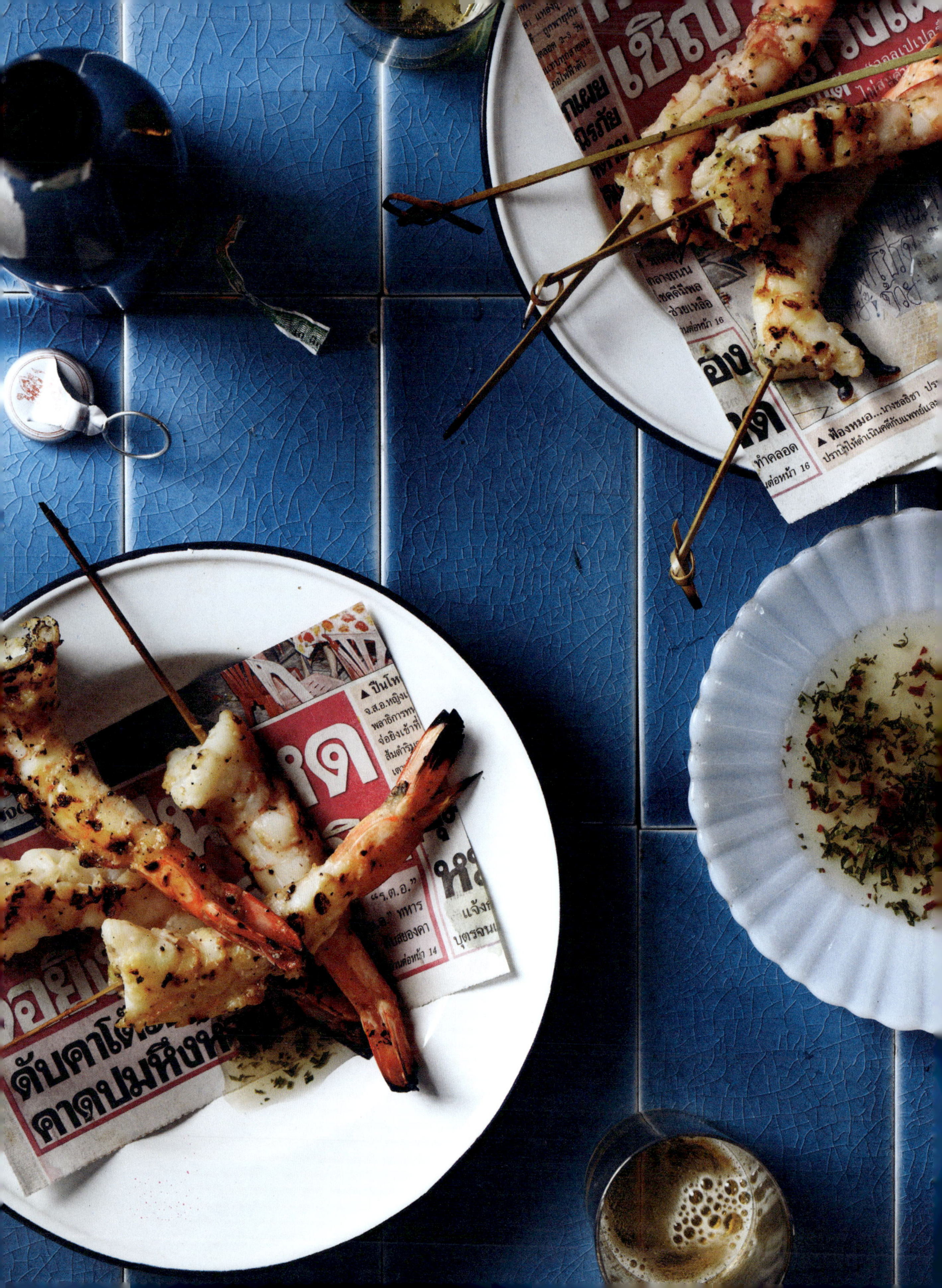

Grilled Prawns with Chilli & Coriander Sauce

The French have their 'mirepoix', the Italians have their soffritto and a 'holy trinity' of vegetables forms the basis of creole cooking. In Thai cuisine, it's a heady paste of garlic, coriander root and peppercorns that forms the foundation of many dishes. The garlicky, peppery paste can be used as a marinade — as it is here — it can be the beginnings of a soup or the start of a slow braise. The root of the coriander is packed with flavour, just be sure to give it a good rinse and scrape away any residual dirt.

4 coriander roots with 4 cm stem attached, cleaned
6 garlic cloves
1 teaspoon black peppercorns
20 raw large prawns, shelled and deveined with tails intact
2 teaspoons fish sauce
1 tablespoon vegetable oil
20 short bamboo skewers, soaked in water for 20 minutes

CHILLI & CORIANDER SAUCE
½ cup white sugar
⅓ cup white vinegar
2 tablespoons fish sauce
½ fresh long red chilli, finely chopped
1 tablespoon finely chopped coriander leaves

Place the coriander root, garlic and peppercorns in a mortar and pound to a rough paste with a pestle. Transfer to a large bowl and add the prawns, fish sauce and vegetable oil. Cover and refrigerate for 15 minutes to marinate.

Meanwhile, make the chilli and coriander sauce. Place the sugar, vinegar, fish sauce and 2 tablespoons of water in a small saucepan over high heat and cook for 3 minutes, or until the sugar has dissolved. Set aside to cool, then stir through the chilli and coriander.

Preheat a barbecue, chargrill plate or large frying pan to medium. Thread each prawn onto a skewer. Grill the prawns for about 2 minutes each side, or until just cooked. Pile onto a platter and serve with the chilli and coriander sauce.

SERVES 4

OYSTERS WITH CORIANDER & GREEN NAHM JIM DRESSING

I'm a little bit in love. I can't help it. A lush, salty oyster; the shock of green chilli spice and then the soothing overture of a creamy French champagne. I'm almost in tears just thinking about it. I love food.

½–1 fresh long green chilli
2 garlic cloves, roughly chopped
6 coriander roots with 4 cm stem attached, cleaned
3 teaspoons white sugar
⅓ cup fish sauce
⅓ cup lemon juice
24 freshly shucked oysters
chilled Champagne, to serve

For the nahm jim dressing, place the chilli (add more or less chilli depending on how spicy you like it), garlic, coriander root, sugar, fish sauce and lemon juice in a food processor and process to a smooth salad-dressing consistency. Set aside until ready to serve (or refrigerate in an airtight container for up to 1 week).

Top each oyster with 1 teaspoon of the dressing and serve with a glass of Champagne.

SERVES 4

SALT & THREE-PEPPER PRAWNS

There are only two types of salt and pepper dishes — the lucky ones and the not-so-lucky ones. The not-so-lucky (and these make up a vast majority) are left to languish in tepid oil and soggy cement-like batter. But there are a lucky few — fresh sweet seafood encrusted with crisp barnacles of salt and peppery crunch. Make yours one of the lucky ones.

- 1 tablespoon Sichuan peppercorns
- 1 teaspoon white peppercorns
- 1 teaspoon black peppercorns
- 1 teaspoon sea salt
- ½ cup plain flour
- vegetable oil, for deep-frying
- 500 g raw large prawns, shelled and deveined with tails intact
- lemon wedges, to serve

WASABI MAYONNAISE
- ½ cup Japanese mayonnaise, such as Kewpie *(available from an Asian grocer or the Asian section of most supermarkets)*
- 1 teaspoon wasabi paste

For the wasabi mayonnaise, combine the mayonnaise and wasabi together in a small bowl and refrigerate until ready to serve.

Heat a small frying pan over medium heat, add the Sichuan, white and black peppercorns and toast, keeping the spices moving in the hot pan, for 2 minutes, or until they start to release their lovely aromas. Transfer to a mortar, add the salt and grind to a powder. Reserve 1 teaspoon of the spice powder for serving. Place the remainder in a large bowl and combine with the flour.

Heat 10 cm of vegetable oil in a wok or large heavy-based saucepan to 180°C. You can tell if the oil is hot enough by dipping a wooden spoon into it – if furious little bubbles form around the spoon, then the oil's ready to go. Coat each prawn in the flour mixture and shake to remove the excess. Gently slide 4–5 prawns at a time into the oil and cook for about 2 minutes, or until pink and opaque. Remove with tongs and drain on paper towel. Sprinkle over the reserved spice powder and serve with the wasabi mayonnaise and the lemon wedges.

SERVES 4

DEEP-FRIED EGGS WITH SMOKED EEL MASH

My smoked eel mash is loosely based on a French provincial classic called 'brandade de morue'. In its simplest form, a brandade is a rich emulsion of salt cod, olive oil and garlic. My version uses smoked eel instead of salt cod. The secret to this decadent brandade lies in the vigorous mixing of the potatoes and fish as you incorporate the olive oil and cream.

2 tablespoons white vinegar
6 eggs, at room temperature
½ cup plain flour
3 eggs, lightly beaten
2 cups panko (Japanese) breadcrumbs — *available from an Asian grocer or the Asian section of most supermarkets*
vegetable oil, for deep-frying
sea salt
¼ cup basil leaves

SMOKED EEL MASH
150 ml pouring (single) cream
100 ml extra-virgin olive oil, plus extra for drizzling
2 garlic cloves, slightly bruised and peeled
2 sprigs thyme
1 kg floury potatoes (such as sebago, coliban or spunta), peeled and quartered
1 tablespoon salt
250 g smoked eel, skin and bones removed — *available from delicatessens or fishmongers*
1 tablespoon sea salt, plus extra to taste
¼ teaspoon freshly ground white pepper

For the deep-fried eggs, you will need to poach them first. Fill a large deep frying pan with water, add the vinegar and place over medium heat, until little bubbles start to form and rise from the base of the pan. You want the water to be hot but not simmering rapidly otherwise the eggs may break up. Crack each egg into a cup or small bowl, then slide into the water. Poach for about 4 minutes, or until the eggwhite is just set but the yolk is still wobbly like soft-set jelly. You may need to poach the eggs in 2 batches. Scoop out each egg with a slotted spoon and gently place in a bowl of iced water to cool. Lift each egg out with a slotted spoon and drain well. Coat each egg with the flour, then dip in the beaten egg and coat with the breadcrumbs. Set aside.

For the smoked eel mash, place the cream, oil, garlic and thyme in a small saucepan over low heat and heat until just simmering. Remove from the heat and leave to infuse while you cook the potato.

Place the potato in a large saucepan, cover with cold water and add the salt. Bring to the boil and cook for 20 minutes, or until cooked through. Drain and mash. Cover to keep warm.

Break up the eel with a fork and mash well in a large bowl. Add the mashed potato and mix vigorously with a wooden spoon. Strain the cream mixture and reheat until just warm. Gradually add the cream to the eel mixture while beating continuously. You'll need a bit of elbow grease for this – you want the mixture to emulsify into a thick, creamy but slightly lumpy paste. Throw in the sea salt and all of the pepper. Cover to keep warm while you tend to the eggs.

Heat 10 cm of oil in a large heavy-based saucepan to 180°C. You can tell if the oil is hot enough by dipping a wooden spoon into it – if furious little bubbles form around the spoon, the oil's ready to go. Gently slide the crumbed eggs into the oil, in 2 batches if necessary, and cook for about 3 minutes, or until golden all over. Remove with a slotted spoon and drain on paper towel. Season to taste with the sea salt.

To serve, place a good dollop of warm smoked eel mash on serving plates. Drizzle with a little olive oil, top with a deep-fried egg and scatter with the basil leaves.

SERVES 6

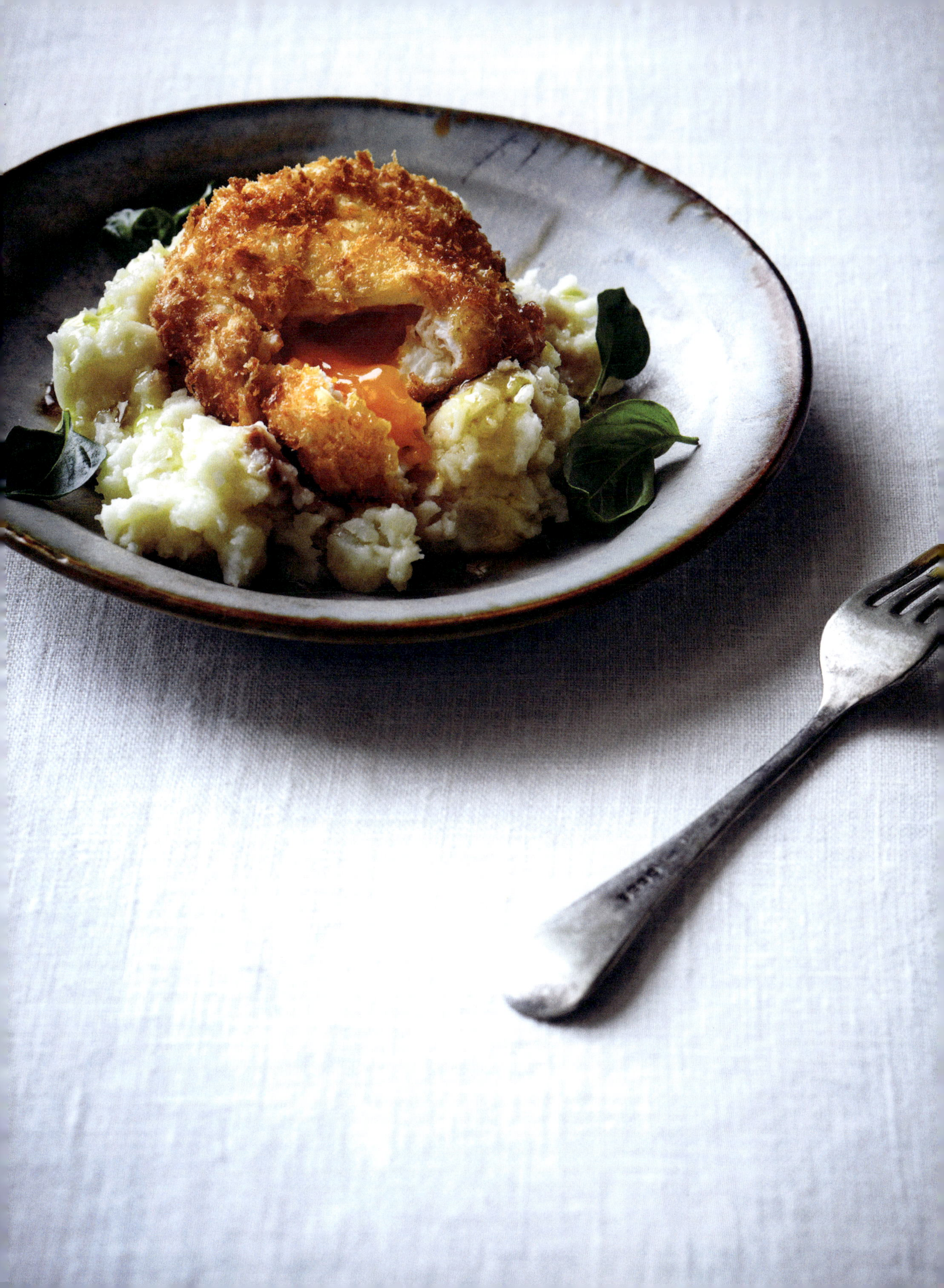

THAI FISHCAKES WITH CHILLI, CUCUMBER & CORIANDER SAUCE

The secret to a good fishcake lies in the squelching. Once you've made the fishcake paste, you need to get your hands dirty by squeezing, massaging and kneading the mixture for a good couple of minutes. I'm sure there's some technical, scientific explanation as to why squelching produces the right texture in a fishcake, but all I'm concerned about is that it works. If squelching fish isn't your thing, then leave the fish paste to whiz around in the food processor for a couple of extra minutes to get the same effect. What you're aiming to achieve here is a fishcake that's smooth and spongy in texture, not crumbly and flaky.

500 g firm white fish fillets (snapper, swordfish, ling or barramundi work well), skinned, pin-boned and cut into chunks
2 tablespoons Thai Red Curry Paste (see page 110)
1 eggwhite
8 snake beans, trimmed *available at Asian grocers but you could substitute green beans*
6 kaffir lime leaves, thinly sliced *[see note]*
1 teaspoon sea salt
vegetable oil, for shallow-frying

CHILLI, CUCUMBER & CORIANDER SAUCE
½ cup white sugar
⅓ cup white vinegar
2 tablespoons fish sauce
½ fresh long red chilli, halved, seeded and finely chopped (optional)
2 tablespoons finely chopped coriander stems and leaves
¼ cup seeded and finely diced cucumber

For the chilli, cucumber and coriander sauce, place the sugar, vinegar, fish sauce and 2 tablespoons of water in a small saucepan over high heat and cook for about 3 minutes, or until the sugar has dissolved. Set aside to cool, then stir through the chilli, coriander and cucumber. Pour into a small serving bowl and set aside until ready to serve.

For the fishcakes, place the fish, curry paste and eggwhite in a food processor and process for about 2 minutes, or until you get a smooth paste. Tip into a large bowl. Slice the beans into 2-mm-thick discs and add to the fish mixture with the kaffir lime leaves and salt. Give it a good mix with your hands, squelching and squeezing it for a few minutes. Shape into little rounds, 5 cm in diameter and 1 cm thick – you don't want whopping great patties. You should get about 24 fishcakes.

Heat about 2 cm of vegetable oil in a large frying pan over medium heat. Shallow-fry the fishcakes, in batches, for about 1 minute each side, or until golden. Drain on paper towel.

Serve with the chilli, cucumber and coriander dipping sauce.

SERVES 6

NOTE: To thinly slice the kaffir lime leaves into delicate shards, stack the leaves on top of each other, roll them up into a cigar shape and slice. Discard any bits of stalk.

SMOKED TROUT & GOAT'S CHEESE DIP

You could use any smoked fish you like in place of the smoked trout in this recipe. I like to search out the biggest smoked fish I can find. I flake off all the lovely pinky flesh and use half of it in a salad with rocket, a squirt of lemon juice and a drizzle of olive oil. The rest goes into this incredibly moreish dip.

200 g hot-smoked trout, skin and bones removed, flesh flaked (about 1 tightly packed cup)
120 g goat's cheese
¼ cup chopped dill
½ cup chopped basil leaves
2 tablespoons lemon juice
¼ teaspoon sea salt
extra-virgin olive oil, for drizzling
freshly ground black pepper
thin slices toasted baguette, fresh bread or crackers, to serve

Place the trout, cheese, dill, basil, lemon juice and salt in a food processor and process for a few seconds until well combined but still a little chunky. Spoon onto a serving plate, drizzle with the olive oil and grind over some pepper. Serve with toasted baguette, fresh bread or crackers.

MAKES ABOUT 1½ CUPS

SMALL PLATES

PIGGY PATTIES WITH WASABI MAYONNAISE & APPLE SALAD

I adore New York chef David Chang's introduction to the pig's head 'torchon' recipe in his book 'momofuku'. He basically says, pigs have heads, so deal with it. These sorts of recipes remind us that pork chops, steaks and chicken drumsticks don't simply come from the fridge section of the supermarket. The meat we eat comes from real, living, breathing animals — something you certainly can't forget when you've got a whole pig's head sitting in your kitchen sink. Before you even attempt this recipe, check that you have a stockpot big enough to fit a pig's head. My stockpot is 28 cm wide x 24 cm high (11-litre-capacity), which fits a pig's head snugly. These piggy patties are quite rich, so one or two per person as an entrée is perfect.

you'll need to order this in advance from your butcher →

3 kg whole pig's head
2 carrots, roughly chopped
1 brown onion, roughly chopped
3 stalks flat-leaf parsley
¼ cup finely chopped coriander leaves
1 teaspoon Chinese five-spice
1 tablespoon soy sauce
sea salt and freshly ground black pepper
1 cup plain flour
3 eggs, lightly beaten
2 cups panko (Japanese) breadcrumbs
vegetable oil, for shallow-frying

available from an Asian grocer or the Asian section of most supermarkets →

WASABI MAYONNAISE
¼ cup Japanese mayonnaise, such as Kewpie *← available from an Asian grocer or the Asian section of most supermarkets*
½ teaspoon wasabi paste
juice of ½ lemon

APPLE SALAD
1 green apple, peeled, cored and cut into matchsticks
juice of ¼ lemon
2 teaspoons olive oil
frehly ground black pepper
50 g wild rocket (about 1 large handful)

Place the pig's head in a clean sink. Take a sharp knife or an unused disposable razor and shave off any hairy bits. Place the head in a stockpot and throw in the carrot, onion and parsley. Cover with water, bring to the boil, reduce the heat to low and gently simmer for 3 ½ hours, or until the skin is soft and gelatinous. Remove from the heat and let the pig's head cool in the liquid for about 30 minutes.

Lift the pig's head out of the stockpot and place on a large tray. Discard the cooking liquid and vegetables. Once the pig's head is just cool enough to handle (but still a little warm), it's time to slice and dice.

Cut off the ears and place in a large bowl — this is your meat bowl. Use a paring knife to peel back the skin of the pig's head to reveal the fat and meat underneath. Cut and pull off chunks of fat and place them in another large bowl — this is your fat bowl. Continue picking through the meat and fat, sorting each into their respective bowls. You will need to feel your way through this process. The fat will look and feel like fat, whereas the meat will be pale and stringy when pulled apart. Discard anything that doesn't look or feel like fat or meat. There will be a big chunk of fat on the surface of the cheek and a good amount of meat beneath it.

Finely dice the meat and ears and place in a large bowl. Take a handful of fat and chop into small chunks. Have a look at how much meat is in the bowl and add just under half that amount in chopped fat, so the ratio of meat to fat is about half and half but with slightly more meat than fat.

The hard part is over. Now, to make the piggy patties. Add the coriander, five-spice and soy sauce to the meat and fat mixture and season to taste with some pepper. Use your hands to mix and squelch everything together. Check for seasoning and add salt to taste; it will probably need at least 1 teaspoon.

Roll ¼-cup amounts of the mixture into balls, then flatten slightly between the palms of your hands. Place on a tray, cover with plastic wrap and refrigerate for at least 2 hours, or until firm.

Now it's time to crumb. Place the flour on a large plate, the beaten egg in a shallow bowl and the breadcrumbs on a separate large plate. Dip each patty in the flour, then in the egg and then the breadcrumbs. Place on a tray and pop in the fridge while you make the wasabi mayonnaise and apple salad.

For the wasabi mayonnaise, place the mayonnaise, wasabi and lemon juice in a bowl and mix well. Cover with plastic wrap and set aside.

For the apple salad, place the apple, lemon juice and olive oil in a bowl, season to taste with the pepper and toss to combine. Add the rocket to the salad just before serving so it remains lovely and crisp.

Heat 2 cm of vegetable oil in a large heavy-based frying pan until hot. Shallow-fry the patties for about 2 minutes each side, or until golden. You don't want to overcrowd the pan, so shallow-fry them in 2 batches if you need to. Remove with tongs and drain on paper towel. Serve hot with the apple salad and wasabi mayonnaise.

MAKES ABOUT 12

SMALL PLATES

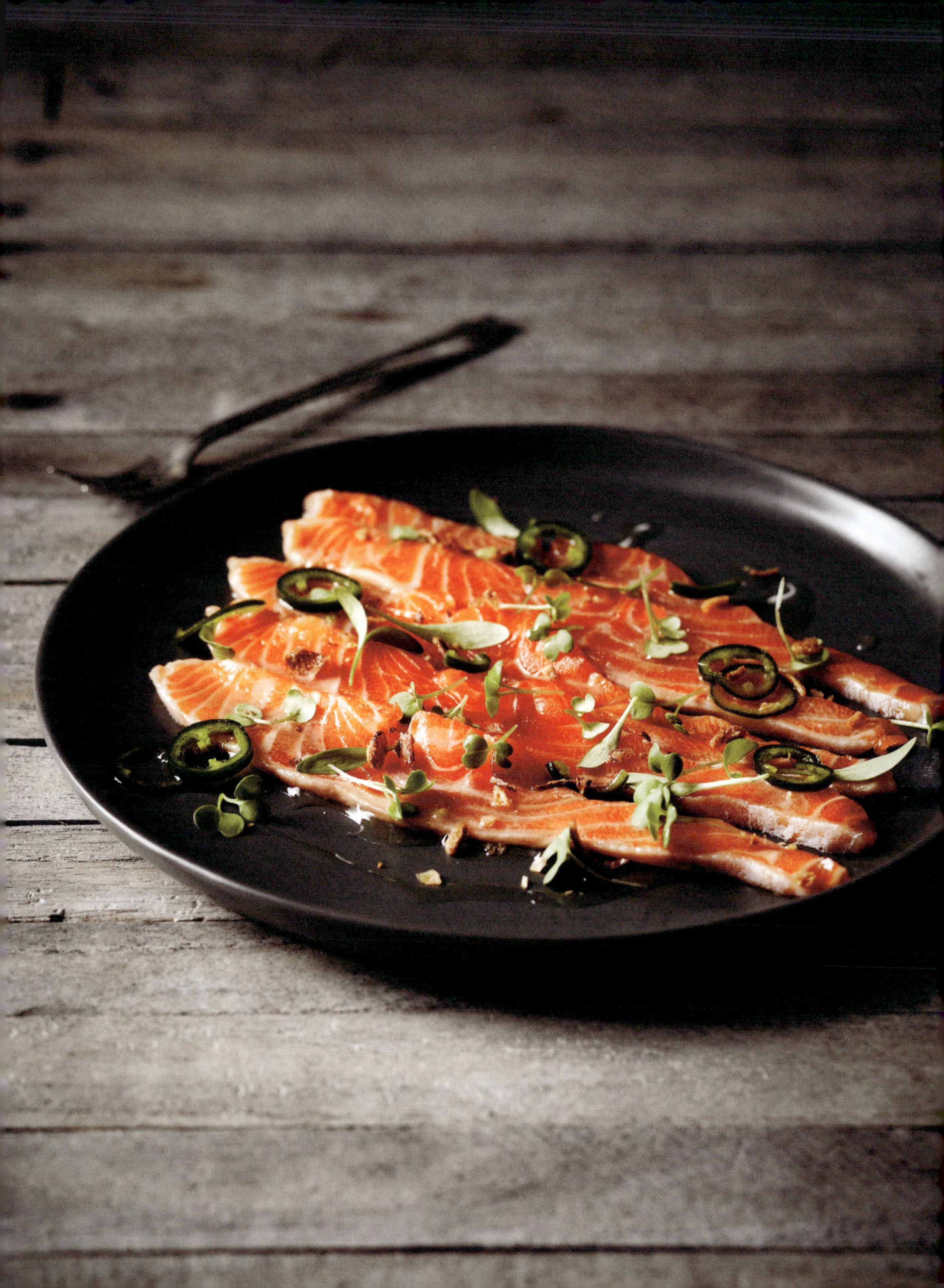

OCEAN TROUT WITH JALAPEÑO DRESSING

Make sure your ocean trout is sashimi grade when you buy it from your fishmonger. Sashimi grade means the fish has been caught and handled in a way that makes it suitable for eating raw. It should be a lovely firm, blushing pinky-orange fillet that smells faintly of the sea. Keep the fish in the fridge until just before serving because it will be more difficult to slice as it gets warm.

2 tablespoons fish sauce
2 tablespoons lemon juice
1 teaspoon white sugar
1 jalapeño chilli, finely sliced
300 g sashimi-grade ocean trout fillet, skinned and pin-boned
1 teaspoon fried shallots ← available from an Asian grocer or the Asian section of most supermarkets
2 tablespoons baby herbs, such as coriander or mustard cress

For the jalapeño dressing, whisk together the fish sauce, lemon juice, sugar and chilli in a small bowl to make a dressing.

Use a very sharp knife to cut 3-mm thick slices of ocean trout. Arrange on a serving plate. Spoon over generous amounts of the dressing and sprinkle the whole lot with the fried shallots and baby herb leaves. Serve immediately.

SERVES 4

SMALL PLATES 67

BEEF CARPACCIO

There are butchers and then there are 'butchers'. Richard Gunner from Feast! Fine Foods in South Australia is in the 'butcher' category, as well as being a lamb and beef producer. I knew he was dedicated when he asked, 'Marion, what do you reckon about a meat dessert?'

It was Richard who let me in on the secret to the best carpaccio ever — big statement, I know. It's all in the cut of meat. Most recipes call for beef fillet, but Richard says you get more flavour out of secondary cuts such as topside. The more work a muscle does, the more flavour it has. And that's really important in a dish such as carpaccio where the beef is the star performer.

Chefs often talk about how important it is to establish good relationships with producers and suppliers in order to get the best ingredients and I think the same should apply for us home cooks. Find yourself a 'butcher' butcher and make friends. Have a chat about all things meaty whenever you pop in: which cut of meat is suitable, where it comes from, how best to cook it. These guys are experts and you'll more than likely learn something new every time. For this recipe, a good butcher will be able to cut you the smallest muscle from the topside, called the eye.

1 teaspoon coriander seeds
2 teaspoons black peppercorns
¼ teaspoon sea salt
1 tablespoon finely chopped dill, plus extra to serve
1 tablespoon finely chopped flat-leaf parsley, plus extra to serve
300 g piece of good-quality eye of topside
¼ cup finely shaved parmesan

DRESSING
¼ cup extra-virgin olive oil
1 teaspoon Dijon mustard
½ teaspoon sea salt
1 golden (French) shallot, finely chopped
1 tablespoon lemon juice

First let's make a herby, peppery coating for the beef. Heat a small frying pan over medium heat, add the coriander seeds and peppercorns and toast, keeping the spices moving in the hot pan, for 2 minutes, or until you can just smell their lovely aroma. Transfer to a mortar, add the salt and grind to a powder with a pestle. Pour onto a plate and mix with the dill and parsley. Roll the beef in the herb mixture to evenly coat.
Wrap tightly in plastic wrap and pop in the freezer for about 30 minutes to partially freeze — this will make it easier to slice.

Unwrap the beef and thinly slice, using a sharp knife. Aim to cut whole slices — don't worry if they're a little thick because we'll take care of that. Sandwich each slice between plastic wrap and use the flat side of a meat mallet, rolling pin or even a wine bottle to gently pound or roll the slices to about 1 mm thick. Arrange on a serving plate, cover with plastic wrap and refrigerate until ready to serve.

For the dressing, whisk together the olive oil, mustard, salt, shallot and lemon juice in a small bowl. Set aside until ready to serve.

To serve, drizzle the beef with the dressing, season to taste with salt and top with the parmesan and extra dill and parsley.

SERVES 6

GRILLED QUAILS

I like to encourage finger food whenever possible. Yes, we must be mindful of our table manners, which is why I stipulate that the licking of fingers must be done 'quietly'. I find picking at a quail with a knife and fork to be a joyless exercise. You could go to the trouble of boning each quail before you cook it, but then you wouldn't have an excuse to lick your fingers at the table.

8 x large quails
4 garlic cloves, peeled
4 sprigs thyme
1 sprig rosemary
2 teaspoons sea salt
finely grated zest and juice of 1 lemon
½ cup extra-virgin olive oil
freshly ground black pepper

Working with one quail at a time, use kitchen scissors or a sharp knife to cut down both sides of the backbone of the quail, then discard the bone. Open up each quail and flatten it out a bit so you can cut the bird in half through the breastbone. Give the quail halves a quick rinse and pat dry with paper towel.

Place the garlic, thyme, rosemary and salt in a mortar and pound to a rough paste with a pestle. Transfer to a large bowl, add the lemon zest and juice, olive oil and generous grindings of pepper. Add the quail and rub the marinade into the flesh using your hands. Cover and refrigerate for at least 1 hour to marinate.

Preheat a barbecue grill plate or large frying pan until piping hot. Cook the quail, in batches, if necessary, for 3 minutes each side. Baste as you go with a little extra marinade. Pile onto a serving platter and serve with napkins.

SERVES 8

FIGS, GORGONZOLA & PROSCIUTTO

we don't need to have a chat here. no long-winded instructions, no childhood recollections. some things are just too perfect for words.

fresh plump little figs
wafer thin slices prosciutto
big wedge Gorgonzola dolcelatte ← [see note]

Preheat the oven to 180°C.

Slice the stems off the figs. Make 2 cuts, in the shape of a cross, about halfway through each fig and stuff with a little of the Gorgonzola. Wrap each fig in a slice of prosciutto and bake until the cheese melts and oozes. Eat warm.

SERVES AS MANY AS YOU WANT

NOTE: Gorgonzola dolcelatte is lovely and soft and slightly sweeter than its picante cousin. If you can't get Gorgonzola dolcelatte, subsitute any other soft, creamy blue.

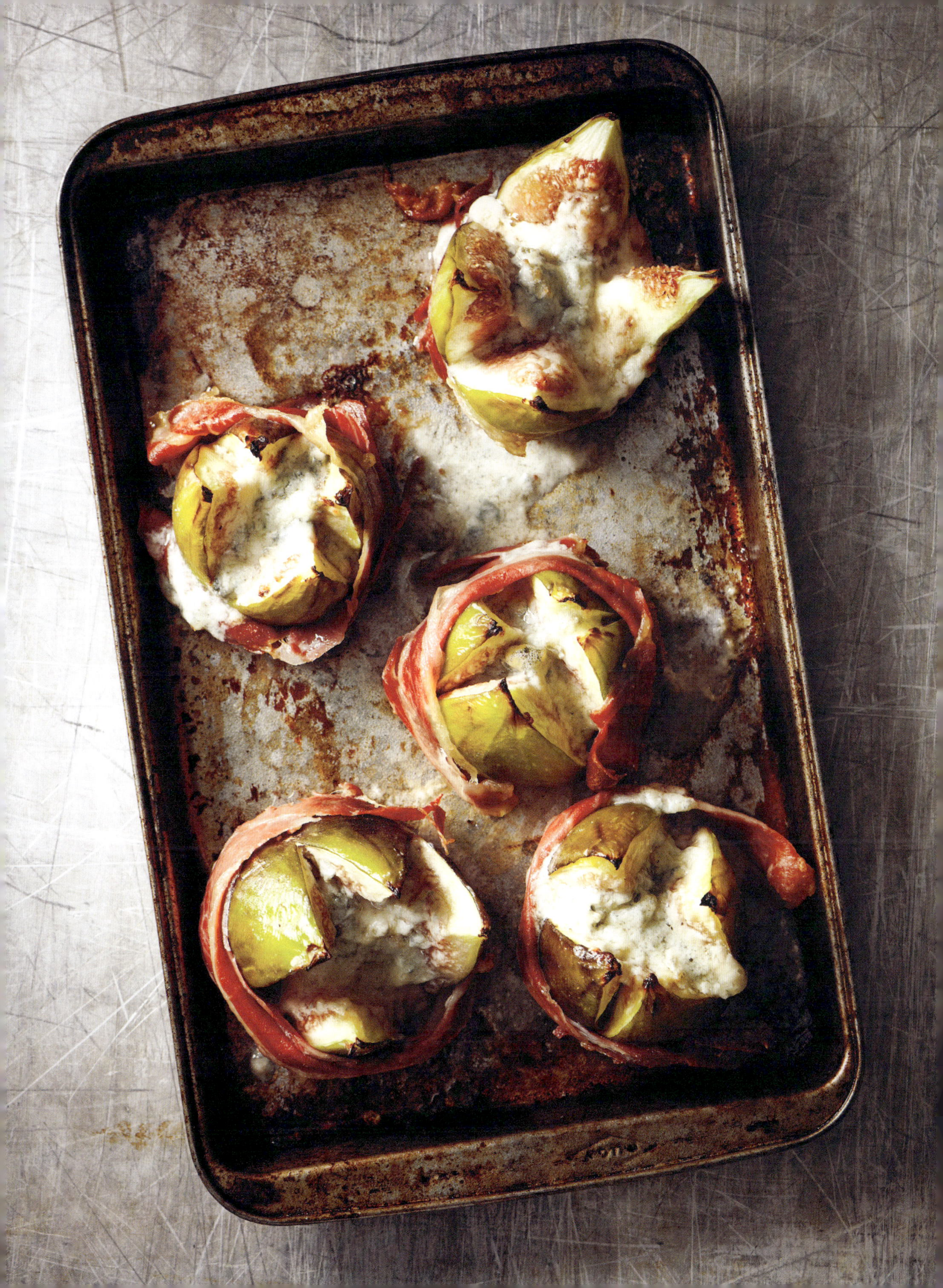

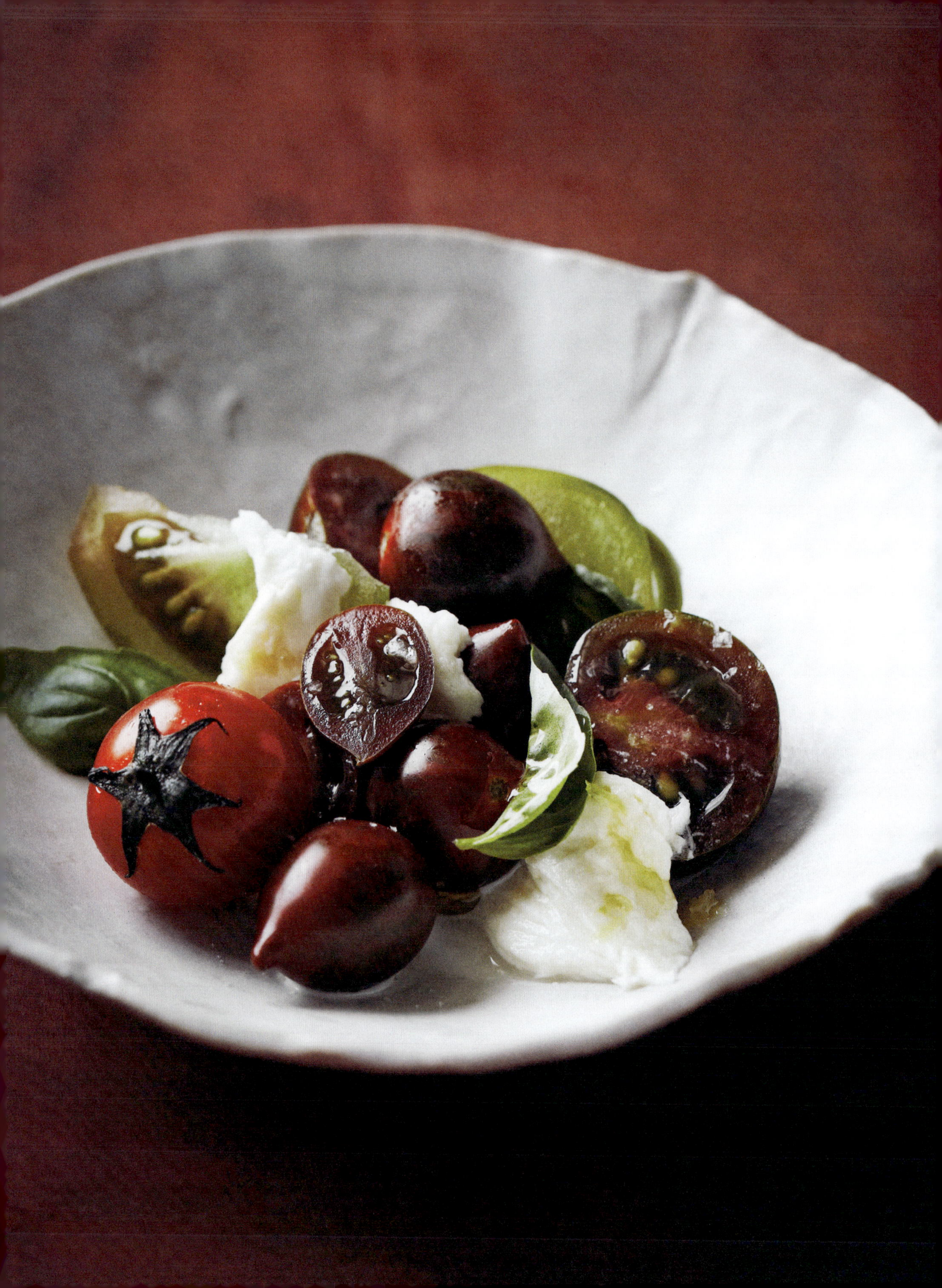

BUFFALO MOZZARELLA & TOMATO SALAD

Pedestrian versions of this salad can be made all year round: unripe tomatoes, crunchy and devoid of flavour, paired with hard, yellow balls of some sort of plastic cheese masquerading as mozzarella. Yes, you can make this salad any time of year. But it's only when the stars align that this little salad ascends to the divine.

The first problem to overcome is finding fresh buffalo mozzarella. A good cheese providore may have imported Italian mozzarella, but there are some Australian producers who also craft this magnificent cheese. Whether Italian or Australian, the buffalo mozzarella should be a milky white colour with a smooth shiny surface and a soft interior that yields into chunks of fine strands when you break it open.

Your final mission is to find tomatoes. I'm talking about good tomatoes — the ones that actually taste like tomatoes. Wait until the height of summer and search out the most audacious sun-ripened beauties you can find. Black Russians, big red beafsteaks or green zebras — it doesn't matter what variety you choose, just as long as they're juicy and packed with flavour.

⅓ cup good-quality extra-virgin olive oil
finely grated zest of 1 lemon
2 anchovy fillets, finely chopped
1 kg assorted ripe juicy tomatoes
sea salt and freshly ground black pepper
250 g ball buffalo mozzarella (the real stuff)
¼ cup basil leaves

Whisk together the olive oil, lemon zest and anchovies in a small bowl to make a dressing.

Cut large tomatoes into thickish slices but leave any small cherry tomatoes whole or halved. Arrange your beautiful tomato pieces on a serving platter or individual plates. Season the tomatoes liberally with the salt and pepper.

Break the ball of mozzarella into rough chunks, like lovely little puffs of cloud, and scatter them over the tomato. Fling the basil over the top and splash around generous spoonfuls of dressing. Season with a little more salt and pepper and devour.

SERVES 4

SMALL PLATES

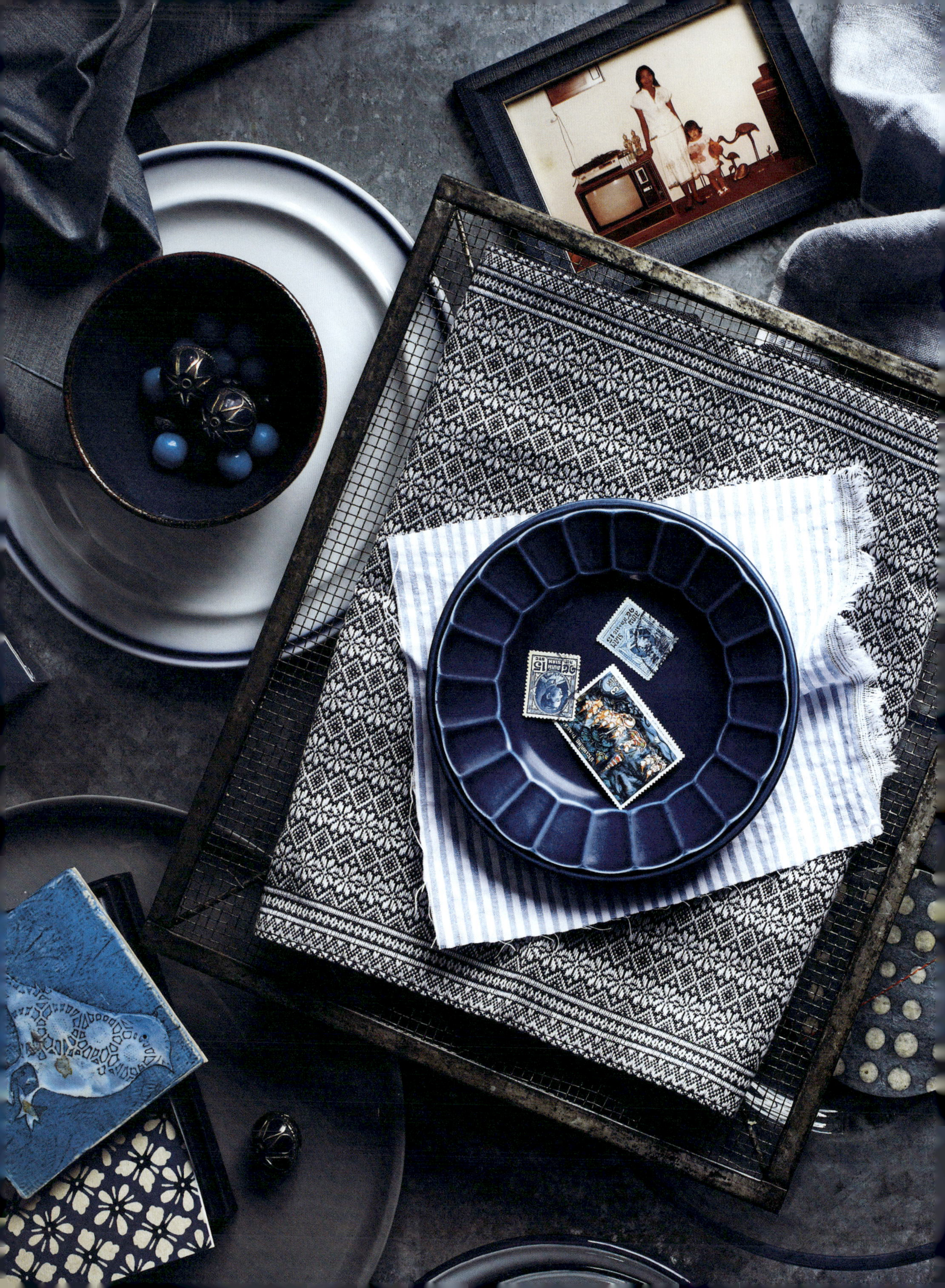

BIG PLATES

THE PLEASURES OF PREPARING

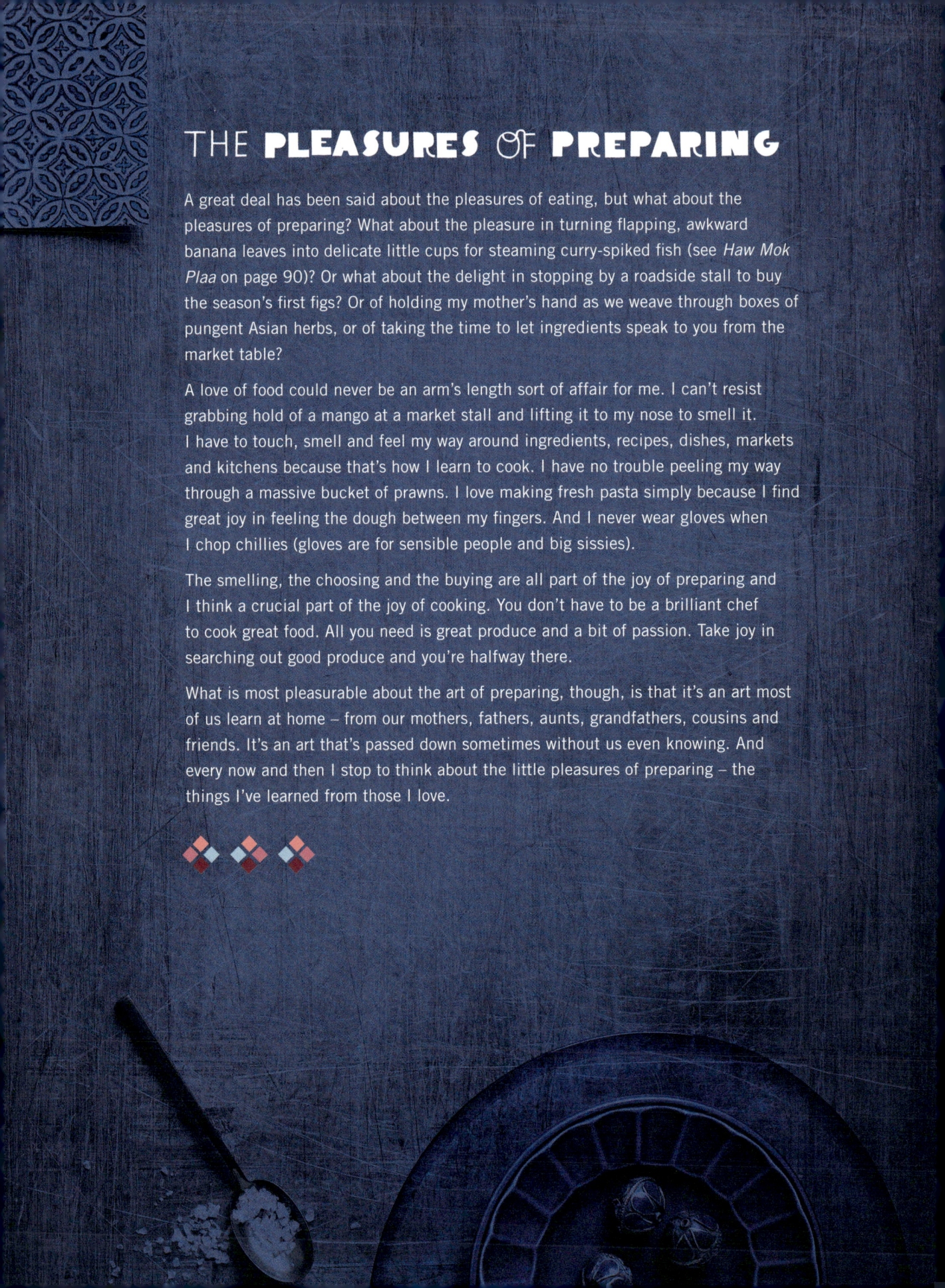

A great deal has been said about the pleasures of eating, but what about the pleasures of preparing? What about the pleasure in turning flapping, awkward banana leaves into delicate little cups for steaming curry-spiked fish (see *Haw Mok Plaa* on page 90)? Or what about the delight in stopping by a roadside stall to buy the season's first figs? Or of holding my mother's hand as we weave through boxes of pungent Asian herbs, or of taking the time to let ingredients speak to you from the market table?

A love of food could never be an arm's length sort of affair for me. I can't resist grabbing hold of a mango at a market stall and lifting it to my nose to smell it. I have to touch, smell and feel my way around ingredients, recipes, dishes, markets and kitchens because that's how I learn to cook. I have no trouble peeling my way through a massive bucket of prawns. I love making fresh pasta simply because I find great joy in feeling the dough between my fingers. And I never wear gloves when I chop chillies (gloves are for sensible people and big sissies).

The smelling, the choosing and the buying are all part of the joy of preparing and I think a crucial part of the joy of cooking. You don't have to be a brilliant chef to cook great food. All you need is great produce and a bit of passion. Take joy in searching out good produce and you're halfway there.

What is most pleasurable about the art of preparing, though, is that it's an art most of us learn at home – from our mothers, fathers, aunts, grandfathers, cousins and friends. It's an art that's passed down sometimes without us even knowing. And every now and then I stop to think about the little pleasures of preparing – the things I've learned from those I love.

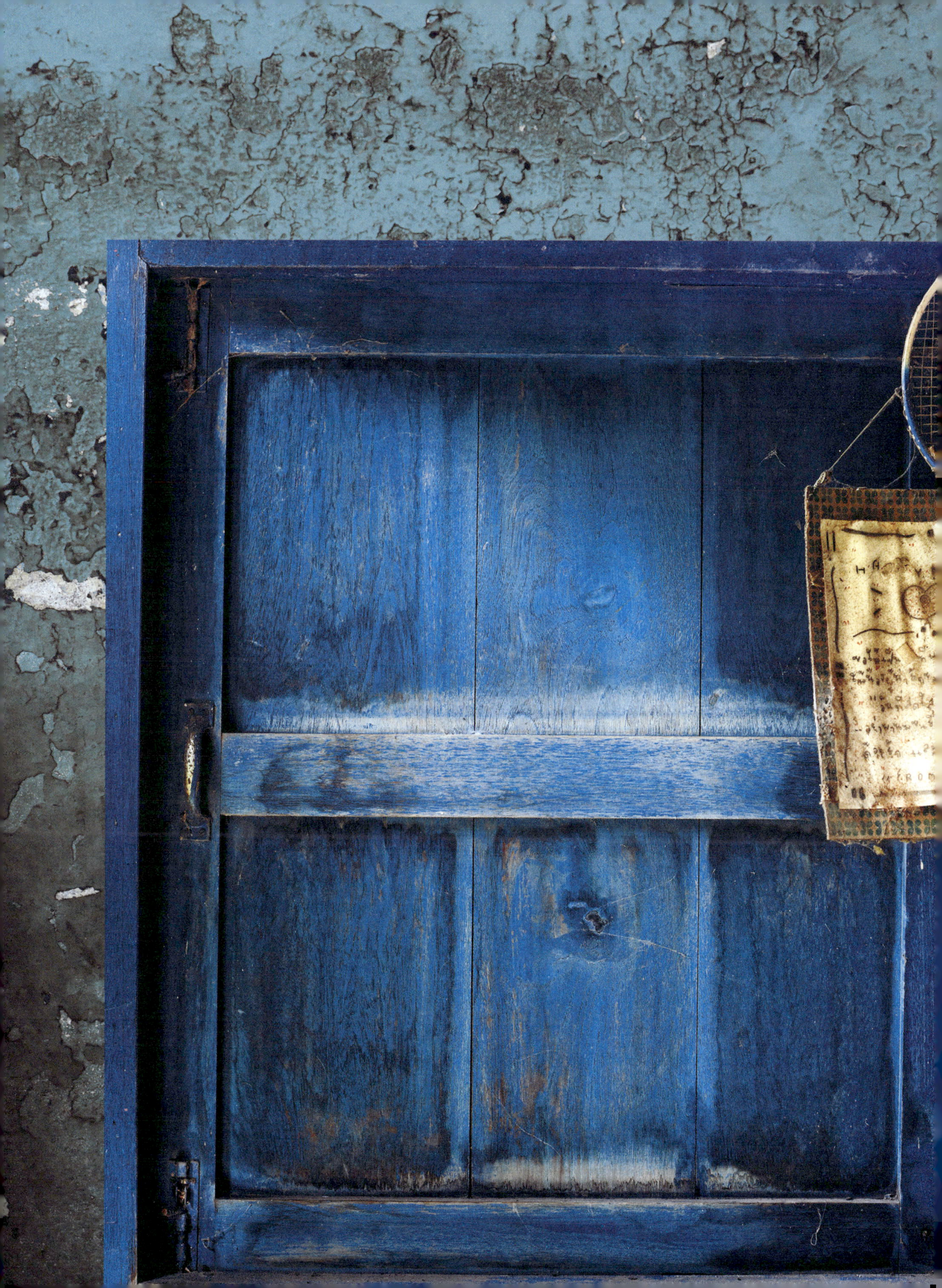

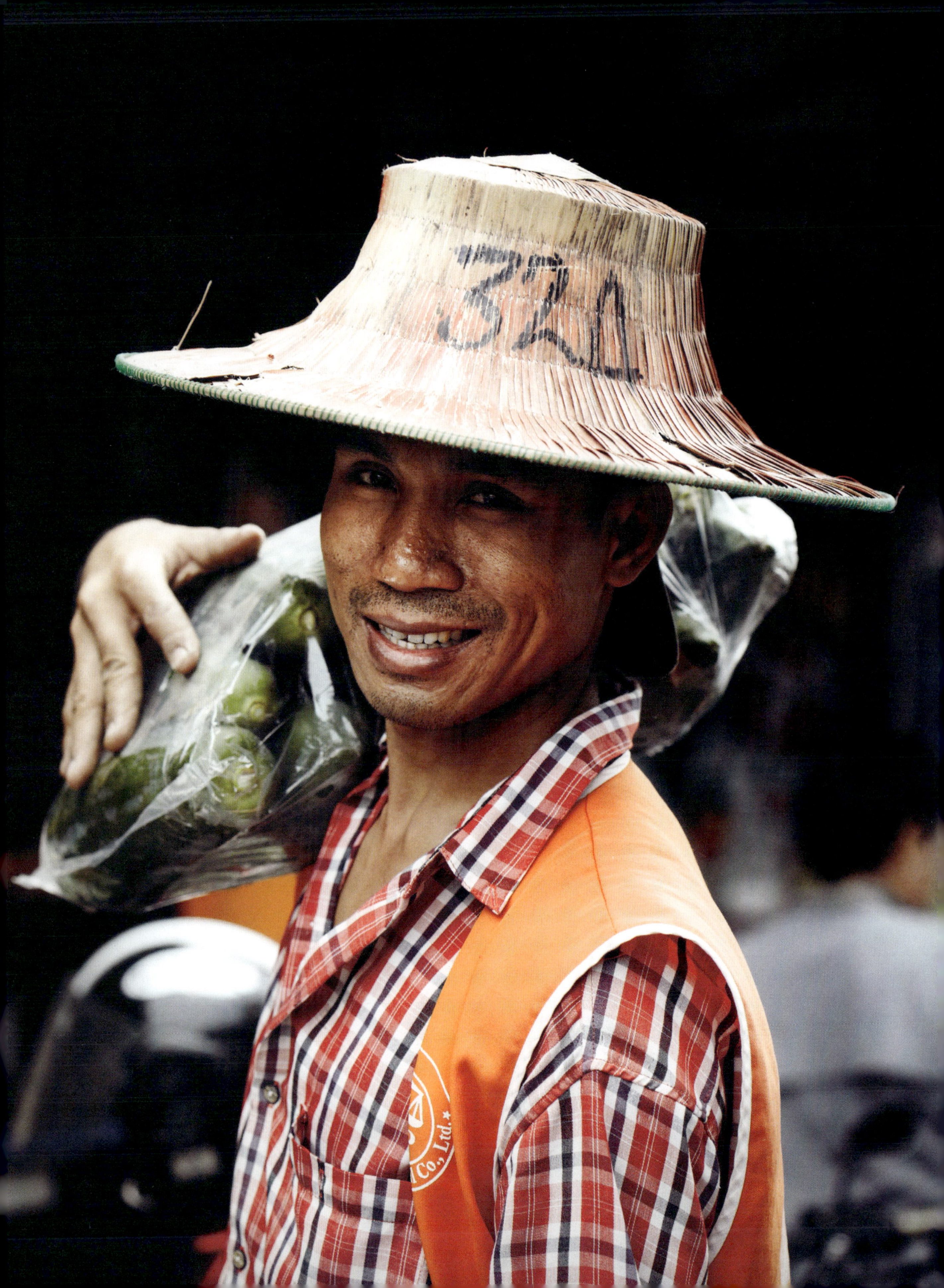
Co., Ltd.

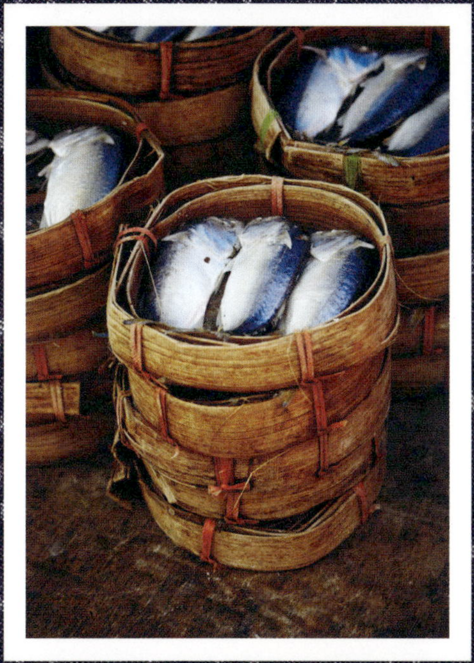

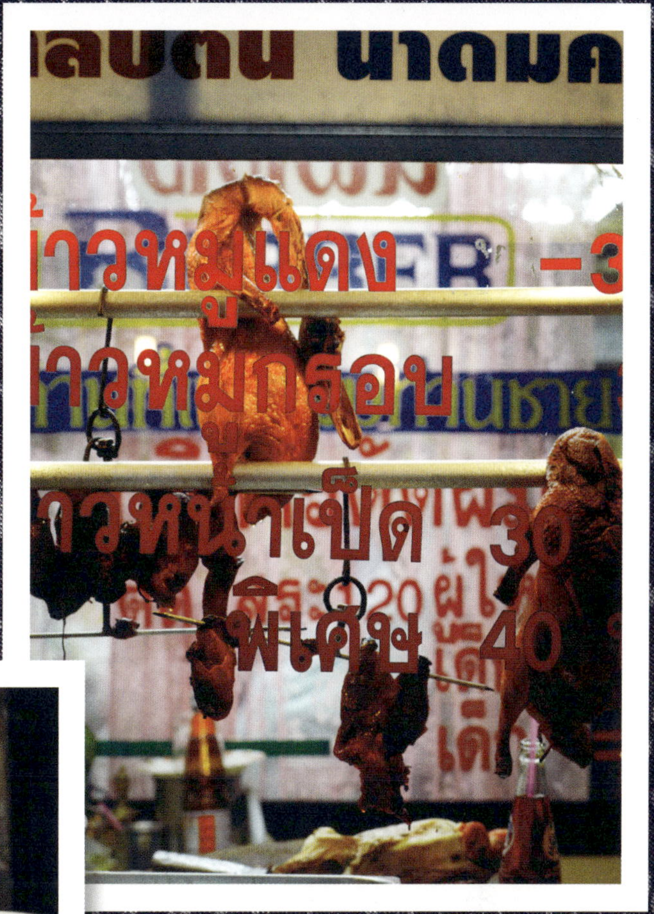
าวหมูแดง
าวหมูกรอบ
าวหน้าเป็ด 30
พิเศษ 40

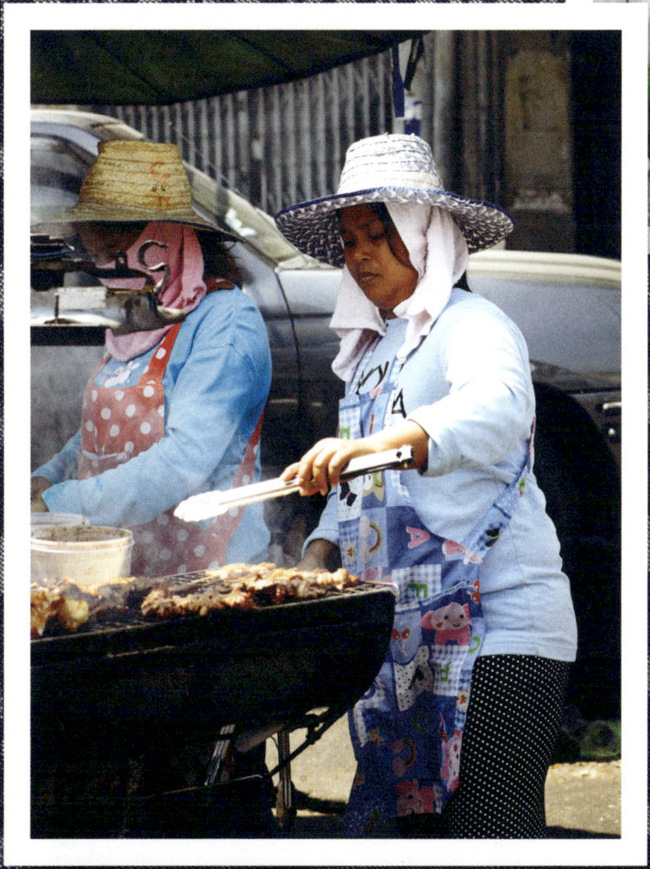

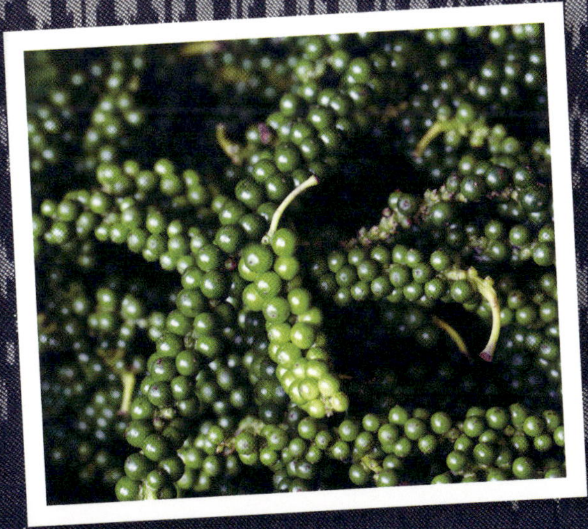

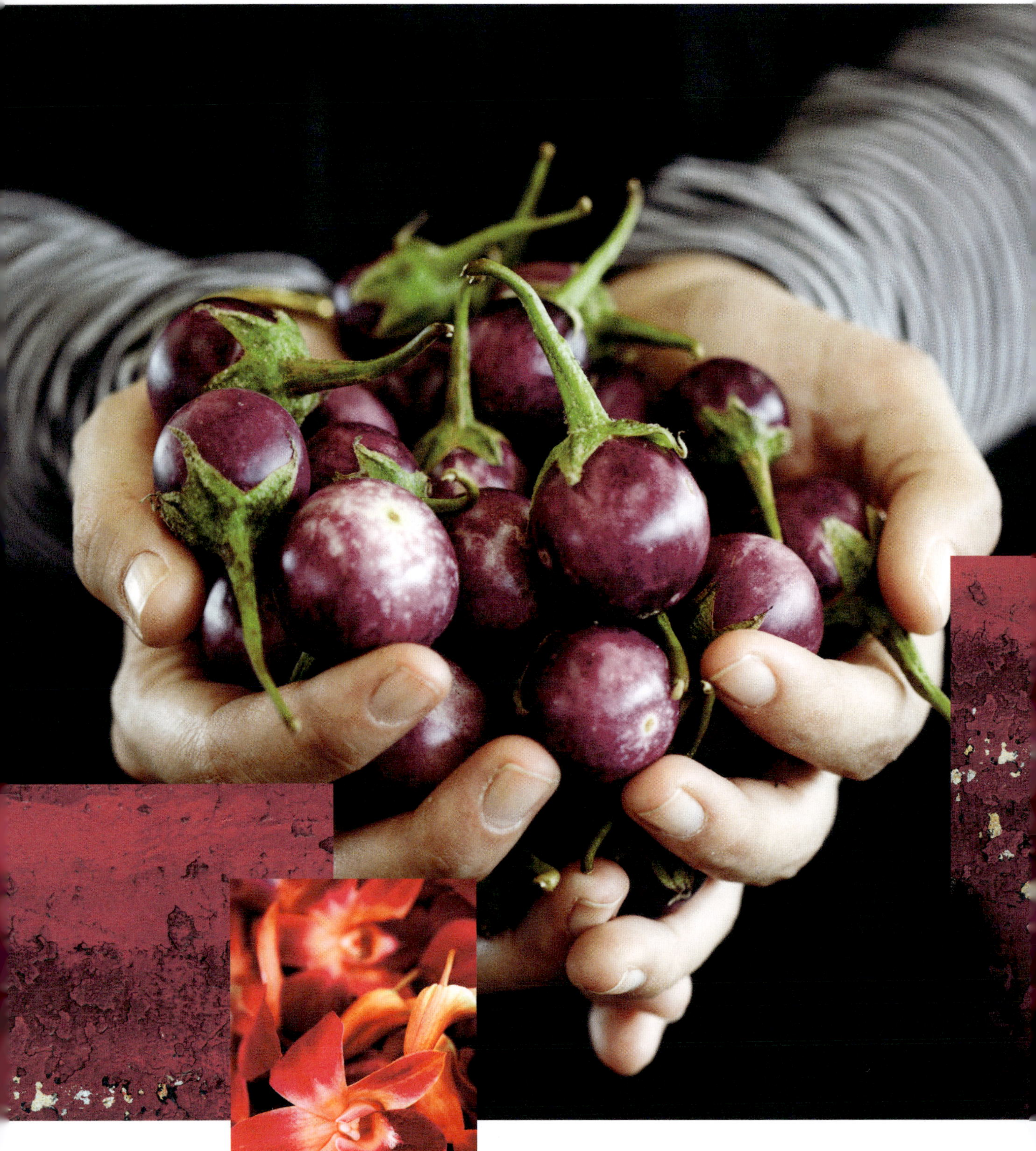

นายวิชัย สถาพรประสาธน์
นางสุธาทิพย์ สถาพรประสาธน์
และบุตร-ธิดา ถวายให้
วัดใหญ่นครชุม

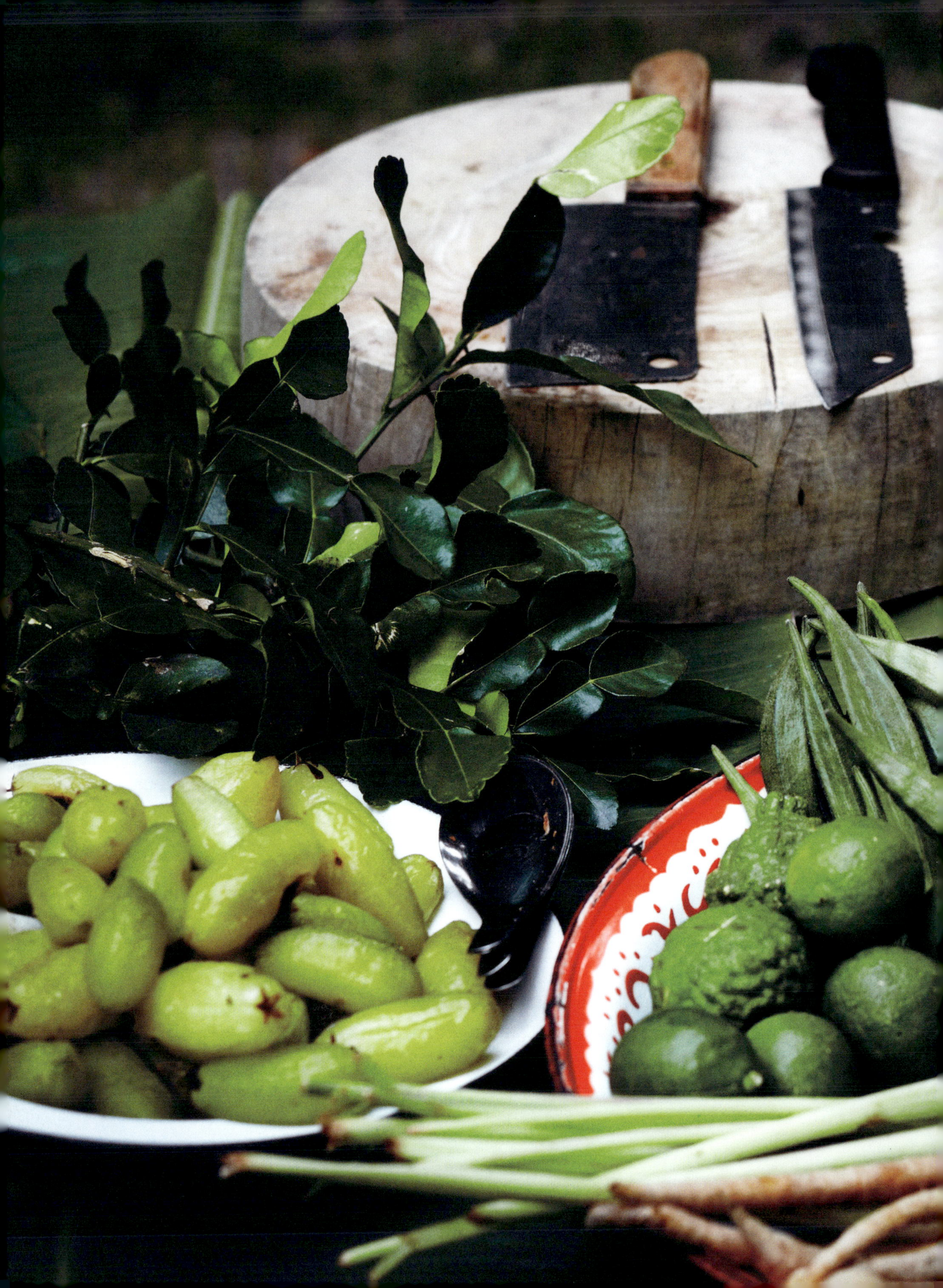

Ingredients for a meal in my mother's village in Thailand.

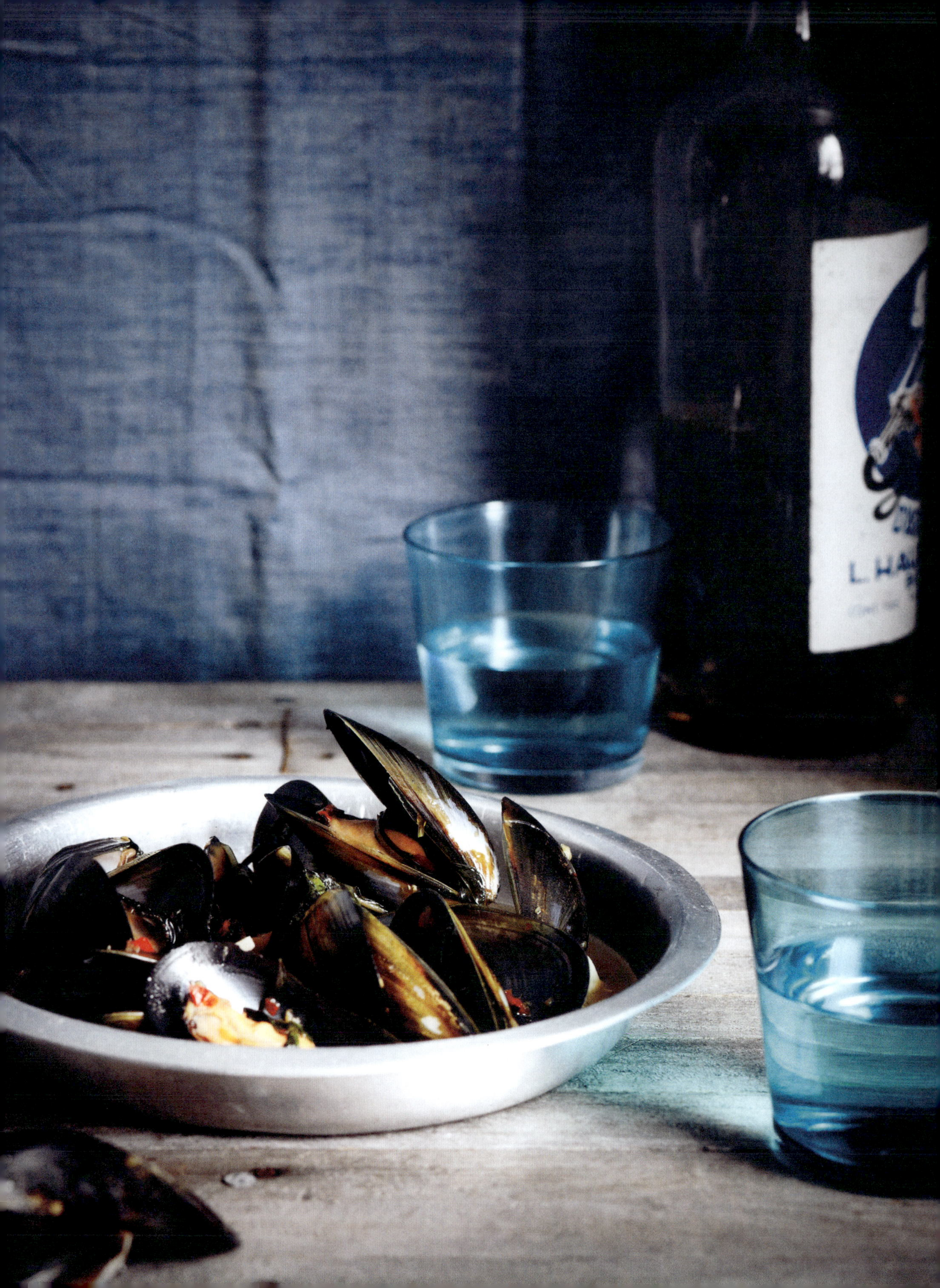

MY FIRST MUSSELS

I'm sitting with my parents at a little riverside restaurant somewhere in Thailand. I must be very small because I'm straining to see over the tabletop as a lady comes by with a steaming plate of mussels. My dad puts a mussel on my plate and shows me how to use an empty shell as a spoon to scoop out the mussel meat along with the basil-spiked broth. That first smell, that first taste of something new and truly wonderful is so ingrained that many years and many restaurants later I can still remember my first mussels.

1 kg mussels
2 tablespoons vegetable oil
2 garlic cloves, finely chopped
2 tablespoons finely chopped fresh ginger
1 fresh long red chilli, finely chopped
2 tablespoons soy sauce
1 tablespoon fish sauce
1 tablespoon oyster sauce
1 teaspoon white sugar
1 bunch Thai basil, leaves picked ← [see note]

Rinse the mussels in cold water and scrub off any barnacle bits from the shells. To debeard the mussels, grab hold of the tuft of hair sticking out of each shell and shake it from side to side until it comes loose. Discard the hairy bits.

Heat the vegetable oil in a large saucepan over medium heat. Add the garlic, ginger and chilli and cook for about 1 minute, or until it starts to smell delicious. Pour in the soy sauce, fish sauce, oyster sauce and sugar and stir to combine.

Add the mussels and give them a quick stir to coat in the sauce. Cover and let the mussels steam for about 4 minutes, or until they have all opened up. Discard any that remain tightly closed. Stir through the basil leaves. Scoop the mussels into a large bowl and pour over as much saucy broth as you like.

SERVES 2 GREEDY MUSSEL LOVERS OR 4 AS A PART OF A BANQUET

NOTE: You may need to go for a wander through an Asian grocer to find Thai basil. It has small green leaves and purple stems and has a slight aniseedy, minty sort of flavour.

BIG PLATES SEAFOOD

FISH PARCELS WITH FENNEL & CHERRY TOMATOES

cooking fish in its own little parcel means it steams and juicifies (yes, I 'know' that's not a word, mr spellchecker) to tender perfection. The cherry tomatoes melt into the wine and fish juices to become a tasty sauce just begging to be mopped up with some roasted potatoes.

1 fennel bulb, cored and thinly sliced
4 x 200 g white fish fillets, skinned ← my favourites are barramundi, trevalla, john dory or snapper
200 g cherry tomatoes, halved
¼ cup lemon juice
½ cup white wine
2 tablespoons extra-virgin olive oil
1 teaspoon sea salt
freshly ground black pepper
¼ cup basil leaves, roughly torn

Preheat the oven to 180°C. First let's make the foil parcels. Tear off a 40-cm length of aluminium foil. Fold it in half, then fold in the sides to form a pocket with one open side. Repeat so you have 4 parcels.

Divide the fennel between the parcels, place a snapper fillet on top, then divide the tomato between the parcels.

Whisk the lemon juice, wine, olive oil, salt and pepper together in a small bowl and spoon into the parcels. Throw in the basil leaves, then fold over the open side to seal.

Place the parcels on a baking tray and bake for 15 minutes, or until the snapper is cooked through. Open a parcel up to have a little peek and check it is tender and flaky.

You can serve these fishy parcels a couple of ways: take the sealed parcels to the table so everyone has the pleasure of tearing open their dinner like kids on Christmas morning or, if you'd like to be a little more fancy, scoop out the fish and fennel onto serving plates – be sure to spoon over the juices. I like to serve this with Roasted Kipfler Potatoes (see page 161) and Wild Rocket Salad (see page 157) – roast the potatoes first, then pop the snapper parcels in the oven for the last 15 minutes of the potato cooking time.

SERVES 4

DEEP-FRIED WHOLE SNAPPER WITH THREE-FLAVOURED SAUCE

I know you're probably looking at the list of ingredients for the three-flavoured sauce and thinking, 'Geez that girl can't count.' Well smarty pants, the name of the sauce comes from the three primary flavours that come through in the finished sauce and not the number of ingredients. And besides, six-ingredient sauce just doesn't have the same ring to it. Sweet, sour and spicy — that's what we're aiming for here.

1.5–2 kg whole snapper, cleaned, scaled and gutted
2 teaspoons sea salt
2 tablespoons plain flour
vegetable oil, for deep-frying
¼ cup coriander leaves
Steamed Rice (see page 157), to serve

THREE-FLAVOURED SAUCE
6 garlic cloves
2 fresh long red chillies, seeded and roughly chopped
1 teaspoon sea salt
¼ cup fish sauce
2 tablespoons tamarind concentrate
2 tablespoons white sugar

For the three-flavoured sauce, place the garlic, chilli and salt in a mortar and pound to a very rough paste using a pestle – you still want chunks of smashed chilli and garlic. Set aside. Combine the fish sauce, tamarind and sugar in a small bowl, stirring to dissolve the sugar, and set aside.

Pat the snapper dry with paper towel, both inside and out. Make 3 deep diagonal cuts in the snapper on both sides. Rub with the salt and lightly dust with the flour.

Fill a wok one-third with oil, place over high heat and heat until 180°C. You can tell if the oil is hot enough by dipping a wooden spoon into it – if furious little bubbles form around the spoon, then the oil's ready to go. Slide the fish into the hot oil and cook for about 4 minutes each side, or until the skin is crisp and the flesh cooked through. (I use a combination of spatula and tongs to gently flip the fish over in the oil.) Remove from the wok, drain on paper towel and keep warm.

Carefully pour off most of the oil in the wok, leaving about a 2-cm layer of oil. Return the wok to the heat, add the garlic paste and cook for about 2 minutes, making sure to scrape up any crisp bits of fish from the base of the wok. Add the fish sauce mixture and let the sauce bubble away for 2 minutes.

Pour the sauce over the snapper, top with the coriander leaves and serve with the steamed rice.

SERVES 4

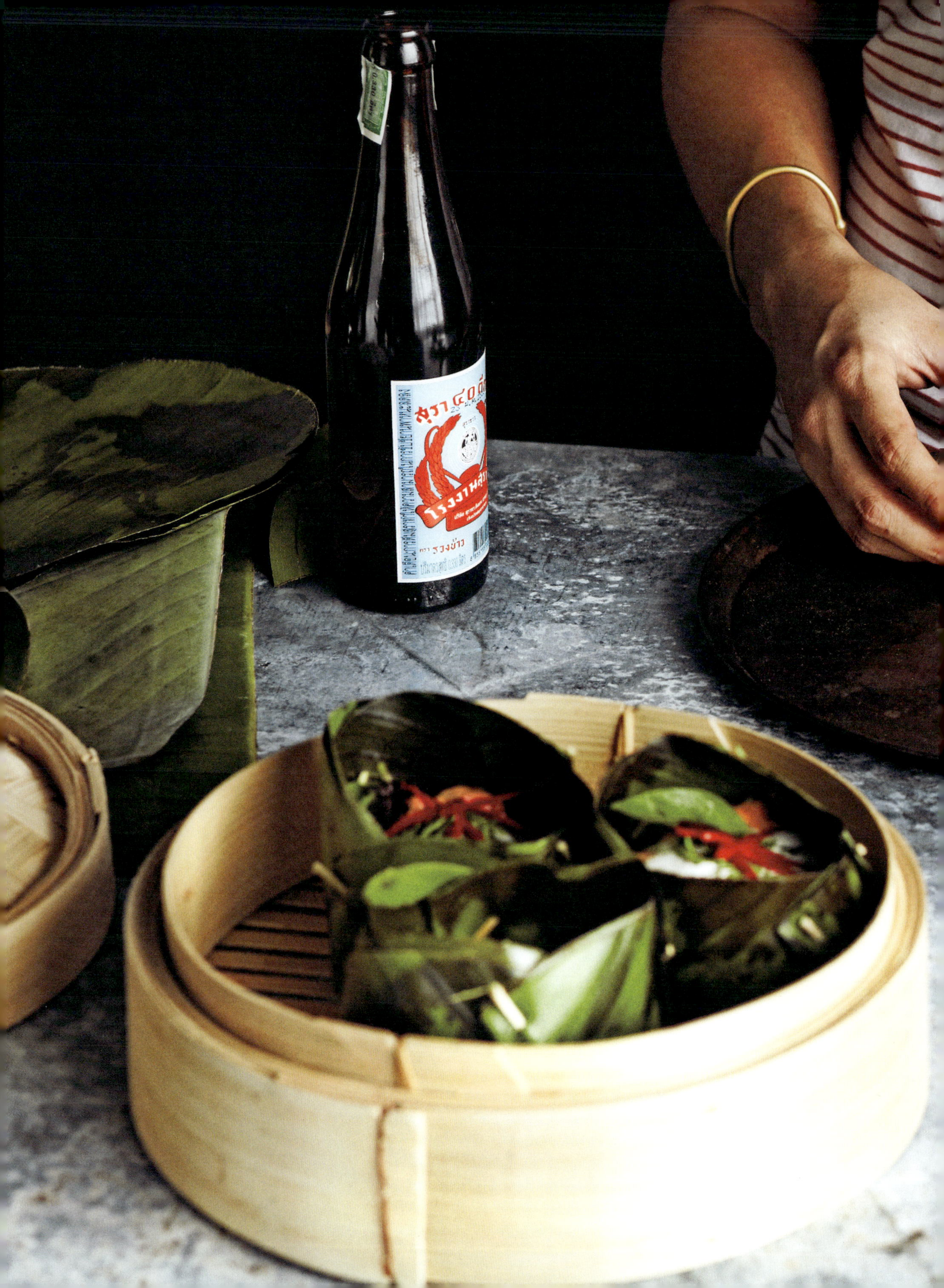

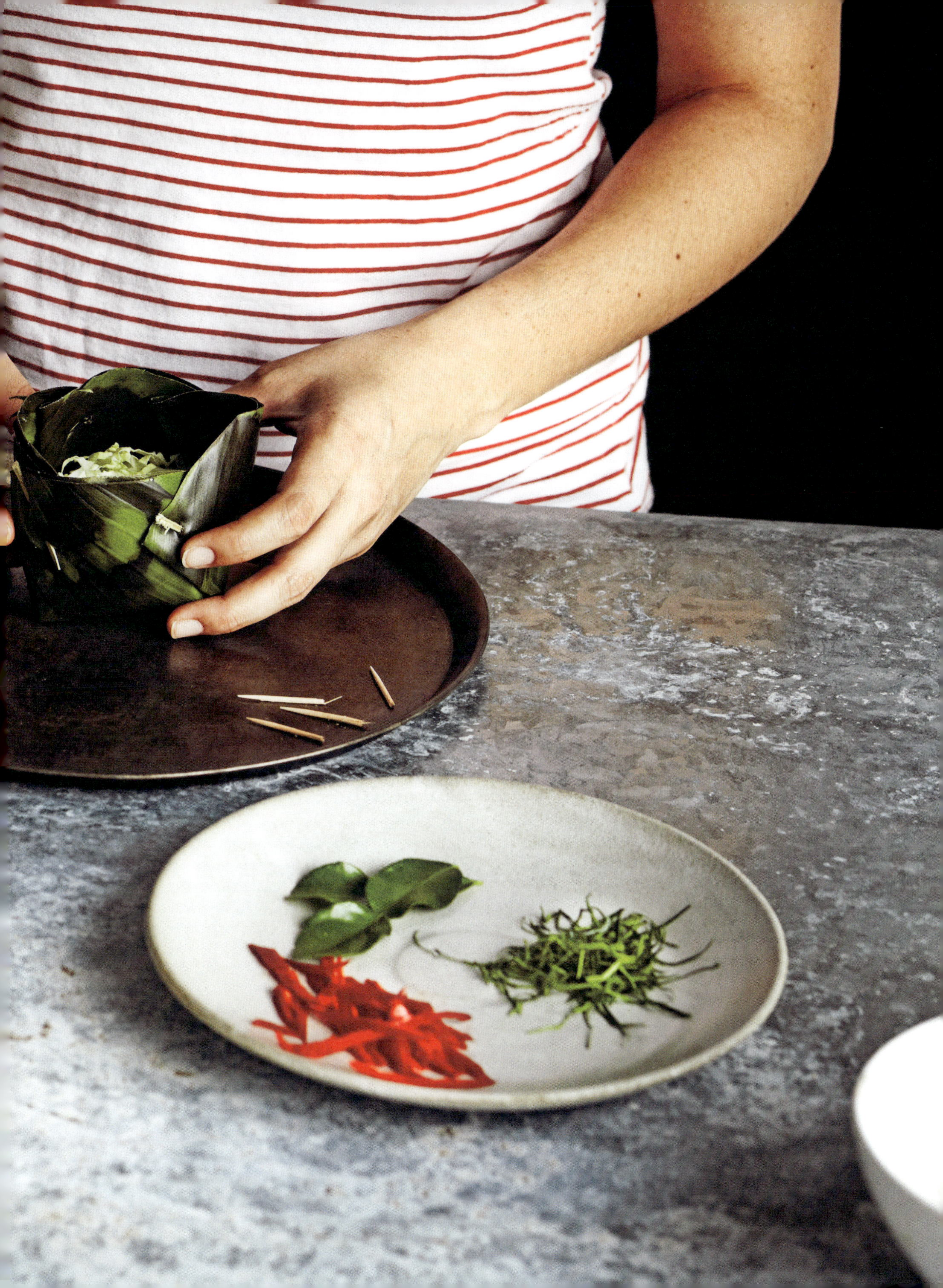

HAW MOK PLAA
[STEAMED FISH IN BANANA LEAVES]

This is my mother's recipe, as observed by me. I love the way she cooks — with splashes of this and sprinklings of that, until the flavour is just right. She has a natural ability to balance flavours and textures. This is her language after all... the language of Thai food. It takes a little practice to make the banana leaf cups, but persevere because the banana leaf imparts flavour to the fish as it steams.

12 toothpicks
6 banana leaves ← [see notes]
¼ cup Thai Red Curry Paste (see page 110 if you'd like to make your own)
1 cup coconut milk
¼ cup fish sauce
1 tablespoon white sugar
1 tablespoon plain flour, plus 1 teaspoon extra
2 eggs
500 g snapper fillets, cut into 4 cm chunks ← you could also use barramundi, trevalla or any other firm white fish
¾ cup coconut cream
½ teaspoon sea salt
2 cups thinly sliced cabbage
¼ cup Thai (or regular) basil leaves
3 kaffir lime leaves, thinly sliced ← [see notes]
3 fresh long red chillies, seeded and thinly sliced into long strips
Steamed Rice (see page 157), to serve

To make the banana leaf cups, break the toothpicks in half. Wipe the banana leaves with a damp cloth and pat dry with a tea towel. Use kitchen scissors to cut out 12 x 20-cm rounds from the leaves. If your banana leaves are fresh they will be quite stiff, so you need to heat them to soften them. I find the best way is to wave them over a naked flame from your gas burner or you could heat them in a dry frying pan. If you've used packet banana leaves they will already be soft and pliable so you won't need to heat them.

To assemble the cups, stack 2 rounds together. Make a small pleat in the round and secure the pleat with a toothpick piece. Repeat to make 3 more pleats to form a square cup. Repeat to make 6 cups. Set aside.

Whisk the curry paste, coconut milk, fish sauce, sugar, the tablespoon of flour and the eggs together in a large bowl. Add the snapper and, using a wooden spoon, stir the sauce vigorously for 5 minutes to thicken and ensure the snapper absorbs the flavours. Set aside until you're ready to assemble.

Place the coconut cream, salt and the extra teaspoon of flour in a small saucepan over low heat and whisk for about 1 minute, or until thickened. Remove from the heat and set aside.

Now let's assemble. Place a small handful of cabbage in the base of each banana leaf cup, spoon in 2–3 pieces of snapper and cover with the curry sauce. Top with a spoonful of the coconut cream mixture, 1–2 basil leaves, a pinch of kaffir lime leaves and a couple of strips of chilli.

Place the cups in a large bamboo steamer, cover and steam over a saucepan of boiling water for 25–30 minutes, or until the snapper is just cooked through. Serve with the steamed rice.

SERVES 6

NOTES: You can buy fresh or packet banana leaves at Thai and Asian grocers. If you can't find them, use small ramekins to hold the fish mixture instead.

To thinly slice the kaffir lime leaves into delicate shards, stack the leaves on top of each other, roll them up into a cigar shape and slice. Discard any bits of stalk.

QUICK-GRILL TROUT

Who's afraid of the big bad fish? Not I, said the little girl. I don't remember eating many fish fillets at our family table and the only memory I have of fish fingers comes from my time at boarding school. We were a whole fish kinda family. My dad and I would share the eyes and cheeks while my mum liked the crisp fins and tail. I would hold on to my mum's hand as we picked our way through the fish markets looking for our dinner. My mum would describe what we were looking for — clear, glistening eyes and bright red gills. And as we moved from place to place the fish on our dinner table would change. In Darwin it was pearly, pink red snapper; in Papua New Guinea, it was often a flat moon-shaped fish my mum called pomfret; in Queensland we loved the lady in red, coral trout; and in South Australia it became the freshwater trout from the inland farms near my house. You can use not only trout but also snapper, barramundi, rainbow trout or just about any whole fish you fancy. Roasted kipfler potatoes (see page 161) or pomegranate & fennel salad (see page 133) marry particularly well with this dish.

2 x 700 g whole trout, cleaned, scaled and gutted
¼ cup extra-virgin olive oil, plus extra for drizzling
2 lemons, zest finely grated and fruit sliced
2 teaspoons sea salt
freshly ground black pepper
4 sprigs rosemary
2 tablespoons chopped dill
¼ cup roughly chopped flat-leaf parsley
lemon wedges, to serve

Preheat the oven grill to high.

Score the trout with 6 deep diagonal cuts on each side. Place in a large roasting tray, pour over the olive oil, sprinkle with the lemon zest and season with the salt and generous grindings of the pepper. Rub the mixture into the fish on both sides to coat. Stuff the cavity of each trout with the lemon slices and rosemary sprigs.

Place the trout under the grill for about 6 minutes each side, or until the skin is crisp, golden and blistered and the flesh is cooked through. You could also cook the fish on a barbecue.

Remove from the grill, season with some salt, drizzle with a little olive oil and sprinkle over the dill and parsley. Serve with plenty of lemon wedges to squeeze over just before eating.

SERVES 4

Skate with Caper & Lemony Burnt Butter Sauce

Would skate by any other name taste as sweet? Perhaps not when you find out that skate is actually stingray. Stingray with caper and lemony burnt butter sauce just doesn't sound as enticing. Whatever you want to call it, this fish has such a beautiful sweetness and a deep earthy flavour. I adore it. It often comes in long lengths that taper from thick and meaty at one end to thin and delicate at the other. I like to cut the fillet so you have two meaty bits and two skinny bits. This allows you to take the skinny bits out earlier than the meaty ones to avoid overcooking. Any kind of potato side will go well with this dish as will the wild rocket salad (see page 157) or Pomegranate & Fennel Salad (see page 155).

400 g piece of skate
2 tablespoons extra-virgin olive oil
¼ cup plain flour
100 g butter, diced
⅓ cup lemon juice
2 tablespoons salted or brined capers, finely chopped *(if using brined capers, be sure to rinse them first to remove excess salt)*
2 tablespoons finely chopped dill

Take hold of the piece of skate and halve it lengthways so you've got 2 long pieces. Now halve each long piece widthways so that you've got 2 thick rectangular fillets and 2 thinner ones.

Heat the olive oil in a large frying pan over high heat. Lightly coat the skate in the flour and slide it into the hot oil. The thicker fillets will need about 4 minutes each side to cook through, while the thinner bits will only take about 2 minutes each side. To check if the skate is done, gently prod a fork into the flesh; if it flakes away easily, then the fish is cooked. When the skate is golden and just cooked through, transfer to serving plates.

Return the pan to high heat and add the butter. Let it foam up, then turn a deep brown colour – it should take less than 1 minute, depending on how hot the pan is. Now add the lemon juice to stop the butter from cooking further, then stir through the capers and dill. Drown the skate fillets in the deliciously nutty, lemony burnt butter sauce and serve.

SERVES 2

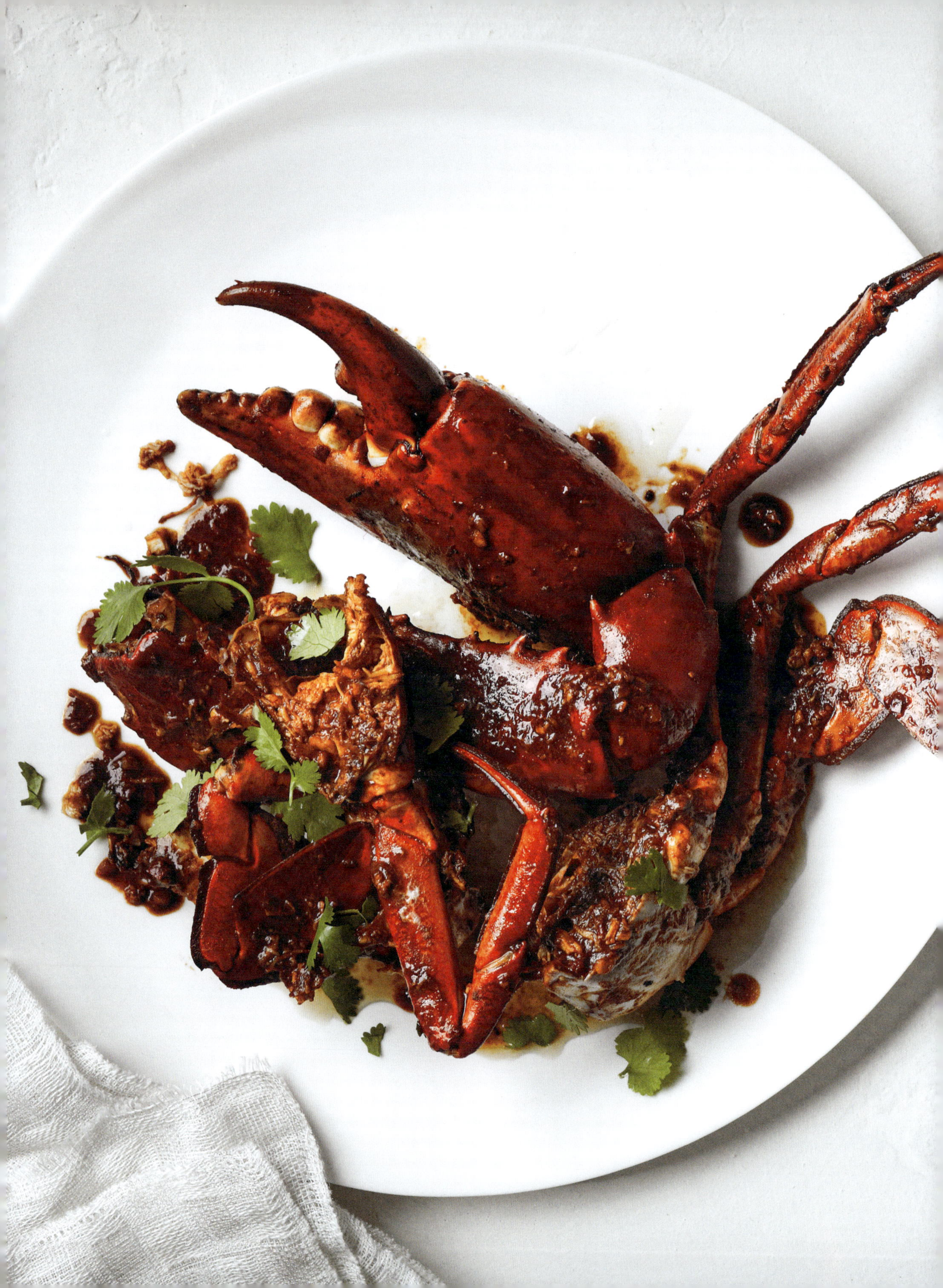

CHILLI MUD CRAB

I was born in Darwin, raised in Papua New Guinea and schooled in Queensland, so my memories of eating mud crab span two states, two countries and nearly three decades. Heading out of Darwin you can pick up a live mud crab from a roadside stall. In Papua New Guinea you must brave the local outdoor markets and swat the flies as you take your pick. But it was in Queensland that mud crab became my weekly addiction. Mum, Dad and I would head out to a hole-in-the-wall Vietnamese restaurant in Darra, in the outer suburbs of Brisbane, at least once a week for our mud crab fix, sitting at a lino-covered table, listening to the wait-staff screaming orders into the kitchen and being engulfed in that wok-fried Asian restaurant smell that clings to your clothes long after you leave. Every week we made the half-hour trip because once you've gotten your hands dirty, once you've splattered chilli sauce all over your new white top, once you've tasted that sweet wok-fried mud crab, there's just no going back.

2 x 1 kg live mud crabs ← [see note]
½ cup tomato sauce
¼ cup white sugar
¼ cup fish sauce
2 tablespoons tamarind concentrate
¼ cup Shaoxing (Chinese rice) wine → *Find this at Asian grocers*

⅓ cup vegetable oil
8 garlic cloves, finely chopped
1 fresh long red chilli, finely chopped
¼ cup coriander leaves, roughly chopped
lemon wedges, for fingerbowls

Tuck the mud crabs in the freezer for about 1 hour to put them to 'sleep'. To clean the crabs, lift the flap on the underside and pull off the top shell. Remove and discard the grey spongy finger-like gills and rinse the crabs quickly under cold water to get rid of any gunk.

Use a heavy knife or cleaver to cut each crab in half down the centre, then cut each piece into thirds. Use the back of the knife to crack the claws and legs to let the sauce seep in while they cook.

Place the tomato sauce, sugar, fish sauce, tamarind concentrate, Shaoxing wine and ¼ cup water in a bowl and stir to combine.

Heat the oil in a large wok over high heat. Add the garlic and chilli and fry for about 30 seconds. Add the crab pieces and give everything a bit of a mix. Add the tomato sauce mixture and toss the crabs around to coat them well. Cover with a lid, reduce the heat to low and cook for about 10 minutes, or until the shells turn orange and the crab is cooked through, removing the lid to toss and shake them around after about 5 minutes.

Pile the crab and sauce into a large serving bowl and sprinkle over the coriander. Serve with lots of napkins and small bowls of water with lemon wedges to clean sticky fingers.

SERVES 4

NOTE: If you can't get a hold of mud crabs, you could use blue swimmer crabs instead.

BIG PLATES SEAFOOD

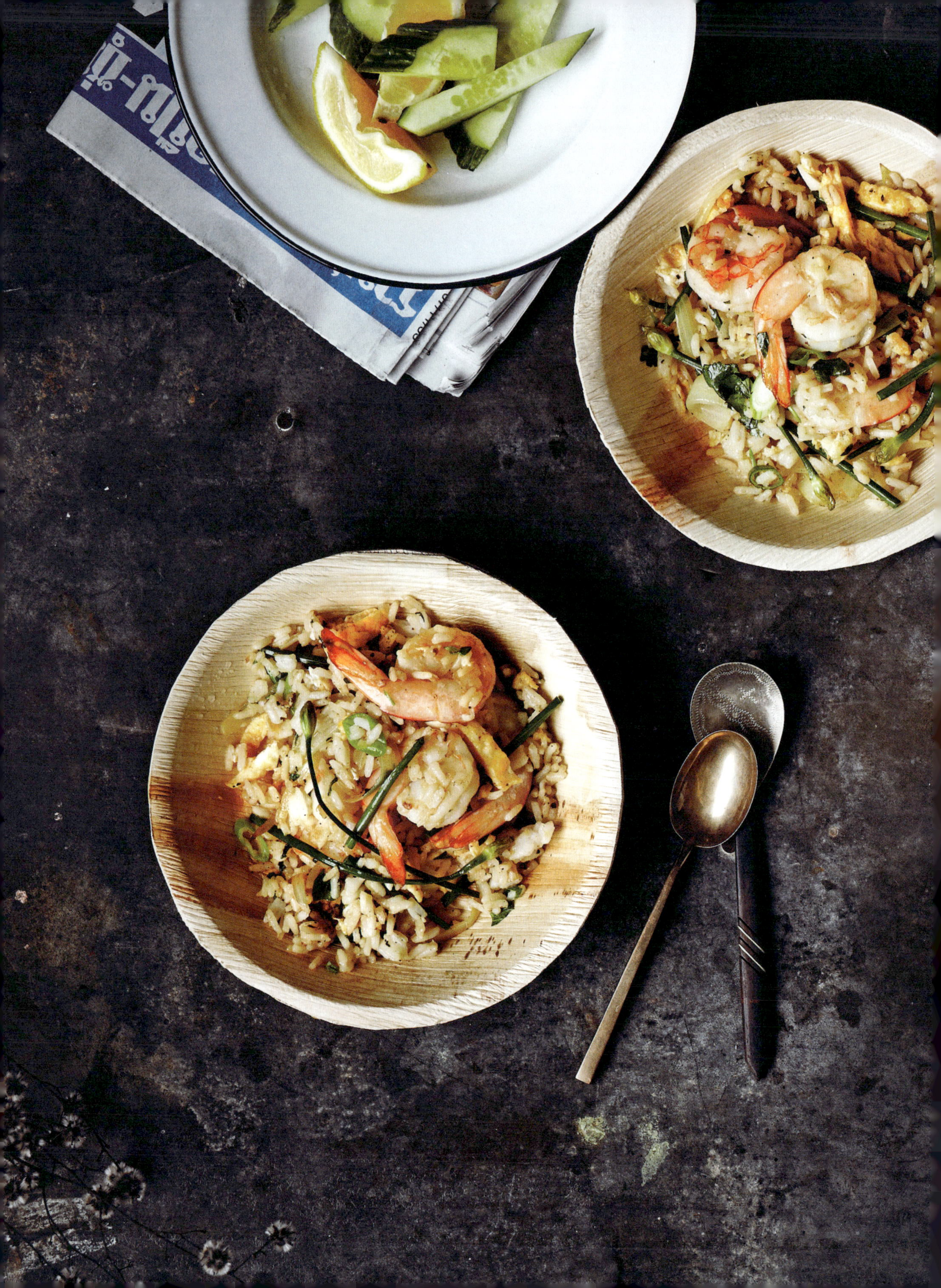

KHAO PAD GOONG
[PRAWN FRIED RICE.]

No peas here. No crimped slices of carrot. None of those pallid prawn pretenders. And certainly no stray bits of ham. The fried rice I grew up eating was never a bedraggled bridesmaid and always the star of her very own show: smoky, wok-fried rice, laced with eggs and garnished with coriander and spring onion. Prawns are my favourite addition when I'm cooking this for dinner at home but, on the streets of Bangkok, I always order the crab version, 'khao pad poo'.

4 eggs
¼ cup vegetable oil
1 brown onion, sliced
3 garlic cloves, finely chopped
500 g raw medium prawns, shelled and deveined
5 cups cold cooked long-grain or jasmine rice ← [see note]
¼ cup fish sauce
2 tablespoons soy sauce

1 teaspoon white sugar
½ cup coriander leaves, roughly chopped
½ cup sliced spring onion
½ cup garlic chives, sliced into 4-cm batons (optional)
freshly ground black pepper
1 cucumber, thickly sliced
lemon wedges, to serve

Whisk the eggs and 1 tablespoon of water together in a bowl until just combined. Heat 1 tablespoon of the vegetable oil in a wok over high heat. Pour in the egg and leave to bubble and blister for about 2 minutes, or until lightly golden. Flip the omelette over and cook the other side for 30 seconds. Remove from the wok and slice into slivers.

Heat the remaining vegetable oil in the wok. Add the onion and garlic and stir-fry until slightly softened and aromatic. Add the prawns and stir-fry until just opaque. Add the rice, fish sauce, soy sauce and sugar and stir-fry for about 1 minute, using a spatula to mix and break up the rice. Remove from the heat and toss through the omelette slivers, coriander, spring onion and garlic chives and season with a generous grinding of pepper.

Pile the fried rice into bowls and serve with the slices of cucumber and the lemon wedges to squeeze over just before eating.

SERVES 4

NOTE: It's a good idea to cook the rice the day before so it's dry and won't be gluggy when you stir-fry it. See page 157 for a recipe for Steamed Rice. This makes more than you will need but I usually make up a big batch of rice to serve for dinner one night and save the rest for my fried rice the next night.

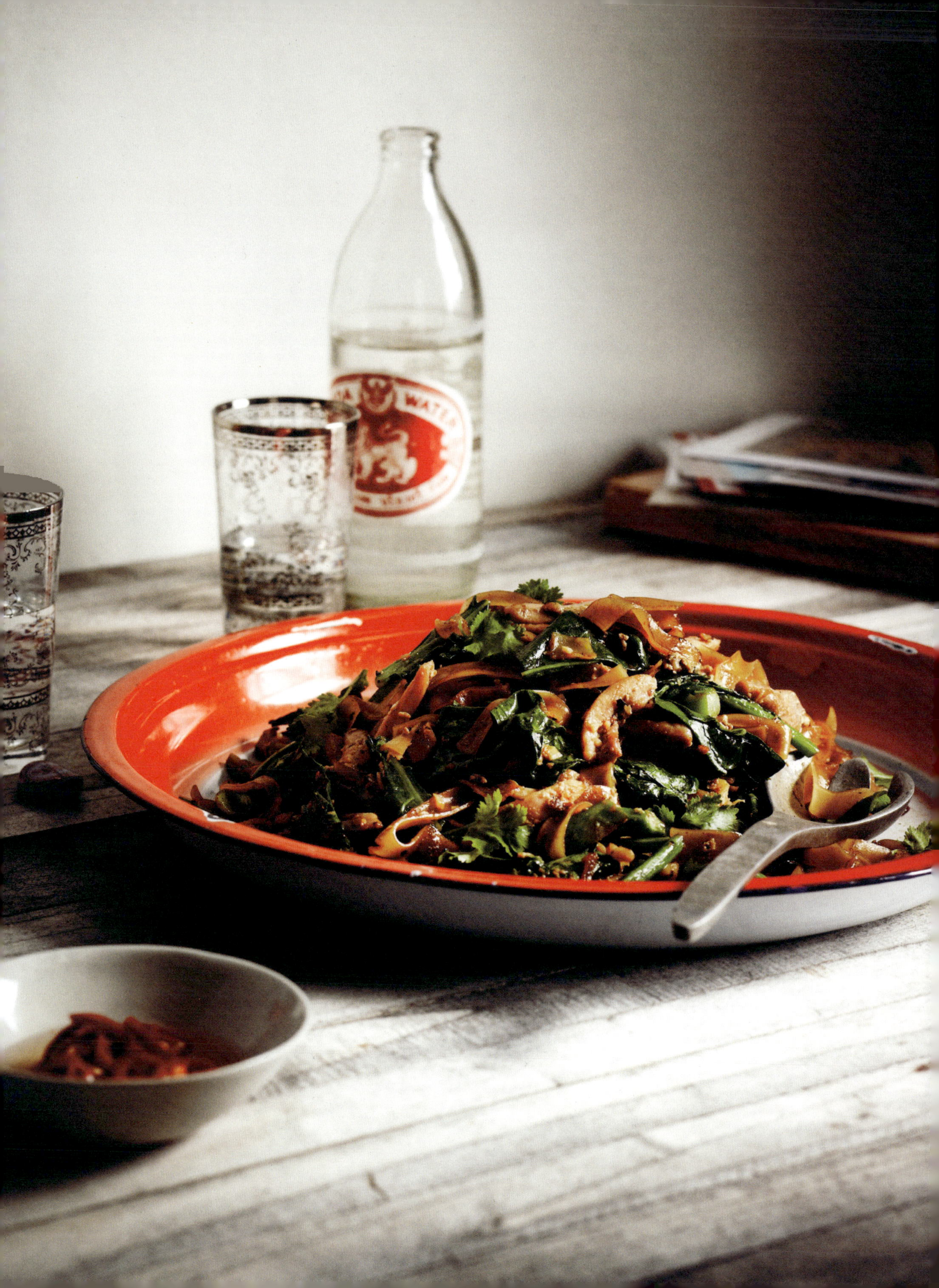

PAD SIEW [WOK-FRIED NOODLES WITH CHILLI VINEGAR]

Pronounced 'p-ah-d see-eeww', this was the spag bol of my childhood, the dish my mum cooked just about every week. I like to cook the ingredients separately instead of piling everything into the wok all at once — that way you can control the crunch of the broccoli and the char of the noodles. As with any good wok dish you need to get everything chopped and prepared before you start cooking because the stir-frying part should be super quick.

300 g chicken thigh fillets, thinly sliced
3 tablespoons fish sauce
¼ teaspoon sesame oil
1 tablespoon oyster sauce
200 g dried rice stick noodles
3 tablespoons peanut oil
250 g Chinese broccoli (gai lan) or broccolini, cut into bite-sized pieces

2 tablespoons kecap manis ← a dark, thick and sweet soy sauce available from the Asian section of most supermarkets or an Asian grocer
3 garlic cloves, finely chopped
1 tablespoon white sugar
1 egg
freshly ground black pepper
¼ cup roughly chopped coriander leaves

CHILLI VINEGAR
¼ cup white vinegar
1 fresh long red chilli, thinly sliced

Combine the chicken, 1 tablespoon of the fish sauce, the sesame oil and oyster sauce in a bowl, mix to coat well and refrigerate for 15 minutes to marinate.

Soak the noodles in warm water for about 10 minutes, or until rubbery and pliable but still firm to the touch. It's important not to let the noodles get too soft or you'll have a soggy mess in the wok when you go to fry them. Drain well and pat dry with a tea towel.

Meanwhile, make the chilli vinegar. Combine the vinegar and chilli in a small bowl and set aside until ready to serve.

Heat a wok over high heat until just smoking, add 1 tablespoon of the peanut oil and the Chinese broccoli. Toss for about 1 minute, or until the broccoli leaves have just wilted, then transfer to a large plate.

Return the wok to the heat and add 1 tablespoon of the peanut oil. Add the noodles and toss to coat in the oil. Add 1 tablespoon of the kecap manis and 1 tablespoon of the fish sauce and stir-fry for about 3 minutes, or until the noodles soften and start to char around the edges. Use your tongs to separate the noodles while they cook. Scoop out the noodles and add to the Chinese broccoli.

Return the wok to the heat and add the remaining 1 tablespoon of peanut oil. Throw in the garlic, marinated chicken and the sugar. Stir-fry for about 3 minutes, or until the chicken is just cooked through. Push the chicken to one side of the wok and crack the egg onto the empty side. Let the egg set for a couple of minutes, then break it up with a spatula and toss through the chicken. Add the Chinese broccoli and noodles and mix everything together with tongs. Add the remaining fish sauce and kecap manis, grind over a generous amount of pepper and mix to combine.

Pile onto a large serving plate, drizzle over a couple of spoonfuls of the chilli vinegar and scatter with the coriander. Serve with the remaining chilli vinegar on the side for everyone to help themselves.

SERVES 4

BEGGAR'S CHICKEN

My dad calls this the world's best chicken. My mum calls it Beggar's chicken. I call it 'that chicken you do in the dark soy soup'. I guess this is my family's roast chicken — it's the dish we've always loved to cook and share for as long as I can remember. A pot of the simmering broth on the stove smells like home to me. We serve the chicken whole on a deep platter at the table with steaming bowls of rice to soak up the dark savoury broth. Unlike a roasted chicken, there's no carving to be done here. The chicken is so soft and tender that we simply use tongs to pull apart the bird at the table.

1 bunch coriander
10 garlic cloves
1 teaspoon black peppercorns
2 tablespoons vegetable oil
1.4 kg whole free-range chicken
½ cup dark soy sauce, plus extra to taste
¼ cup fish sauce
5 star anise
1 tablespoon white sugar
Steamed Rice (see page 157), to serve

Cut the bunch of coriander about 4 cm from its root end. Rinse the coriander roots with water to remove any grit. Reserve the leaves for garnishing. Place the roots in a mortar, add the garlic and peppercorns and pound to a rough paste using a pestle. (You can also use a food processor, but I love using a mortar and pestle so I can smell and feel my way through the process.)

In a saucepan large enough to hold the chicken, heat the vegetable oil over medium heat. Add the coriander root paste and cook for 1 minute, or until it starts to smell fragrant. Add the whole chicken and cook for about 2 minutes each side, or until lightly browned. Add the soy sauce, fish sauce, star anise, sugar and enough water to cover the chicken completely. Reduce the heat and simmer gently for about 1 hour, or until the chicken is soft and the legs are just about falling off the bone.

Carefully lift the chicken out of the stock – I find a combination of spatula and tongs useful here. Taste the stock and add more soy sauce if it needs to be a little saltier. Place the chicken on a large deep serving plate, ladle over some of the stock, scatter over the reserved coriander leaves and serve with the steamed rice.

SERVES 6

NOTE: You'll have loads of leftover broth, which you can use for noodle soups. Simply strain the stock and refrigerate it for up to 4 days. To serve, reheat the stock and cook your noodles in the broth until soft. Pile the noodles into a bowl, ladle over the soup and top with sliced spring onion.

HERB & PARMESAN CHICKEN SCHNITZELS

I'm a sucker for a good schnitter — those crunchy colossal schnitzels at the pub are always tempting when there's a cold beer in my hand. At home, I like to give my schnitzels the herb and cheese treatment. I often make a double or sometimes triple batch and store them in the freezer as a weeknight dinner back-up. The Cabbage & Almond Coleslaw (see page 156) or the Wild Rocket Salad (see page 157) are the perfect wingmen for these herby cheesy schnitzels.

4 x 200 g chicken breast fillets
3 cups stale bread, torn into small pieces
¼ cup rosemary leaves
1 tablespoon thyme leaves
½ cup roughly chopped flat-leaf parsley leaves
1 garlic clove, roughly chopped
½ cup grated parmesan
2 teaspoons sea salt, plus extra to serve
½ cup plain flour
3 eggs, lightly beaten
vegetable oil, for shallow-frying
lemon wedges, to serve

Cut each chicken breast in half, slicing through the middle so you get two thin fillets. Place each piece between plastic wrap and, using a meat mallet, pound to an even 1-cm thickness.

Place the bread, rosemary, thyme, parsley and garlic in a food processor and process until you have green-hued fine breadcrumbs. Combine with the parmesan and salt in a large shallow dish.

Place the flour and beaten egg in separate shallow dishes. Dust each piece of chicken in the flour, dip in the egg, then coat in the breadcrumb mixture. (At this stage, you can wrap each schnitzel in plastic wrap and freeze for up to 3 months.)

Heat enough vegetable oil to just coat the base of a large frying pan over medium heat. Add the schnitzels, you may need to do this in batches, and cook for about 4 minutes each side, or until cooked through. Drain on paper towel and season with salt. Serve with the lemon wedges and your choice of wingman.

SERVES 8

CINNAMON CHICKEN TAGINE

Forget flowers, diamonds or perfume. The way to my heart is an oversized aubergine-coloured tagine. My lovely partner, Tim, gave me a tagine for my 26th birthday and it's become a well-used fixture in my kitchen ever since. Tagines are traditionally made from clay and have a round base with a conical-shaped lid. It's that cone-shaped lid that allows steamy juices to collect back into the simmering sauce in the tagine base. I love to serve this with the Rosy Israeli couscous (see page 158) or steamed rice (see page 157).

¼ cup extra-virgin olive oil
2 red onions, sliced
3 garlic cloves, finely chopped
2 teaspoons ground ginger
1 teaspoon ground cumin
1 cinnamon stick
8 chicken drumsticks or
4 x 200 g chicken marylands
300 g pitted prunes
pinch saffron threads
2 teaspoons sea salt
¼ cup flaked almonds

Heat the oil in a tagine or large casserole dish over medium heat. Add the onion, garlic, ginger, cumin and cinnamon and cook for about 3 minutes, or until the onion has softened. Add the chicken and stir to coat. Scatter over the prunes, pour over 3 cups of water and give everything a bit of a stir. Add a pinch of saffron and the salt and cover with the tagine top or casserole lid. Reduce the heat to low and simmer for about 1 hour, or until the chicken is falling off the bone and the prunes have dissolved to make a thick sauce.

Meanwhile, place the almonds in a small dry frying pan over medium heat and toast until they just start to turn golden. Sprinkle over the chicken and serve.

SERVES 4

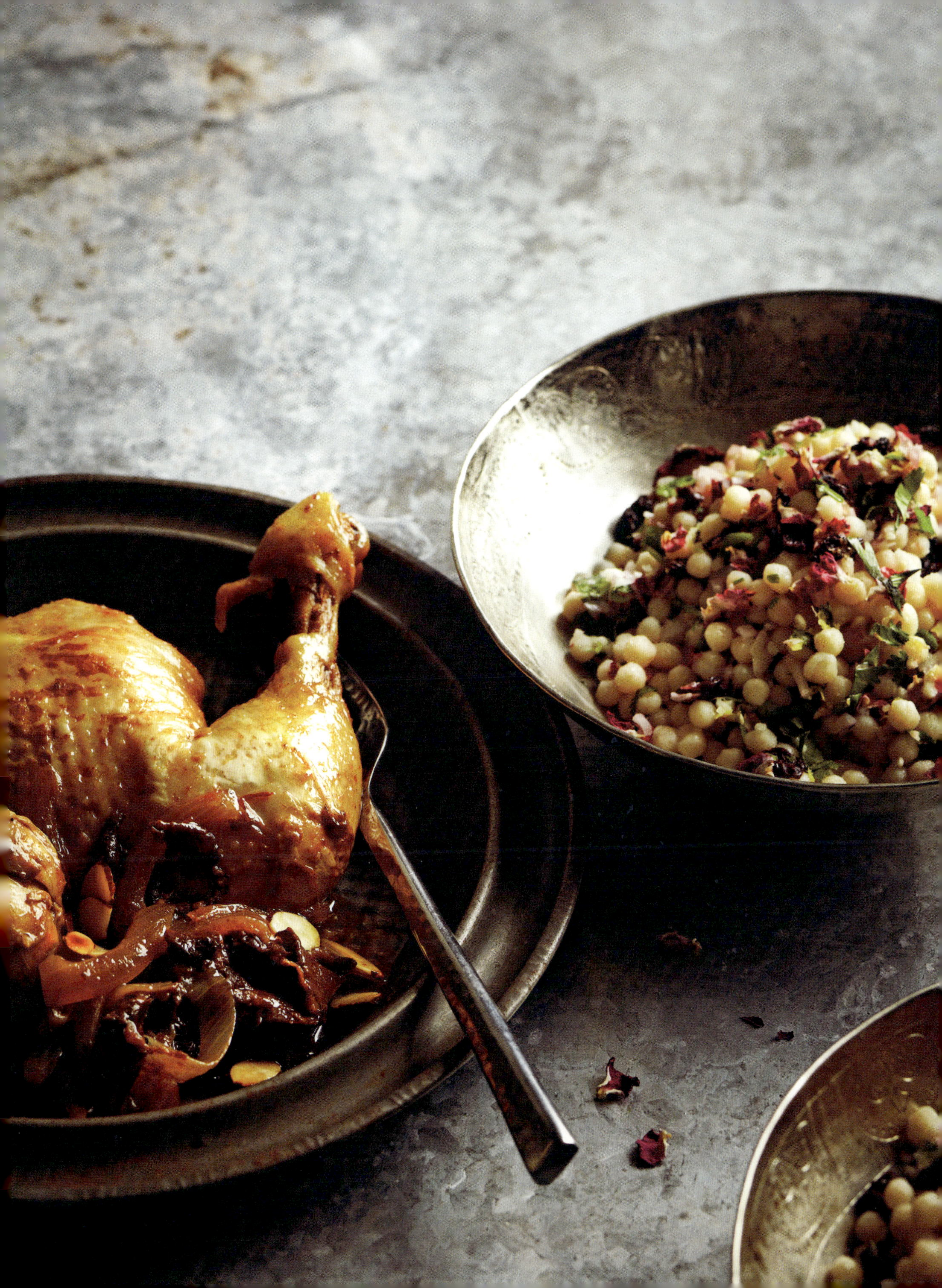

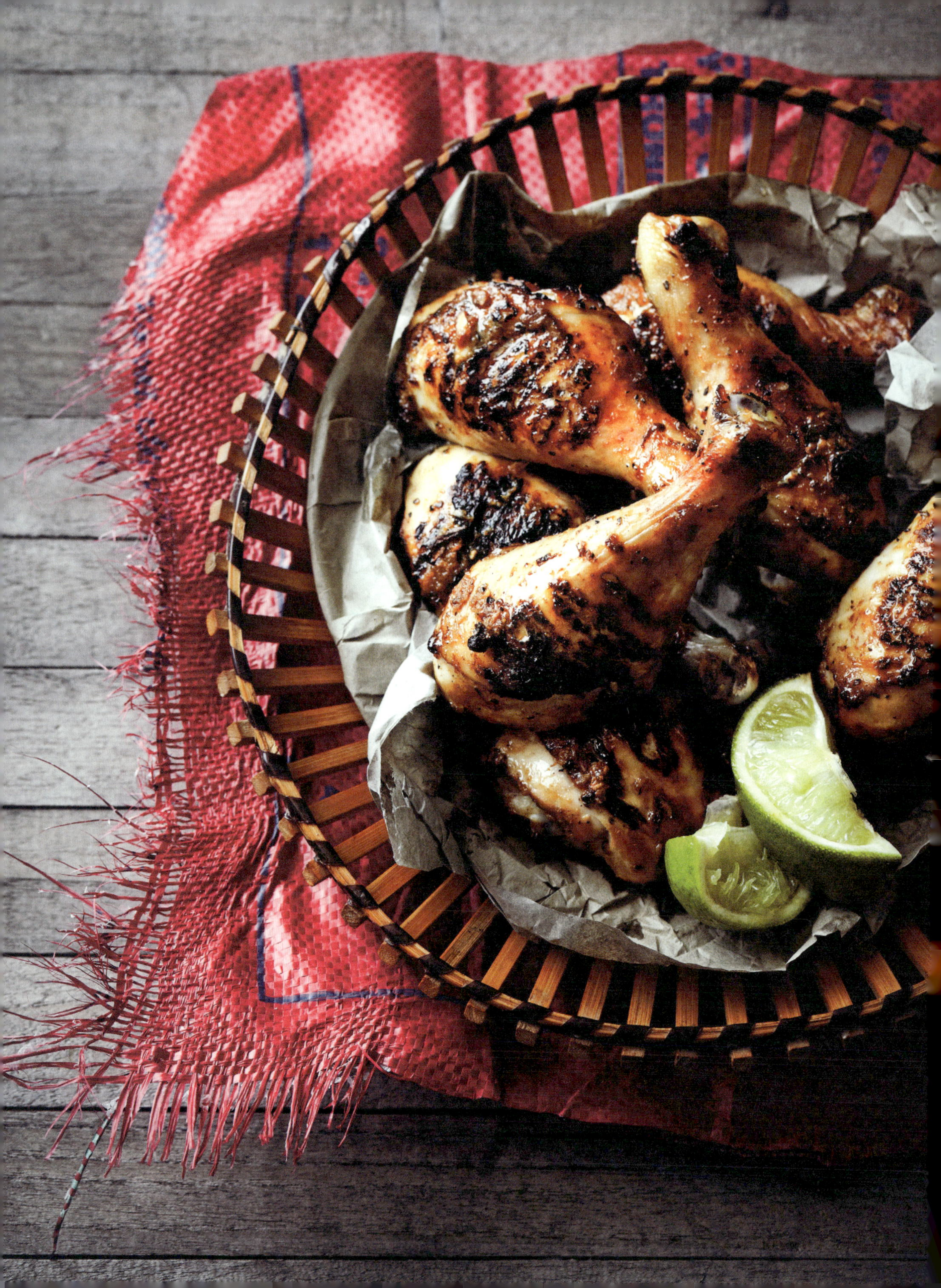

SWEET PEPPER CHICKEN

I find it hard to resist a sweet, sticky grilled hunk of chicken. My mum would often make this for dinner, served with steamed rice (see page 157) and 'som tum' (see pages 138–9). I had no idea she added sweetened condensed milk until I was old enough to pay attention in the kitchen. It adds just the right amount of sugary stickiness. I often make up a batch of this to serve alongside my barbecued sausages and chops.

4 garlic cloves
1 teaspoon black peppercorns
1 teaspoon sea salt
4-cm piece of fresh ginger, peeled and roughly chopped
2 tablespoons dark soy sauce
2 tablespoons sweetened condensed milk
1 kg chicken pieces, such as drumsticks, marylands or wings
2 star anise

Place the garlic, peppercorns, salt and ginger in a mortar and pound to a rough paste using a pestle. Mix in the soy sauce and condensed milk to make a marinade.

Place the chicken in a large bowl or container and pour over the marinade. Throw in the star anise and massage the marinade into the chicken with your hands, breaking up the star anise as you go. Cover with plastic wrap and refrigerate for about 1 hour to marinate.

Heat your barbecue, chargrill plate or large frying pan to medium–high. Cook the chicken pieces for about 25 minutes until they've got lovely dark grill marks and are cooked through. Turn the pieces every 5 or so minutes to stop the skin from burning too much – you want a bit of charry goodness but not charry badness. If you're cooking the chicken on a stove top and not on your barbecue you could also pop them into a 180°C oven for 10–15 minutes to cook them through after you've seared them in your frying pan.

SERVES 4

BIG PLATES POULTRY

Rosemary & Garlic Roasted Chicken with Braised Lentils

One of the things I love about food is that it can engage and seduce you long before you sit down to eat. There are some dishes that reach out and tell you how delightfully satisfying they're going to be as they roast, simmer and fry. Hello chicken, hello garlic and hello rosemary roasting away in my oven.

4 x 300 g chicken marylands
2 sprigs rosemary, leaves picked
5 garlic cloves, unpeeled
1 teaspoon sea salt
1 tablespoon extra-virgin olive oil
½ cup white wine

BRAISED LENTILS
1 cup Puy or tiny blue-green lentils, rinsed
1 tablespoon extra-virgin olive oil
1 brown onion, finely chopped
2 garlic cloves, finely chopped
4 rashers bacon, finely diced
1 teaspoon ground cumin
400 g can diced tomatoes
1 cinnamon stick
1 fresh or dried bay leaf
½ cup currants
1 tablespoon finely chopped flat-leaf parsley

Preheat the oven to 180°C. You've got a couple of options for preparing the chicken marylands. Leave them as they are if you're making a casual dinner. But if you'd like to get a little bit fancy, you can trim the drumsticks. Cut the skin around the bone end of each drumstick, then use a cleaver to remove the bottom joint of the drumstick. Preparing the marylands this way means the meat will shrink down during roasting, leaving a lovely clean drumstick bone. Place the chicken in a baking dish.

Use a mortar and pestle to lightly pound the rosemary, garlic and salt. Give everything a bit of a bruising without creating a paste – you want the garlic cloves to be just popping out of their skins. Stir through the olive oil.

Pour the rosemary mixture over the chicken and massage into the meat with your hands. Pour over the wine and cover with aluminium foil. Roast for 20 minutes. Remove the foil and roast for a further 40 minutes, or until golden and cooked through. Pour off the juices and reserve. Keep all the roasted garlic and rosemary bits in a separate bowl, as well.

Meanwhile, make the braised lentils. Place the lentils in a saucepan with 1 litre of water. Bring to the boil over high heat, then reduce the heat and simmer for about 25 minutes, or until just tender. Drain well. Heat the olive oil in a separate saucepan over medium heat, add the onion, garlic, bacon and cumin and cook for about 5 minutes, or until the onion has softened and the bacon starts to brown. Add the lentils, tomato, cinnamon, bay leaf, currants and 2 cups of water and simmer for 30 minutes. Stir through the reserved juices from the roasted chicken for a final kick of flavour. Stir through the parsley.

To serve, place a generous scoop of lentils on each plate, top with a piece of chicken and scatter with the reserved roasted garlic and rosemary.

SERVES 4

CONFIT DUCK WITH STAR ANISE & CHERRY SAUCE

There's nothing like duck cooked in duck fat. Or potatoes cooked in duck fat. Or onions cooked in duck fat. Or pork belly cooked in duck fat. Hmmm, duck fat. I think fat is a wonderful thing. I like my steak fatty, my pork fatty and my bacon — you guessed it — fatty. Fat is flavour. In our low-fat, low-GI, high-protein, vita-supplemented eating world I think we can sometimes forget that simple fact. It's almost blasphemous to talk of cooking with fat these days and yet our televisions are filled with advertisements tempting us with meal deals that wheel and deal in just that. Don't get me wrong, I haven't got a problem with meal deals and I will admit to loving a chicken nugget or six on occasion, but I try to forgo the regular eating of meal-deal fat so I can afford to indulge in a little home-cooked fat every now and then... or a little more often. For extra decadence, I like to serve this with duck fat potatoes. Simply boil quartered potatoes until just tender, drain, then cook in a large non-stick pan with a big spoonful of duck fat until golden.

- 2 tablespoons sea salt
- 3 garlic cloves, peeled
- 1 teaspoon black peppercorns
- 1 star anise
- 6 thyme sprigs
- 6 duck marylands (about 200 g each)
- 2 kg duck or goose fat, plus olive oil for topping up

Buy duck or goose fat from butchers and gourmet food shops

CHERRY SAUCE
- ¼ cup red wine
- 680 g jar morello cherries, drained, ¼ cup syrup reserved
- 2 tablespoons white sugar
- 2 star anise
- 1 cinnamon stick

Available in the canned fruit section of most supermarkets

First we need to get together a flavoured salt. Lightly pound the salt, garlic, peppercorns, star anise and thyme springs in a mortar using a pestle. You want the garlic to be slightly crushed and the spices cracked. Rub the salty mixture into the duck pieces, cover with plastic wrap and refrigerate overnight to marinate.

Now for the confit bit. Preheat the oven to 120°C.

Rinse the duck under cold water to remove the salt mixture. Pat dry and place in a casserole dish or deep roasting tray that's just large enough to fit the duck in one snug layer.

Heat the duck or goose fat in a saucepan until just melted. Pour over the duck, making sure all the pieces are completely covered — top up with a little olive oil, if you don't quite have enough.

Bake for 2 hours, or until the meat is soft and shrinking back from the bone. Remove from the oven. At this stage you can crisp up the duck skin and enjoy immediately or store the confit duck for later. If you'd like to store it, transfer the pieces to a large sterilised jar (see note on page 200) or container. Strain the fat into the jar to completely cover. Cool, then store in the fridge until you're ready to serve. You can store the confit duck like this for up to 2 weeks.

[continued overleaf] →

CONTINUED...

Ready to eat now? Preheat the oven to 120°C. Heat a heavy-based frying pan over medium heat. Remove the duck pieces from the fat. You will need to scrape away the excess fat, if you've been storing them in the fridge. Add to the pan, skin-side first, and sear for 3–4 minutes, or until the skin is golden and crisp. Turn the duck pieces over and cook on the other side for about 2 minutes, or until warmed through. Transfer to a roasting tray and keep warm in the oven while you make the cherry sauce.

Pour off most of the fat from the pan, leaving about 1 tablespoon and put it back on medium heat. Pour in the red wine and let it sizzle for half a minute, using a wooden spoon to scrape off any crisp duck bits from the base of the pan. Add the cherries and reserved syrup, sugar, star anise and cinnamon. Simmer for about 15 minutes to infuse the flavours and let the cherries collapse and thicken the sauce slightly.

Serve the duck with generous spoonfuls of sweet cherry sauce.

SERVES 6

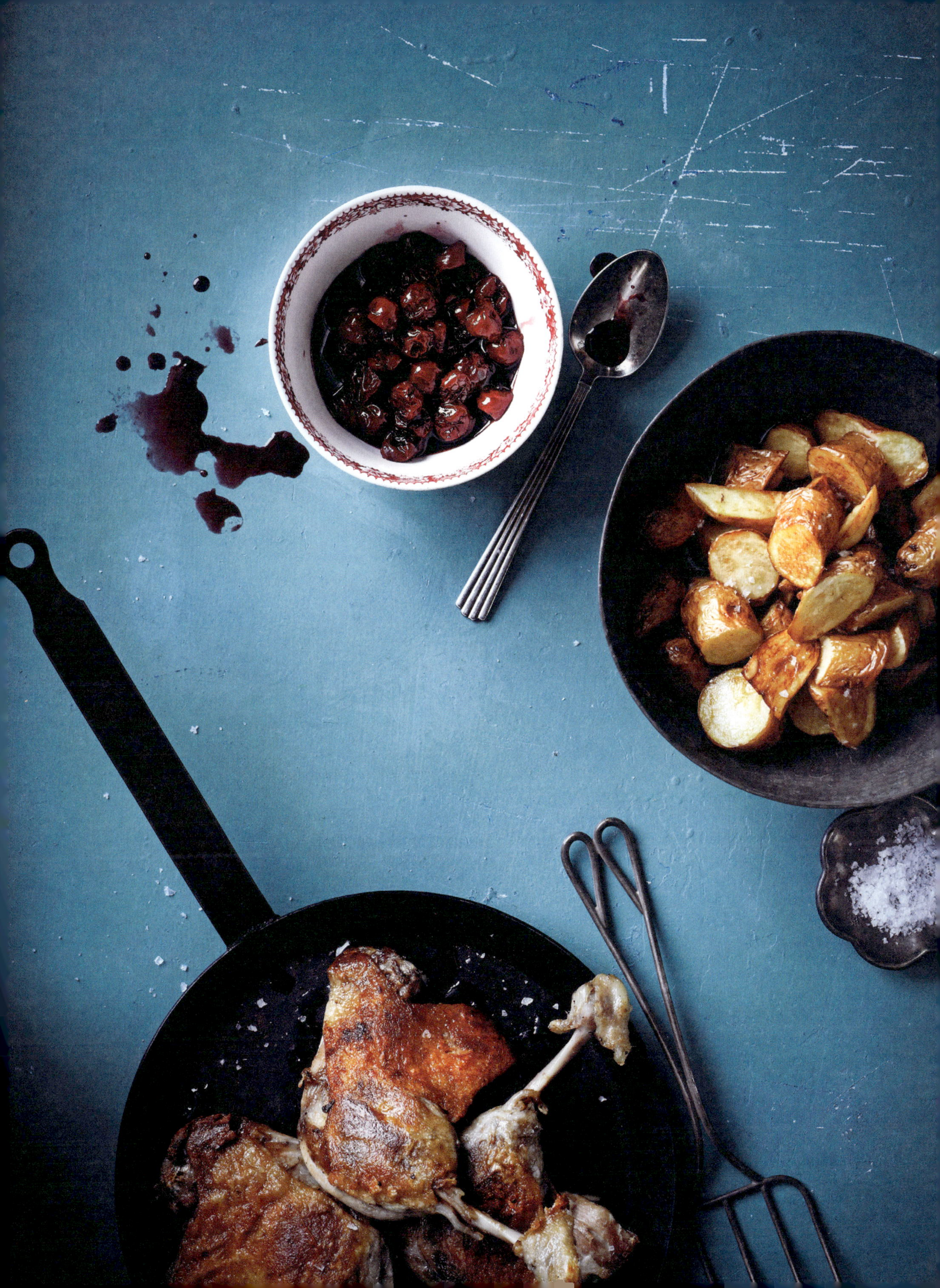

Roast Duck & Pineapple Curry

Okay so I'm not going to pretend that making fresh curry paste is something I do every day — or even every month. I always keep a jar of ready-made paste in my fridge because it means I can indulge in my love of Thai curry without breaking a sweat, so feel free to use a good-quality store-bought curry paste (you'll need about 2 tablespoons) instead of making your own. But do try this fresh version when time is not your enemy. A homemade paste always has a lovely spiced complexity. Use a pestle to bruise and bash the ingredients in a mortar for as long as you can. This initial bruising will break down some of the tough fibres of ginger and lemongrass that might catch in a food processor. You could do the entire paste using a mortar and pestle, but I find it's easier to blend the chillies in a food processor because I don't enjoy blinding myself with splashes of chilli juice.

1 tablespoon vegetable oil
2 cups coconut milk
2 kaffir lime leaves, whole
1 Chinese roast duck, chopped into pieces ← Ask your friendly Chinese barbecue vendor to chop the duck for you
1 cup fresh pineapple, roughly chopped
125 g cherry tomatoes, halved
1 tablespoon fish sauce, or to taste
[see notes] → 2 tablespoons finely shaved palm sugar, or to taste
½ cup basil leaves
Steamed Rice (see page 157), to serve

RED CURRY PASTE
10 dried long red chillies
1 teaspoon coriander seeds
1 teaspoon cumin seeds
1 tablespoon uncooked rice
3 red or golden (French) shallots, chopped
4 garlic cloves, chopped
10-cm piece of fresh ginger, unpeeled, roughly chopped
1 lemongrass stem, white part only, chopped
1 teaspoon sea salt
1 fresh long red chilli, chopped
2 teaspoons shrimp paste ← [see notes]

For the red curry paste, soak the dried chillies in warm water for about 20 minutes to soften. Drain and set aside. Meanwhile, heat a small frying pan over medium heat, add the coriander and cumin seeds and toast, keeping the spices moving in the hot pan, for a couple of minutes, or until you can just smell their lovely aroma. Transfer to a mortar and use a pestle to grind to a powder. Add the rice, shallot, garlic, ginger, lemongrass and salt and pound for as long as your arms will let you. Scoop everything into a food processor, add the dried and fresh chillies and the shrimp paste, and give it a whizz until you get a smooth paste. Open the lid, step back, smell those heady chilli-spice aromas and pat yourself on the back. Homemade curry paste! (See Notes)

Now to make the curry. Heat the vegetable oil in a saucepan over medium heat, add ¼ cup of the curry paste and cook for 1–2 minutes, or until you start to smell all that heady spice. Add the coconut milk and lime leaves and simmer for 1 or so minutes. Stir in ½ cup of water and bring it back to a simmer. Add the duck, pineapple and tomato. Simmer for about 5 minutes, or until the duck is warmed through. Add the fish sauce and palm sugar. Have a taste and add more fish sauce or palm sugar to taste. Remove from the heat and stir in the basil leaves just before serving. Ladle over bowls of steamed rice to serve.

SERVES 6

NOTES: Palm sugar and shrimp paste are available from Asian grocers and in the Asian aisle of some supermarkets. Palm sugar comes in hard blocks and you'll need to run a sharp knife along its edges to finely shave it into soft sugar.

The red curry paste recipe makes about 1 cup but you won't need all of it for this dish. Store the leftover curry paste in an airtight container in the freezer for up to 2 weeks for another night's curry, but do try to use it as quickly as possible as its flavour will diminish the longer you leave it.

OXTAIL RAGÙ WITH FRESH PAPPARDELLE

It's cold outside. I've got a big pot of simmering tomatoey, meaty goodness on the stove and all is good with the world.

2 kg oxtail pieces
2 tablespoons plain flour
3 tablespoons extra-virgin olive oil, plus extra for drizzling
3 garlic cloves, finely chopped
1 brown onion, finely chopped
1 carrot, diced
1 celery stalk, diced
1 cup white wine
400 g can diced tomatoes
1 fresh or dried bay leaf
1 tablespoon thyme leaves
1 tablespoon finely chopped rosemary leaves
2 teaspoons white sugar
sea salt and freshly ground black pepper
grated parmesan, to serve

FRESH PAPPARDELLE
400 g plain flour, plus extra for dusting
4 eggs
1 teaspoon extra-virgin olive oil

Dust the oxtail in the flour. Heat the olive oil in a large saucepan over high heat, add the oxtail, in batches, and sear until lightly browned. Remove from the pan.

Pour off all but about 1 tablespoon of oil and fat from the pan and return to medium–high heat. Add the garlic, onion, carrot and celery and cook for about 5 minutes, or until the onion and celery have softened, scraping up any brown meaty remains from the base of the pan. Return the oxtail to the pan, add the wine, tomato, bay leaf, thyme, rosemary and sugar. Bring to a simmer, then reduce the heat to low, cover and cook for about 2 hours, or until the meat is falling off the bone, stirring every so often. Keep an eye on the ragù and add about 1 cup of water if it starts to look too dry or if it catches on the base of the pan.

Meanwhile, make the fresh pappardelle. Place the flour in a large bowl and make a well in the centre. Crack the eggs into the well and add the oil. Using a fork, whisk the eggs and oil while slowly incorporating the flour. Keep mixing until the fork becomes useless. Now use your hands to knead and smoosh the mixture until it forms a dough. Tip out onto a lightly floured bench and knead for about 10 minutes, or until smooth and Plasticine-like. If it feels too dry or flaky, add 1 teaspoon of water while kneading. Divide the dough into 6 balls, wrap in plastic wrap and refrigerate for at least 10 minutes to rest.

Working with one ball of dough at a time, pass a ball of dough through the widest setting of a pasta machine. Fold the flattened piece in half, then pass through the same setting again. Repeat this 8 times. The fancy name for this process is called 'laminating' the dough to make the pasta shiny and firm when it's cooked instead of limp and soggy. Now pass the dough through each setting of the machine until you reach the second-last setting. Lightly dust the dough with flour between each setting to stop it from sticking. Fold the sheet in half (without pressing down), then in half again to make it easier to cut. Slice into thick strips for pappardelle or thinner ones for tagliatelle or fettuccine. Unravel and toss with flour to keep it from sticking. Repeat with the remaining balls of dough. Leave the pappardelle on the bench to dry slightly until you're ready to cook it.

Take your pan of meltingly tender oxtail off the heat and fish out the bones (the meat should have fallen off the bones at this point). Scoop the marrow from the bones and add back to the oxtail ragù. Discard the bones. Break up any big chunks of meat with a fork and season to taste with the salt and pepper. Cover to keep warm.

Cook the pasta in a large saucepan of boiling water seasoned with plenty of salt. It will only need 2–3 minutes, so watch it carefully. To test if it's ready, scoop out a strip of pasta and taste it. It should be just tender with a little bit of bite to it. Drain, divide into bowls and ladle over the ragù. Top with the parmesan and drizzle with some olive oil.

SERVES 6

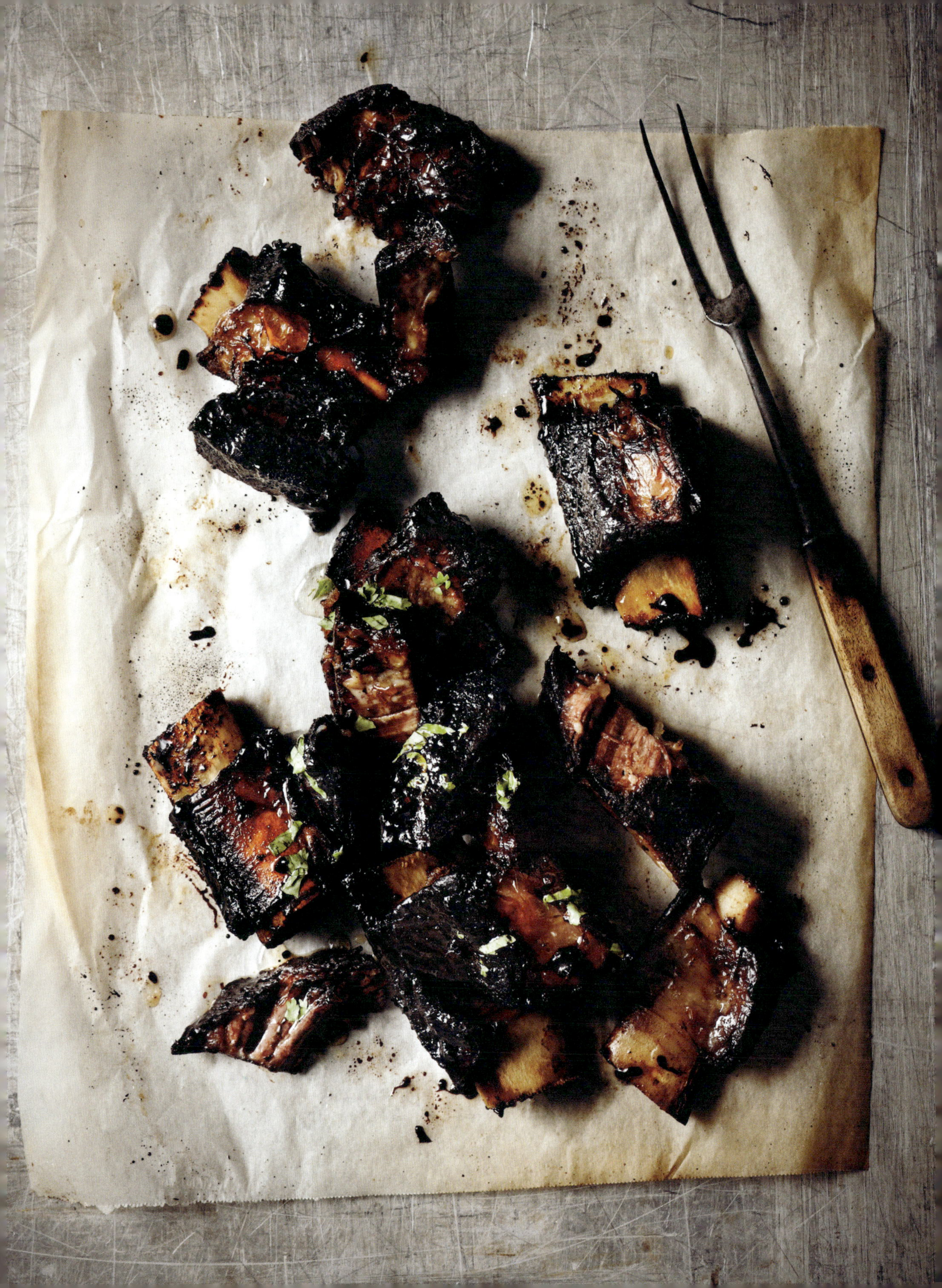

STICKY BEEF RIBS WITH SWEET CORIANDER SAUCE

You don't often see beef short ribs in a supermarket aisle or in a butcher's shop window, but they're well worth asking for. They've got a big hunk of meat on them that just falls away from the bone when slowly cooked. I cook them twice, first braised, then grilled. Cooking them twice means you get melt-in-the-mouth meat from the braising combined with crisp charry goodness from the grilling. You could serve this as part of an Asian banquet, in which case one rib per person will be enough (trust me, they're huge). For a smaller four-person affair, I often serve them as a stand-alone main course with a side of Dutch cream mash (see page 162) and Cabbage & Almond coleslaw (see page 156). You'll need plenty of napkins.

8-rib rack of beef short ribs (about 2 kg)
1 tablespoon sea salt
2 teaspoons Chinese five-spice
1 cup Shaoxing (Chinese rice) wine
¼ cup oyster sauce
¼ cup hoisin sauce
½ cup firmly packed brown sugar
2 tablespoons vegetable oil
4-cm piece of fresh ginger, peeled and finely chopped

3 garlic cloves, finely chopped
1 fresh long red chilli, finely chopped
coriander leaves, for garnishing

SWEET CORIANDER SAUCE
¼ cup white sugar
¼ cup white vinegar
1 teaspoon fish sauce
1 tablespoon chopped coriander stems and leaves

Preheat the oven to 120°C. Cut the rack into 8 individual ribs. Place in a large bowl and rub the salt and five-spice into the meat. Combine the Shaoxing, oyster and hoisin sauces and brown sugar in a separate bowl and set aside.

Heat the vegetable oil in a large frying pan over high heat, add the ribs, in batches, if necessary, and sear until browned on each side. Transfer to a deep baking dish or large casserole dish. Pour all but about 1 tablespoon of fat from the pan and return to the heat. Add the ginger, garlic and chilli and stir-fry for 2 minutes, or until it starts to smell delicious. Add the Shaoxing mixture, bring the sauce to a bubbling simmer, making sure you scrape up any charred beefy bits from the base of the pan. Pour over the ribs, cover with aluminium foil or a lid and bake for 4 hours, turning the ribs every hour.

Meanwhile, make the sweet coriander sauce. Simmer the sugar, vinegar and fish sauce in a small saucepan over high heat until the sugar dissolves. Set aside to cool, then stir in the coriander.

Once you've had 4 hours of drooling over the smell of the braising ribs, take them out of the oven to grill. There are a couple of options. You can heat the barbecue and chargrill the ribs or place them on a baking tray and cook them under an oven grill. Either way, you need to grill them for at least 10 minutes, or until they're just blackened, basting regularly with the braising liquid as you go.

Pile the sticky charred ribs onto a serving plate, spoon over the sweet coriander sauce and garnish with the coriander leaves.

SERVES 4 OR 8 AS PART OF A SHARED BANQUET

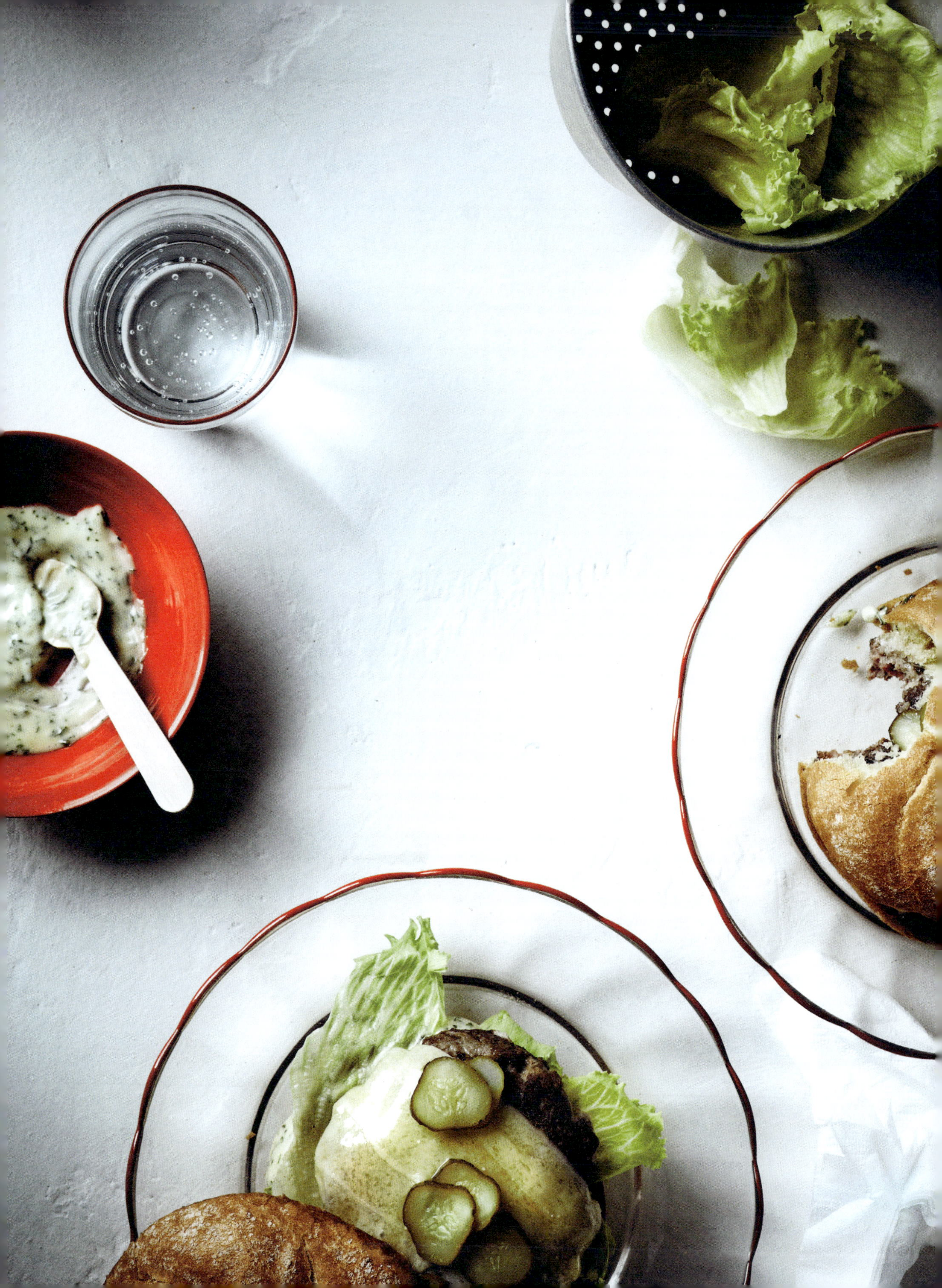

BEEFY BEEF BURGERS

I like an elegant sort of burger — pared back and simply dressed with a fresh mayonnaise, piquant dill pickles and melted cheese. The beauty comes from details such as a hint of aniseed from the fennel seeds in the patty and the tender crunch of a soft bun lightly toasted under the grill. Burger architecture is a critical consideration. It should be a generous construction but amenable to being patted down to a bite-sized thickness. And most important of all is the patty itself. Like any skill worth acquiring, perfecting the beefy beef burger patty took me some time. Well, actually, it took up my butcher's time, as I pestered him about what cuts of meat I should use and in what quantity. And, as usual, the butcher knows best. The navel-end part of the brisket is quite fatty, which keeps the patty moist and juicy, while the skirt steak, being a secondary cut of meat, provides the flavour. If you don't have a meat mincer at home, ask your friendly butcher to mince the beef for you. I like to make a big batch of burger patties so I can freeze some for later. Use a good-quality store-bought mayonnaise if you don't have time to make your own.

4 tablespoons fennel seeds
2 tablespoons sea salt
1 kg navel-end beef brisket, cut into chunks
1 kg beef skirt steak, cut into chunks
1 cup panko (Japanese) breadcrumbs ← available from an Asian grocer or the Asian section of most supermarkets

DILL MAYONNAISE
¼ cup rice bran oil or vegetable oil
¼ cup extra-virgin olive oil
2 egg yolks
2 teaspoons Dijon mustard
1 teaspoon white wine vinegar
2 tablespoons finely chopped dill
1 tablespoon finely chopped parsley

BURGER BITS
soft white buns, halved
softened butter, for spreading
slices of cheese (Gruyère is my favourite)
greenery (I like buttercup or iceberg lettuce)
good-quality dill pickles, thinly sliced

Heat a small frying pan over medium heat, add the fennel seeds and salt and toast, keeping the spices moving in the hot pan, for about 2 minutes, or until you can just smell the lovely aroma. Transfer to a mortar and roughly grind with a pestle.

Mince the beef brisket and skirt steak using the coarse plate on a meat mincer. Place the minced beef, ground fennel mixture and the breadcrumbs in a large bowl and use your hands to squelch it all together until well combined. Take heaped ½-cup amounts of the mixture and shape into 8-cm diameter, 2.5-cm thick patties and place on a tray. (At this point, you can freeze the patties between sheets of freezer film in an airtight container for up to 3 months.) Refrigerate for at least 20 minutes, or until firm.

[continued overleaf] →

CONTINUED...

Meanwhile, make the dill mayonnaise. Combine the oils in a pouring jug. Whisk the egg yolks, mustard and vinegar together in a large bowl. While whisking, add the combined oils, drop by drop. Once the mixture starts to look like thick yellow cream, you can add the oil in a steady stream, while whisking continuously. Alternatively, make the mayonnaise in a food processor. Stir through the dill and parsley.

Preheat your oven grill to high.

Heat a barbecue or large non-stick frying pan over medium heat. Cook the patties, in batches, if necessary, for 3–4 minutes each side, or until cooked through. You shouldn't need to add any oil because there should be enough fat in the patties from the navel-end brisket.

Meanwhile, butter the burger buns, place under the preheated oven grill and lightly toast. Remove from the grill and keep warm in the oven while you finish off the patties.

Top each patty with 1–2 slices of the cheese and pop under the grill until the cheese is bubbling and melted.

To assemble the burgers, spread a good dollop of dill mayonnaise on the toasted burger bun bases, top with some lettuce, a patty and a layer of pickles. Sandwich with the burger bun tops and squish down ever so gently. Devour in big greedy bitefuls and just try to stop yourself from eating more than one!

MAKES 12–14

Sumac-Crusted Scotch Fillet with Chimichurri

I know I talk a lot about the quality of meat, about talking to your butcher and so on, but it's only because I care. I care about your meat tasting just as good as mine. It's not the way I cook it. I'm not, after all, some grand classically trained chef and there are myriad different ways to cook a brilliant steak. No, the key is the way I buy it. Good meat means good eating. It also helps if you live with someone who is obsessed with cooking the perfect steak. From what I can tell it's all about treating your steak with love and a bit of tender care. My partner, Tim, lets the steaks come to room temperature 'so the poor fellas don't get too much of a shock when they hit the pan'. And then finishes the cooking in a low temperature oven, which also allows the steak to rest up a bit before it hits my plate.

4 x 4-cm thick good quality scotch fillet steaks (about 300–350 g each) ← *If you've got smaller steaks, no problem, just reduce the cooking time in the oven*

2 teaspoons sumac ← *A Middle Eastern spice with a lovely lemony sort of flavour and is available in select supermarkets or gourmet food stores*

2 tablespoons extra-virgin olive oil

1 teaspoon sea salt

CHIMICHURRI

1 cup extra-virgin olive oil

¼ cup red wine vinegar

1 cup chopped flat-leaf parsley

2 garlic cloves, chopped

1 teaspoon sea salt

½ teaspoon smoked sweet paprika

½ teaspoon ground cumin

Take the steaks out of the fridge a good couple of hours before you want to cook them so they can come to room temperature. Combine the sumac, olive oil and salt in a small bowl, pour over the steaks and rub all over the meat. Leave to marinate while you wait for them to come to room temperature.

Meanwhile, make the chimichurri. Place all of the ingredients in a food processor and process until smooth. Set aside until ready to serve.

Preheat the oven to 150°C. Heat a barbecue grill plate or large frying pan to high. Sear the steaks for about 2 minutes each side, then transfer to a roasting tray and roast for about 6 minutes for a juicy medium-rare steak, or until cooked to your liking. Rest the steaks for about 4 minutes. Serve with chimichurri sauce and your choice of sides.

SERVES 4

EIGHT-HOUR LAMB ROAST WITH TOMATO & HERB GRAVY

I find slow cooking so incredibly satisfying, not to mention easy. An eight-hour lamb roast may take a while to cook but you don't have to do too much else except wait. The slow roasting produces a melt-in-the-mouth, unctuously delightful lamb that's worth the time in the oven. Serve with a big bowl of Dutch cream mash (see page 162) or the Rosy Israeli couscous (see page 158).

3 anchovy fillets
4 garlic cloves
2 sprigs rosemary
1 teaspoon sea salt, plus extra to taste
2 tablespoons extra-virgin olive oil
2.5 kg lamb shoulder, bone in freshly ground black pepper

TOMATO & HERB GRAVY
2 teaspoons plain flour
2 cups Saturday Afternoon Chicken Stock (see page 30)
3 tomatoes, finely diced
2 tablespoons salted or brined capers, finely chopped
1 tablespoon chopped flat-leaf parsley
2 tablespoons chopped basil leaves

If using salted capers, be sure to rinse them first to remove the excess salt

Preheat the oven to 200°C.

Place the anchovies, garlic, rosemary and salt in a mortar and pound with pestle to a rough paste. Mix in the olive oil. Place the lamb in a deep flameproof roasting tray, pour over the anchovy paste and use your hands to rub it all over the lamb. Add 2 cups of water to the tray (this will keep the lamb moist as it roasts), cover with 2 layers of aluminium foil and seal the edges well. Place in the oven and immediately reduce the temperature to 110°C. Forget about it for 8 hours – well, not quite. Check the lamb after 4 hours and add 1 cup of water, if there's not much liquid left in the base.

After 8 hours, the meat should be falling off the bone. Carefully transfer the lamb to a serving platter and cover with foil to keep warm.

Now for the gravy. Pour off most of the fatty liquid from the tray, leaving about 1 tablespoon. Place over medium heat and stir in the flour. Cook, stirring, for about 1 minute, then add the stock and whisk to combine, making sure there are no lumpy bits. Simmer for 3–4 minutes, or until slightly thickened. Stir in the tomato and capers and simmer for 2 minutes. Remove from the heat and stir through the parsley and basil. Season with salt and pepper to taste.

Serve the big hunk of lamb at the table, so everyone can strip off their own bits of tender meat, with the gravy on the side.

SERVES 6

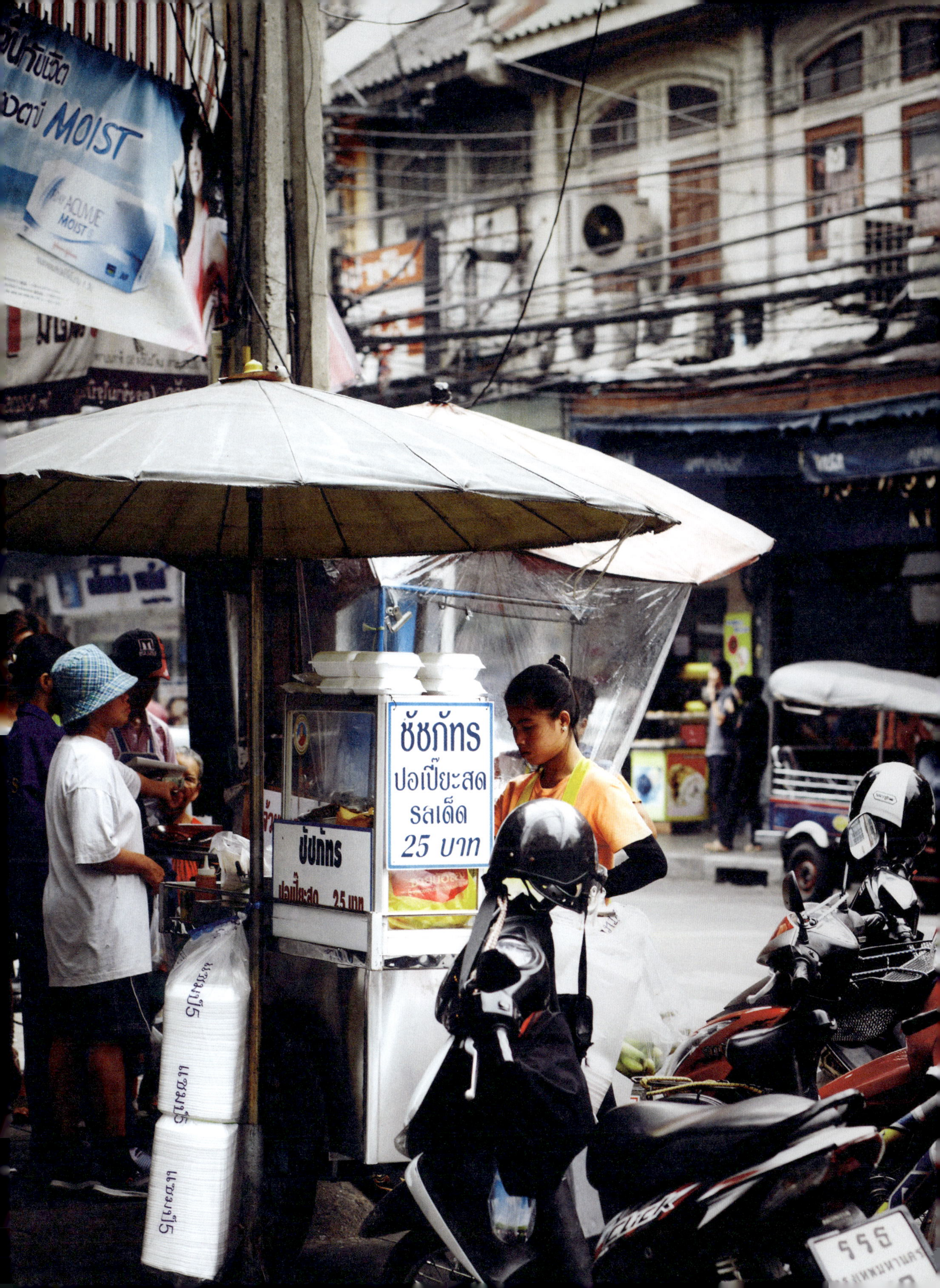
MOIST
ชัชภัทร
ปอเปี๊ยะสด
รสเด็ด
25 บาท

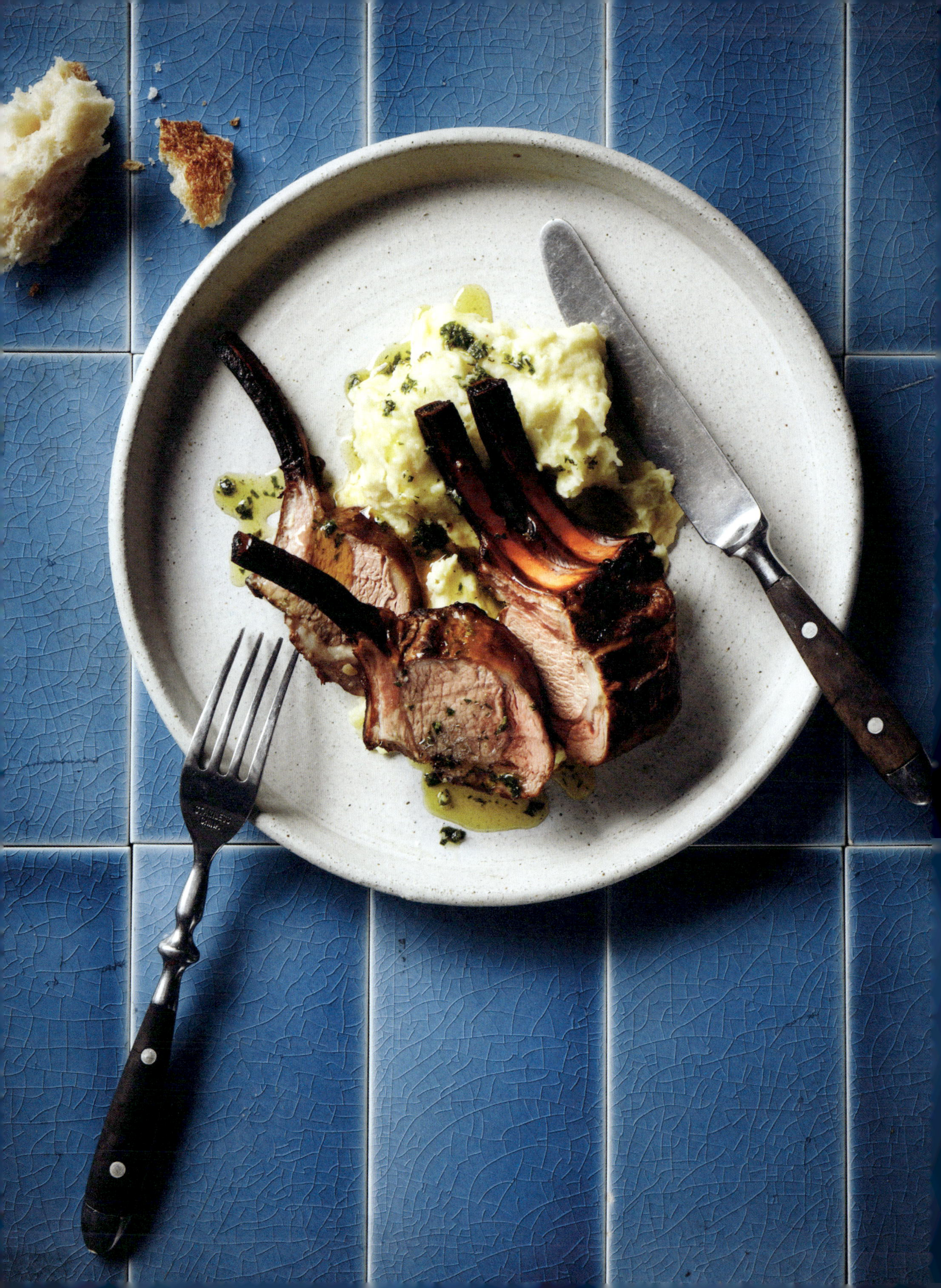

SMOKED LAMB CUTLETS WITH HERB BUTTER SAUCE

Michel Roux taught me how to smoke. In case you're not a food nerd like me, Michel Roux is one of the greats, the godfather, if you will, of French cooking in the UK. He, with his brother Albert, opened iconic restaurant, Le Gavroche, in London in the 1960s. It was the first British establishment to not only gain a Michelin star but also three Michelin stars. His cookbooks have always been my kitchen manuals. I nearly peed my pants when I met him and got to cook with him. We smoked duck breast. My smoking mixes are now forever based on his smoked duck breast recipe and I will be forever grateful. Here I've mixed it up a bit and used Sichuan peppercorns and lamb. But you could use the same smoking mix for duck or even fish. I think you need a large dollop of Dutch cream mash (see page 162) or crushed purple congo potatoes (see page 162) to soak up the buttery, herby sauce that goes with this lamb.

4 x 4-cutlet racks of lamb (about 300 g each)
1 teaspoon sea salt

SMOKING MIX
1 cup firmly packed brown sugar
2 star anise, slightly crushed
2 tablespoons Sichuan peppercorns

HERB BUTTER SAUCE
125 g good-quality unsalted butter, cubed
1 garlic clove, finely chopped
1 tablespoon finely chopped rosemary leaves
2 tablespoons finely chopped flat-leaf parsley
2 tablespoons finely chopped dill
1 teaspoon sea salt

Preheat the oven to 150°C. Season the lamb with the salt and set aside.

For the smoking mix, line a wok with 4 layers of aluminium foil, making sure there is plenty of overhang off the wok. Combine the sugar, star anise and peppercorns in a bowl, then place onto the foil in the wok, spreading to cover the base. Place a round wire cake rack in the wok, so that it rests on the wall of the wok about 2 cm above the smoking mix.

Heat the wok over high heat until it just starts to smoke. Place the lamb on the wire rack, cover with a tight-fitting lid and seal with the overhanging foil. Turn on the rangehood exhaust and open the windows. Now we're smoking. Reduce the heat to medium and leave to smoke for 12 minutes, then turn off the heat and allow the lamb to sit in its smoky enclosure for about 2 minutes – don't be tempted to lift the lid. Remove the lamb from the wok, place on a baking tray and roast in your preheated oven for about 15 minutes for medium-rare, or until to cooked to your liking. Remove the lamb and allow to rest covered in foil for about 4 minutes.

Meanwhile, make the herb butter sauce. Melt the butter in a frying pan over high heat until foaming. Add the garlic and rosemary and stir for about 1 minute, or until the garlic softens. Stir through the parsley, dill and salt and remove from the heat. Set aside and keep warm until ready to serve (the sauce can be gently reheated, if it gets too cold).

Slice each lamb rack in half, arrange the 2 halves on each plate and drizzle with generous spoonfuls of herb butter sauce.

SERVES 4

LAP CHONG OMELETTE

I'm smitten with the omelette: a fluffy, cheesy, buttery omelette; an omelette layered with tendrils of smoked salmon; an omelette stuffed with buttery sautéed mushrooms; or any omelette. Where did it all begin? I suspect it began here, with this Thai omelette I grew up eating at my family table. The Thai omelette is a little different to its European cousin. Cheese is never an ingredient and the omelette itself is never folded or fiddled with. Rather, you let the eggs puff and expand as they hit the hot oil in the wok. This serves two greedy omelette lovers or four as part of a banquet. I often make this for a simple dinner, scoffed with a bowl of steamed rice (see page 157).

6 eggs
2 teaspoons fish sauce, plus extra to serve
freshly ground black pepper
¼ cup vegetable oil
2 lap chong (dried Chinese sausages), thinly sliced *— get these at Asian grocers, Chinese barbecue shops or the Asian section of most supermarkets*
½ brown onion, sliced
1 spring onion, thinly sliced

Place the eggs, 2 teaspoons of the fish sauce, 2 tablespoons of water and heaps (I mean about 10 turns of a pepper grinder) of the pepper in a large bowl. Whisk until just combined.

I find it easier to cook the omelette in 2 batches. Heat half of the vegetable oil in a wok over high heat, add half of the lap chong and onion and stir-fry for 1 minute, or until the onion just starts to brown. Pour in half of the egg mixture and let it bubble and puff up. Let the eggs set for about 2 minutes, or until lightly browned, then flip over and cook for another 10 seconds. By this stage it should be cooked through. Remove from the wok, and cover to keep warm. Repeat with the remaining oil, lap chong, onion and egg.

To serve, sprinkle the omelettes with the spring onion and splash with a little more fish sauce.

SERVES 2–4

KAI PALO
[FIVE-SPICE PORK & EGG STEW]

I love the streets of Bangkok. They can be stinky, grimy and stinking, dirty hot. But everywhere you turn there's food — vats of simmering curries, fiery woks of noodles and charcoal burners topped with sizzling satay sticks. I don't know what the dishes are most of the time and I don't even recognise some of the ingredients, but that's what makes it fun and just a little bit dangerous at times. You simply point and pay for an unknown adventure. One of the dishes I *can* recognise instantly is 'kai palo'. I can smell its earthy, spiced broth metres away. In any given Bangkok street you'll find a colossal steaming pot of 'kai palo' — a dark five-spiced broth with chunks of melting pork and burnished eggs gently bobbing like buoys in a deep murky harbour.

6 coriander roots with 4 cm stem attached, cleaned
8 garlic cloves, peeled
1 tablespoon white peppercorns
1.5 kg pork belly, skin on, cut into 5-cm x 3-cm chunks
1 tablespoon Chinese five-spice
2 teaspoons sea salt
3 tablespoons vegetable oil
¼ cup soy sauce
¼ cup kecap manis
6 star anise
2 cinnamon sticks
¼ cup white sugar
8 eggs
150 g fried tofu ← *You can buy packets of these at Asian grocers. They look like golden fluffy marshmallow squares*
¼ cup roughly chopped coriander leaves
Steamed Rice (see page 157), to serve

Pound the coriander roots, garlic and peppercorns to a rough paste using a mortar and pestle. Place the pork in a large bowl, add the coriander paste, five-spice and salt and mix to coat well. Refrigerate for 30 minutes to marinate.

Heat the vegetable oil in a large saucepan over medium heat, add the pork and cook for about a minute, or until just browned all over. Add the soy sauce, kecap manis, star anise, cinnamon, sugar and 1.25 litres of water and bring to a simmer. Reduce the heat to low and leave to gently bubble away for about 1 hour, or until the pork is tender.

Meanwhile, put the eggs in a saucepan, cover with cold water and place over high heat. Bring to a gentle simmer, then reduce the heat and cook for 8 minutes. Drain and, when cool enough to handle, peel.

When the pork is tender, add the eggs and tofu and simmer for 10 minutes. Remove from the heat, scatter with the coriander and serve with the steamed rice.

SERVES 8

BIG PLATES /MEAT

ROASTED PORK WITH APPLE SAUCE

Some things need no fancy embellishments or inventive additions — the match has been made and there's no need for improvement. I call them the perfect pairs: champagne and oysters, steak and chips and that classic marriage of pork and apples. I cannot eat this roasted pork without a cabbage salad but I tend to swing between the Dutch cream mash (see page 162) and the roasted kipfler potatoes (see page 161) as my potatoes of choice.

I like to buy Berkshire free-range pork because it has a superior juiciness and a sweet porky flavour

1.8 kg boned rolled pork loin, skin on
2 teaspoons sea salt
2 tablespoons extra-virgin olive oil

APPLE SAUCE
50 g butter
2 green apples, peeled, cored and roughly chopped
1 tablespoon white sugar
1 tablespoon lemon juice
¼ teaspoon sea salt

GRAVY
1 tablespoon plain flour
½ cup white wine
1 cup Saturday Afternoon Chicken Stock (see page 30)
sea salt and freshly ground black pepper

Get your pork out of the fridge a couple of hours before you want to roast it so that it comes to room temperature.

Preheat the oven to 220°C. Using a sharp knife, score the pork skin at 1-cm intervals. You want to cut through the skin and just into the fat layer. This is an important part of the crackling process. I find that even if the butcher has done some scoring on my pork, I still add a few extra score lines and cut into the pork fat a little deeper. Pat the pork dry with paper towel – too much moisture is death to crackly crackling. Sprinkle over the salt, drizzle over the olive oil and vigorously rub into the skin using your hands. Place in a large deep flameproof roasting tray and roast for 20 minutes to get the crackling started, then reduce the heat to 160°C and roast for another 1 hour 20 minutes, or until just cooked through.

Meanwhile, make the apple sauce. Place the butter, apple, sugar, lemon juice, salt and ¼ cup of water in a saucepan over medium heat and bring to a simmer. Reduce the heat to low and gently simmer for about 15 minutes, or until the apple has softened. Give everything a bit of a mash with a fork – I like it slightly lumpy. Remove from the heat and transfer to a serving bowl.

Now back to the pork. Remove the tray from the oven, and lift out the pork and place it on a carving plate or chopping board. Let the pork rest for 15 minutes.

Meanwhile, pour off most of the fatty liquid from the tray, leaving about 1 tablespoon. Place over medium heat and whisk in the flour. Cook, whisking, for about 1 minute, then add the wine and stock and whisk to combine making sure there are no lumpy bits. Simmer for 5 minutes, or until slightly thickened. Season to taste with some salt and pepper. Carve thick slices of pork and serve with the apple sauce, gravy and your choice of sides.

SERVES 8

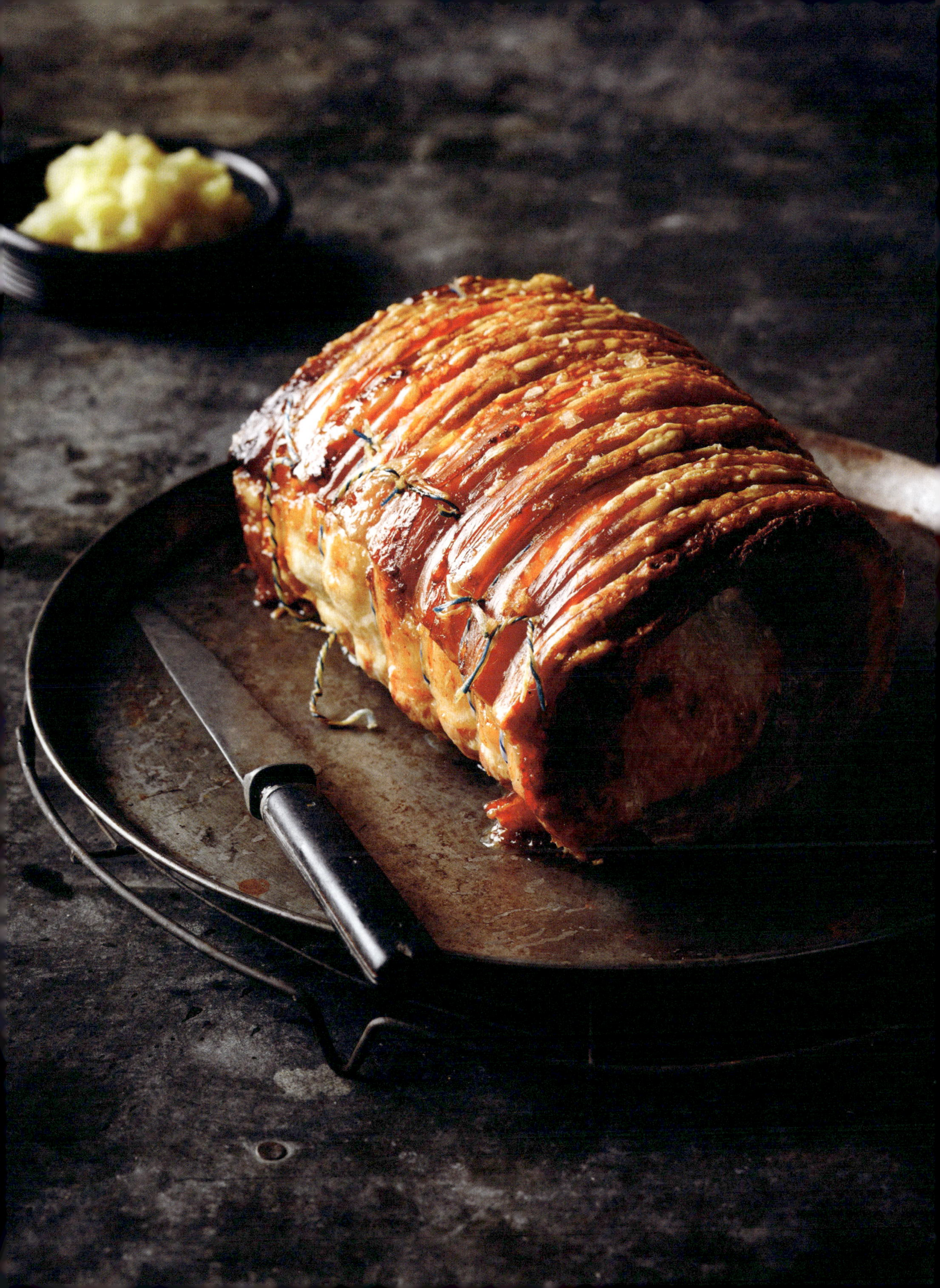

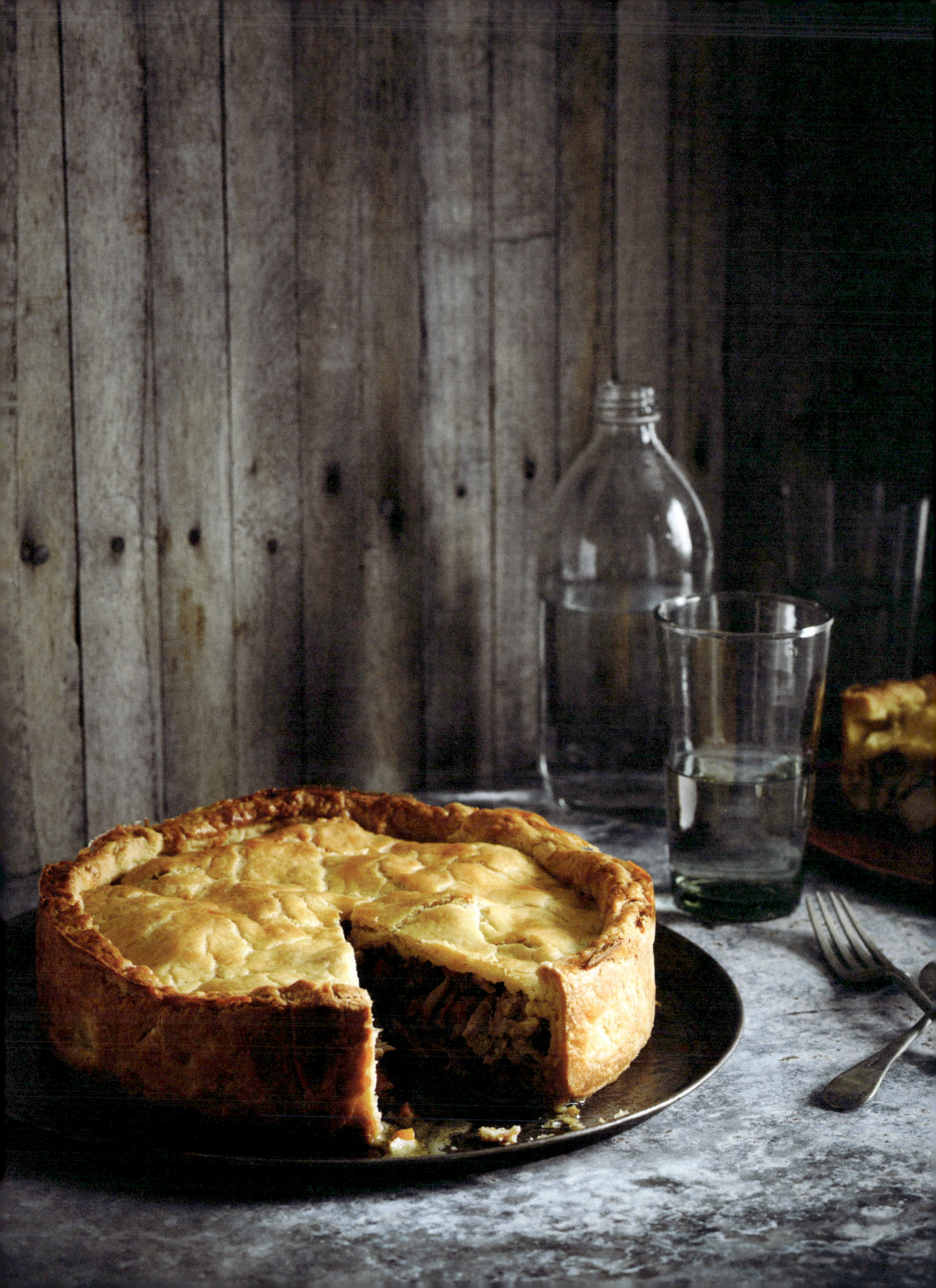

RABBIT PIE WITH MUSTARD SAUCE

I make this rabbit pie for my dad. He's of Australian-British stock and grew up in a small country town in Victoria, where he was sent out to shoot dinner every day from the time he could hold a gun. 'We lived on rabbits,' he says. 'Stewed rabbit, baked rabbit, rabbit pie. Your grandmother made the best rabbit pie.' I love hearing about my grandma and her pies, her scones and sponge cakes. I love hearing about foods and kitchen habits that time forgot — tripe and onions, beef dripping and suet pastry. When I make rabbit pie for my dad, it reminds me of all those things and it's a great pleasure to see him remembering too.

Dad might be my go-to guy for rabbit, but Maggie Beer is my go-to girl for pastry. Her sour cream pastry is impossibly flaky and incredibly forgiving as you roll it out. I love the process of making pastry and I've tried many a different recipe, but Maggie has it just right. I was lucky enough to meet Maggie on the set of 'Masterchef', where she made this pastry for a challenge. I feel incredibly humbled when I meet people like Maggie whose infectious love of food and amazing knowledge has influenced decades of Australian home cooks. Thanks for being you, Maggie, and thanks for a ripper of a pastry recipe.

1.4 kg whole farmed rabbit ← *If you're using wild rabbits, you will need two because they're smaller than the farmed ones*
2 tablespoons butter
2 rashers bacon, finely diced
1 onion, finely diced
1 carrot, diced
2 garlic cloves, finely chopped
1 cup white wine
1 cup Saturday Afternoon Chicken Stock (see page 30)
1 fresh bay leaf
1 tablespoon thyme leaves
¼ teaspoon sea salt

1 tablespoon cornflour
½ cup pouring (single) cream
1 tablespoon Dijon mustard
2 tablespoons finely chopped flat-leaf parsley
finely grated zest of 2 lemons
sea salt and freshly ground black pepper
1 egg

MAGGIE BEER'S SOUR CREAM PASTRY
200 g chilled butter, cubed
2 cups plain flour, plus extra for dusting
½ cup sour cream

Place the rabbit, breast-up, on a chopping board. Using a sharp knife, remove the back legs first, then divide the body of the rabbit in half by cutting across it where the rib cage ends. You should have 4 pieces. Melt the butter in a large saucepan over medium heat. Sear the rabbit until lightly browned all over. Remove the rabbit from the pan. Return the pan to the heat, add the bacon, onion, carrot and garlic and cook for 2 minutes, or until the onion has softened and the bacon has browned. Return the rabbit to the pan and pour over the wine and stock. Add the bay leaf, thyme and salt, reduce the heat to low, cover and simmer for 1 hour.

[continued overleaf] →

CONTINUED...

Meanwhile, make the sour cream pastry. Place the butter and flour in a food processor and process until you get a fine breadcrumb-like texture. Add the sour cream and pulse until it just starts to come together in clumps. If the dough doesn't come together, add 1 teaspoon of water and pulse again. Tip the mixture onto a bench and smoosh the pastry together to form a clump – don't play around with it or knead it or you'll end up with a melted buttery mess. Divide the pastry into two pieces, using one-third for one piece and two-thirds for the other. Quickly pat each into a thick disc, wrap in plastic wrap and refrigerate for 20 minutes to rest and firm up.

Lightly dust the bench with some flour and place the larger disc of pastry on the bench. Lightly dust the top of the pastry and rub flour all over a rolling pin. Now you're good to go. The trick to rolling pastry is to keep the pastry moving so it doesn't stick to the bench. Roll the rolling pin across the pastry a couple of times, then turn the pastry 90 degrees. Roll a couple of times, then turn 90 degrees again. Keep rolling and turning, dusting with flour as you go to stop the pastry sticking, until it is 5 mm thick and at least about 35 cm in diameter. Roll one end of the pastry onto the rolling pin, so the pastry drapes off it, and transfer to a non-stick 23-cm round springform cake tin. Gently line the base and sides with the pastry, then pop it back in the fridge for another rest, about 20 minutes. Roll out the remaining pastry disc, following the above instructions to make a pie lid at least 28 cm in diameter. Place on a large tray and refrigerate for 20 minutes to rest.

Preheat the oven to 200°C. Remove the rabbit from the braising liquid in the saucepan and set aside to cool slightly, then pull off and shred the meat into a large bowl. Discard the bones.

Remove the bay leaf from the braising liquid in the saucepan. Combine the cornflour and 2 tablespoons of water to make a slurry, then whisk into the braising liquid. Simmer over medium heat for about 20 minutes, or until thickened. Stir in the cream and mustard and simmer for another 5 minutes. Strain the mixture over a heatproof bowl. Add the solids to the rabbit meat and reserve the sauce. Add the parsley and lemon zest to the rabbit mixture and give everything a mix. Add about ½ cup of the reserved sauce to just moisten the rabbit mixture without making it too wet because that will make the pastry soggy. Season to taste with the salt and pepper and set aside to cool. Reserve the remaining sauce for serving.

Spoon the filling into the pastry case. Drape the pie lid over the rolling pin and lay the pastry over the top of the filling. Trim the excess pastry with a knife or scissors so there is about a 2-cm overhang, then fold the overhang in toward the centre of the pie, making sure to fold over both the pastry side and the top to seal. Poke a couple holes in the top of the pastry lid to let the steam escape while it bakes. Lightly whisk the egg with 1 tablespoon of water and brush over the top of the pie. Bake for about 30 minutes, or until the pastry is golden and shrinking back from the edges of the springform cake tin. Remove from the oven and allow to rest in the tin for about 15 minutes.

Meanwhile, gently reheat the reserved sauce. Carefully remove the pie from the tin and slide onto a serving plate. Cut into large wedges and serve drizzled with as much of the reserved mustard and cream sauce as you like.

SERVES 6

DEEP-FRIED PEPPERY PORK BELLY

I feel so naughty when I make this dish. Not only are you using a cut of fatty meat but you're also deep-frying it in oil. Even I know that's a little bit wicked. But the resulting dish is packed with so much flavour and not at all oily provided you get your deep-frying technique right. The secret to a good deep-fry is to get the oil hot enough so that it seals the outside of the food instead of being absorbed by it. I use a wooden spoon to test the temperature of the oil. Dip the spoon into the oil and if you get loads of furious little bubbles rolling and fizzing around the spoon then you're good to go. The sweet and sour coriander sauce has just the right amount of acid to cut through the rich pork belly. I guess this is my naughty version of sweet and sour pork, which tastes great with steamed rice (see page 157) and wok-fried kang kong (see page 160).

choose a piece with a good layer of meat and not too much fat (as much as I love being naughty, you don't want to overdo it) →

700 g pork belly
4 coriander roots with 4 cm stem attached, cleaned
4 garlic cloves
1 tablespoon white peppercorns
1 tablespoon soy sauce
1 tablespoon fish sauce
1 teaspoon white sugar
vegetable oil, for deep-frying
2 tablespoons plain flour

SWEET & SOUR CORIANDER SAUCE
¼ cup white sugar
¼ cup white vinegar
1 tablespoon fish sauce
1 tablespoon finely chopped coriander leaves

Use a sharp knife to remove the tough skin from the pork belly. Discard the skin, cut the pork belly into 3-cm cubes and place in a large bowl.

Place the coriander roots, garlic and peppercorns in a mortar and pound with a pestle to a rough paste – you don't want a smooth paste, in this case, because the lumpy bits of garlic will turn sweet and crisp when you fry it. Add to the pork belly with the soy sauce, fish sauce and sugar. Refrigerate for 30 minutes to marinate.

Meanwhile, make the sweet and sour coriander sauce. Simmer the sugar, vinegar and fish sauce in a small saucepan over high heat until the sugar dissolves. Set aside to cool, then stir in the coriander.

Heat 10 cm of vegetable oil to 180°C in a wok or large heavy-based saucepan. Toss the pork belly in the flour to coat, then carefully drop the pork, in batches, into the oil and cook for about 5 minutes, or until golden. Remove with a slotted spoon and drain on paper towel. Serve with a bowl of sweet and sour coriander sauce on the side, ready to drizzle over the pork.

SERVES 4

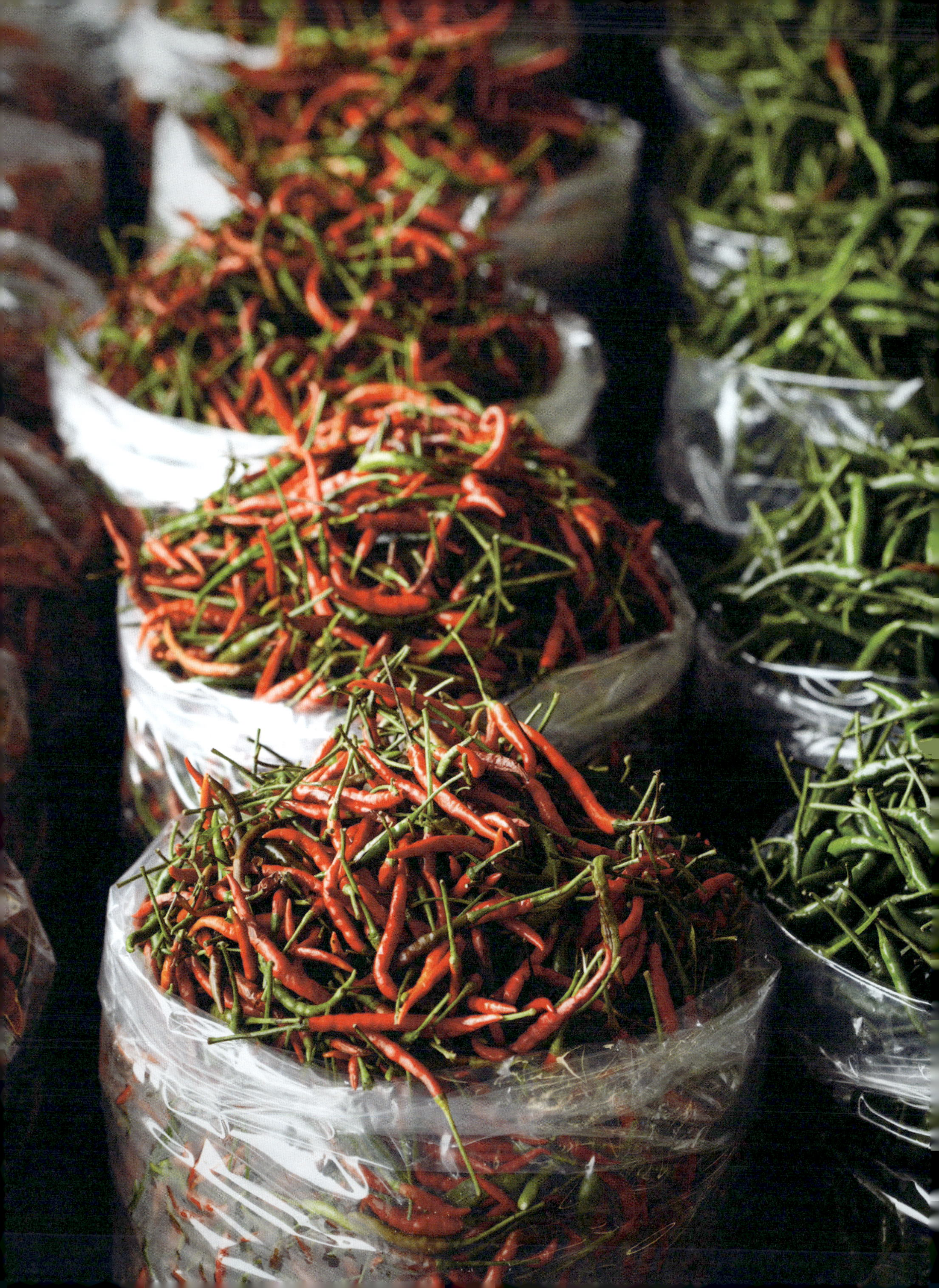

CHILLI, GARLIC & ANCHOVY SPAGHETTI

Garlicky, salty and just a little spicy. I crave this dish on a regular basis. It's a good thing it's easy to make and most of the ingredients can be kept on hand at all times.

300 g spaghetti
½ cup extra-virgin olive oil
3 garlic cloves, thinly sliced
6 anchovy fillets
½ teaspoon chilli flakes
1 cup grated parmesan
1 cup basil leaves
sea salt

Bring a large saucepan of salted water to a rolling boil. Add the spaghetti and cook according to the packet instructions.

Meanwhile, heat the olive oil in a large saucepan over medium heat. Add the garlic and anchovies and cook, stirring to break up the anchovies, for about 2 minutes, or until the anchovies have melted, then sprinkle in the chilli flakes.

Drain the pasta and add to the garlic, anchovy and chilli oil. Toss to coat, sprinkle over half of the parmesan and the basil leaves and toss again. Pile into serving bowls and scatter with the remaining parmesan. Season to taste with the salt.

SERVES 4

TUESDAY-NIGHT TRUFFLE TAGLIATELLE

I don't suppose there are many students who can claim truffle pasta as their weeknight dinner of choice. After quitting my career as a journalist to undertake a Master of Gastronomy I found myself manning the phones at an Adelaide gourmet food and wine company called Bottega Rotolo. My partner, Tim, had also quit his day job to follow his own wine dream and we would joke that at least we would never starve with a vegetable patch in our backyard. And starve we certainly did not. Not when I had a cheese room and a warehouse full of imported Italian goodies to play with. And so my hard-earned phone-answering wage was spent on treats such as aged Italian parmesan (Parmigiano-Reggiano) and fresh winter truffles imported from Italy. So it was, on many a Tuesday night, we found ourselves sitting down to a bowlful of fresh tagliatelle smothered in truffled butter.

½ quantity fresh pasta (see pages 112–3)
½ cup grated Parmigiano-Reggiano

TRUFFLE BUTTER
250 g good-quality unsalted butter, at room temperature
15–20 g fresh black winter truffle, ← [see note] roughly chopped

For the truffle butter, place the butter and truffle pieces in a bowl and mix until well combined. Spoon onto a large piece of plastic wrap and roll into a thick bonbon-shaped log. Twist the ends to seal tightly and place in the freezer until firm.

Cook the fresh pasta in boiling salted water for 2–3 minutes, or until al dente.

Meanwhile, cut off a whopping chunk of frozen truffle butter, about one-quarter, and heat in a large saucepan over low heat until just melted.

Drain the pasta and add to the melted butter. Toss well, scatter over the Parmigiano-Reggiano and toss again. Pile into large bowls and scoff.

SERVES 2

NOTE: Winter truffles are available from specialty providores. I prefer winter truffle to its summer cousin because it has a more intense flavour. For European winter truffles, you'll need to wait until about December, while Australian winter truffles hit their straps from about June to August. The truffle butter recipe makes more than you will need. It will keep in the freezer for up to 6 months but use it sooner rather than later as the flavour becomes less intense.

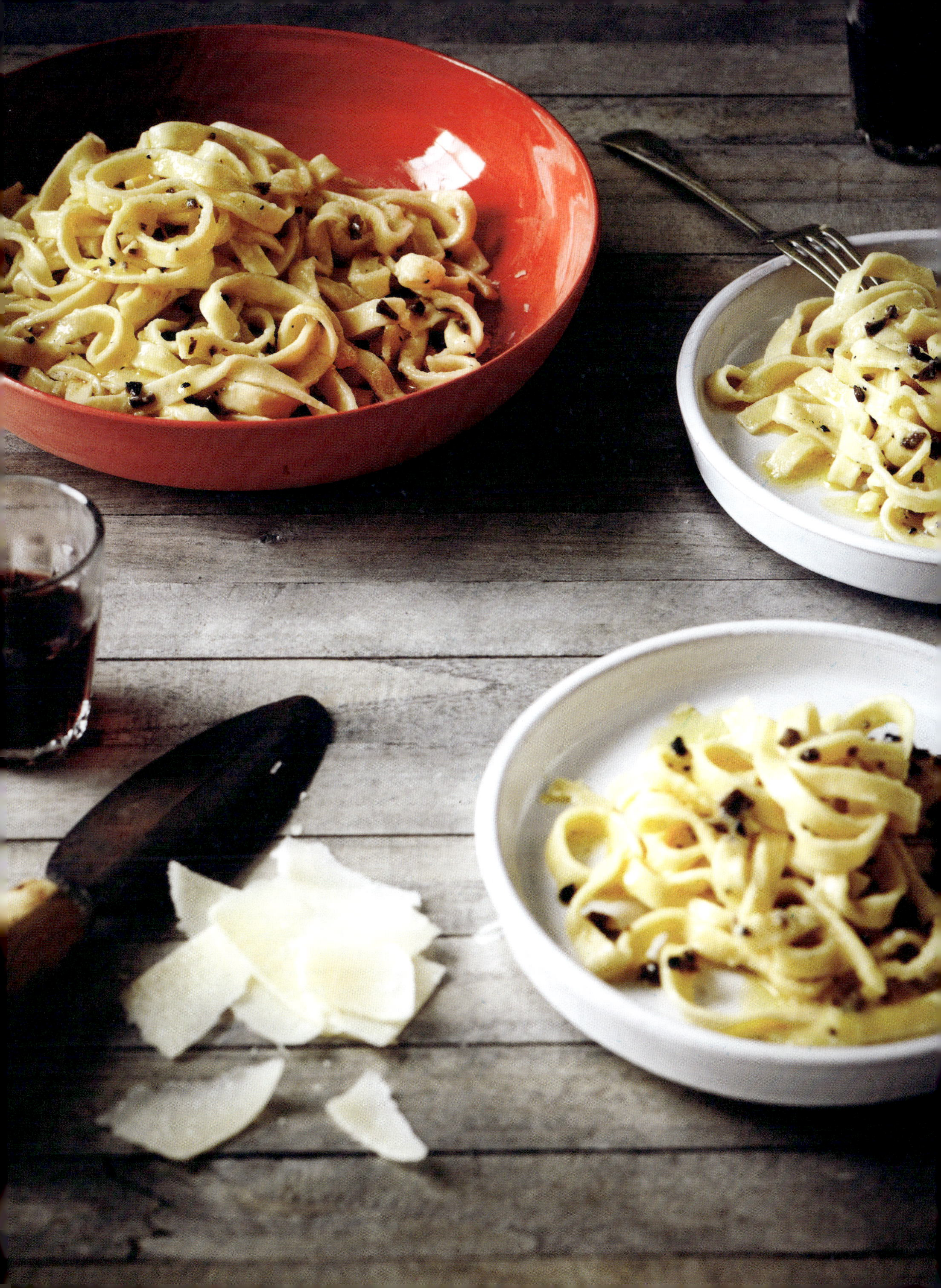

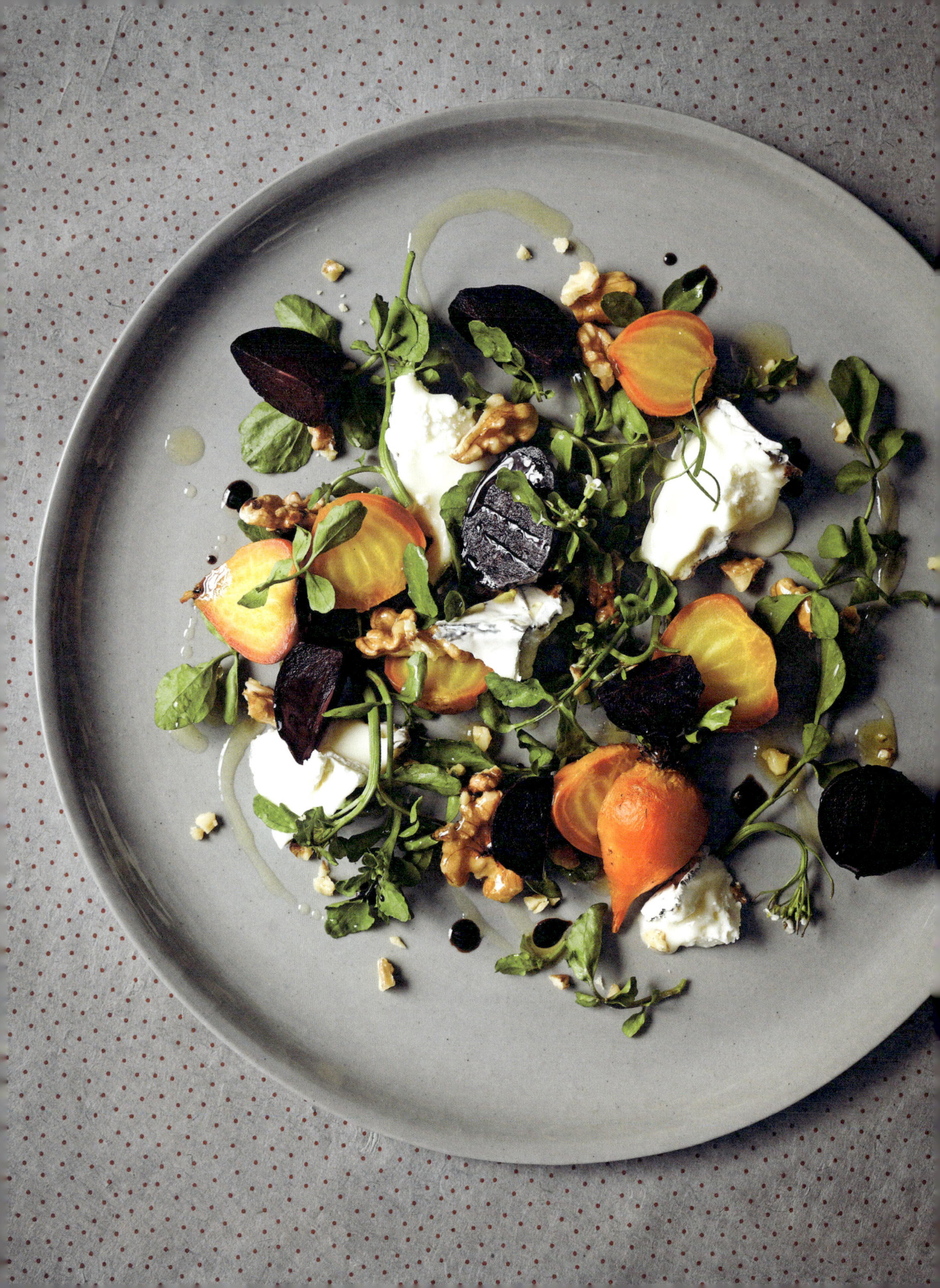

COLOUR-ME-AUTUMN SALAD

It was the Willunga Farmers' market in South Australia that changed me. I was a city girl who had just moved to the country and it all seemed a little too quiet, a little too far removed. But come Saturday morning, all that was forgotten as I wandered through the farmers' market, chatting and piling fresh goodies into my giant basket. I became a reformed city girl and the change of seasons came to mean more than just the excitement of dusting off my beloved leather boots and snuggly jackets. My weekly market visit instilled in me a passion for the fresh palette of produce and ingredients that come with each new season.

12 baby beetroot
12 baby golden beetroot ← *If you can't get hold of these, use 4 large carrots, peeled and cut into thirds*
½ cup walnuts
2 tablespoons honey
100 g ashed goat's camembert ← *use regular goat's cheese if you can't find this*
mixed salad leaves, such as watercress, rocket or frisée (curly endive)
2 tablespoons balsamic vinegar
2 tablespoons extra-virgin olive oil, plus extra for rubbing
sea salt and freshly ground black pepper

Preheat the oven to 180°C. Wrap 3–4 beetroot (or pieces of carrot) in foil and bake the parcels for 45 minutes, or until cooked through. To test, use a skewer or sharp knife to pierce through the foil and if the beetroot feels tender all the way through, then they're cooked.

While the beetroot are cooking, spread the walnuts on a baking tray lined with baking paper and drizzle with the honey. Bake for about 5 minutes, or until toasted and caramelised. Remove from the oven and set aside to cool.

Remove the beetroot from the oven and set aside to cool for a few minutes, then peel off the skins. Rub your hands with a little oil as this will help stop the beetroot staining your skin. Start with the golden beetroot. This will be a bit of a hot potato scenario as the beetroot will still be a little warm, but the skins should come away very easily, if they are cooked. Slice in half or in quarters if they're a little large and place on a serving plate. Repeat with the remaining beetroot.

Break the goat's camembert into chunks and scatter over the beetroot. Scatter over the honeyed walnuts and salad leaves, drizzle with the vinegar and olive oil and season to taste with the salt and pepper.

SERVES 4 AS A LIGHT LUNCH OR 6 AS A SIDE DISH

SOM TUM
[GREEN PAWPAW SALAD]

1 x 800 g green pawpaw
2 garlic cloves, peeled
1 fresh small red chilli *more if you like it spicy*
2 tablespoons unsalted peanuts
2 tablespoons dried shrimp, soaked in water for 5 minutes, drained
2 tablespoons fish sauce, or to taste
2 tablespoons white sugar, or to taste
1¼ cups lemon juice, or to taste
8 cherry tomatoes, halved

1 *peel*
Use a knife to shave off the pawpaw skin. Give the pawpaw a quick rinse and dry with a clean tea towel.

2 Get yourself a big tray and hold the pawpaw in one hand over the tray. Take the knife in your other hand and tap the pawpaw lengthways all over to make lots of little cuts in the flesh.

tap, tap, tap

be careful to keep your fingers clear of the knife

3 *Shave*
Keep tapping and turning the pawpaw until little shreds start falling onto the tray. Now use the knife to 'shave' along the length of the pawpaw to produce long shards. Shave the entire pawpaw, then start tapping again. Repeat until you reach the core of the pawpaw – or until the pawpaw gets so small that it becomes too scary to hold and tap it for fear of losing a finger.

Darwin's food markets are at the very heart of what that hot and humid city means to me. I love the smell of ripe mangoes, Asian herbs, simmering laksa and spicy Som tum (green pawpaw salad) made fresh to order. Each Som tum station has a devoted maker standing at the ready and arguments abound about who makes the best. You order your Som tum by specifying how many chillies you'd like 'Som tum with one please!'

pound

SERVES 4 AS A LIGHT MEAL OR 6 AS PART OF A BANQUET

TASTY

Pound the garlic, chilli, peanuts and dried shrimp using a large mortar and pestle until just bruised and the peanuts are just cracked. Add the pawpaw, fish sauce, sugar, lemon juice and tomato and gently bruise the pawpaw with the pestle, while turning and mixing the salad with a large spoon held in your other hand. You'll get the hang of this after a while. The aim is to soften the pawpaw and slightly bruise everything together without completely crushing the pawpaw. Taste the salad. It should be sweet, sour, salty and spicy. Add more fish sauce, lemon juice or sugar, if you like.

FENNEL RISOTTO WITH TALEGGIO & ROSEMARY PANGRATTATO

A spirit of generosity and a little bit of theatre is what I aim for when I cook for my family and friends. I like to take a colossal pan of risotto straight from under the grill to the table where it sits, with its burnished Taleggio cheese crust, bubbling away. As the smell of toasted cheese steams and wafts across the table, I toss over handfuls of pangrattato that rain down with a pitter-patter crunch onto the risotto's surface. Then I dig out big spoonfuls of creamy, cheesy risotto and pile it onto plates to be passed around the table.

¼ cup extra-virgin olive oil
1 small fennel bulb, trimmed and finely diced
2 garlic cloves, finely chopped
1 small brown onion, finely chopped
2 cups carnaroli or arborio rice [see note]
1 cup white wine
about 2 litres vegetable or Saturday Afternoon Chicken Stock (see page 30)
¼ cup grated parmesan
50 g butter
sea salt
200 g Taleggio, thinly sliced

ROSEMARY PANGRATTATO
1 cup panko (Japanese) breadcrumbs — available from an Asian grocer or the Asian section of most supermarkets
2 anchovy fillets
finely grated zest of 1 lemon
2 garlic cloves
2 tablespoons finely chopped rosemary leaves
1 tablespoon finely chopped flat-leaf parsley
2 teaspoons sea salt
¼ cup extra-virgin olive oil

For the rosemary pangrattato, place all of the ingredients, except the olive oil, in a food processor and process until you get fine breadcrumbs. Heat the oil in a small frying pan over high heat, add the breadcrumb mixture and cook for about 5 minutes, or until golden. Transfer to a bowl and set aside.

For the risotto, heat the oil in a large deep-sided frying pan over low heat, add the fennel, garlic and onion and cook for 15 minutes, or until softened but not coloured. Increase the heat to medium, add the rice and stir to coat in the oil. Keep stirring for 2 minutes, or until the grains look slightly translucent. Pour in the wine and stir while it bubbles away. Keep stirring until the rice has absorbed the wine.

Meanwhile, heat the stock in a saucepan over medium heat until hot, then reduce the heat to low.

Now add a ladleful (about ½ cup) of hot stock to the rice. Give it a bit of a stir and let it simmer until the rice absorbs the stock. Keep adding the stock, a ladleful at a time, and lovingly stir until the rice is tender and the risotto looks creamy. If the stock looks like it's getting low before the risotto is ready, top it up with more stock or hot water. The whole ladling and stirring process should take 20 or so minutes.

At some stage you need to preheat your oven grill to high.

When you're happy with the texture of your risotto, stir through the parmesan and butter. Have a taste and season with the salt to your liking. Remove from the heat and cover the top of your risotto with the Taleggio. Place under the hot grill and cook until the cheese is melted, bubbling and just starts to turn golden. Sprinkle over handfuls of pangrattato to serve.

SERVES 6

NOTE: Carnaroli rice is a type of risotto rice that has a slightly larger grain than arborio. It holds its shape well, while still producing a creamy risotto. It's available from gourmet food stores and Italian grocers.

GREENS & EGGS

During my stint as a journalist I was sent to work in Renmark on the banks of the River Murray in regional South Australia. The hours were long and my dinners were quick. There's no time for long complicated cooking when your radio shift starts before dawn. And so greens and eggs became my favourite after-work dinner. Crisp, crunchy Asian greens and soft-fried eggs that ooze their yellowy yolk into a salty sauce, all in a matter of minutes. Serve with steamed rice (see page 137) for a simple dinner.

1 bunch Chinese broccoli (gai lan)
¼ cup vegetable oil
2 eggs
3 garlic cloves, thinly sliced
1 fresh small red chilli, thinly sliced
1 tablespoon soy sauce
2 tablespoons oyster sauce
1 spring onion, thinly sliced
1 teaspoon fish sauce, to serve
freshly ground black pepper

It's a good idea to separate the Chinese broccoli stems from the leaves because they will cook for different lengths of time. Place the bunch of Chinese broccoli on a chopping board and cut off the leafy section. Cut the leafy section into 4-cm lengths and pop into a bowl. Cut the stalks into 4-cm lengths and pop into a separate bowl.

Heat the vegetable oil in a wok over high heat. Carefully crack the eggs into the oil. As the eggs bubble and puff up, using a spatula, gently flick some of the oil over the tops of the eggs. After about 2 minutes the eggwhites should have crisp edges but the yolks should still be soft and a little runny. Scoop out the eggs or leave in for a bit longer, if you don't like runny eggs. Place on a plate, and cover with aluminium foil to keep warm.

Carefully pour half of the oil out of the wok – I pour it into a heatproof bowl and deal with it later once it's cooled. Return the wok to the heat, add the garlic and chilli and stir-fry for a few seconds or until fragrant. Add the Chinese broccoli stems and stir-fry for about 1 minute. Pour in the soy and oyster sauces and stir-fry for about 2 minutes, or until the stems are tender but still have some bite. Add the leaves and stir-fry until just wilted.

Remove from the heat and scoop the greens onto a serving plate. Perch the eggs on top, scatter with the spring onion, drizzle with the fish sauce and grind over loads of pepper.

SERVES 1–2 FOR A QUICK DINNER OR 4 AS PART OF A BANQUET

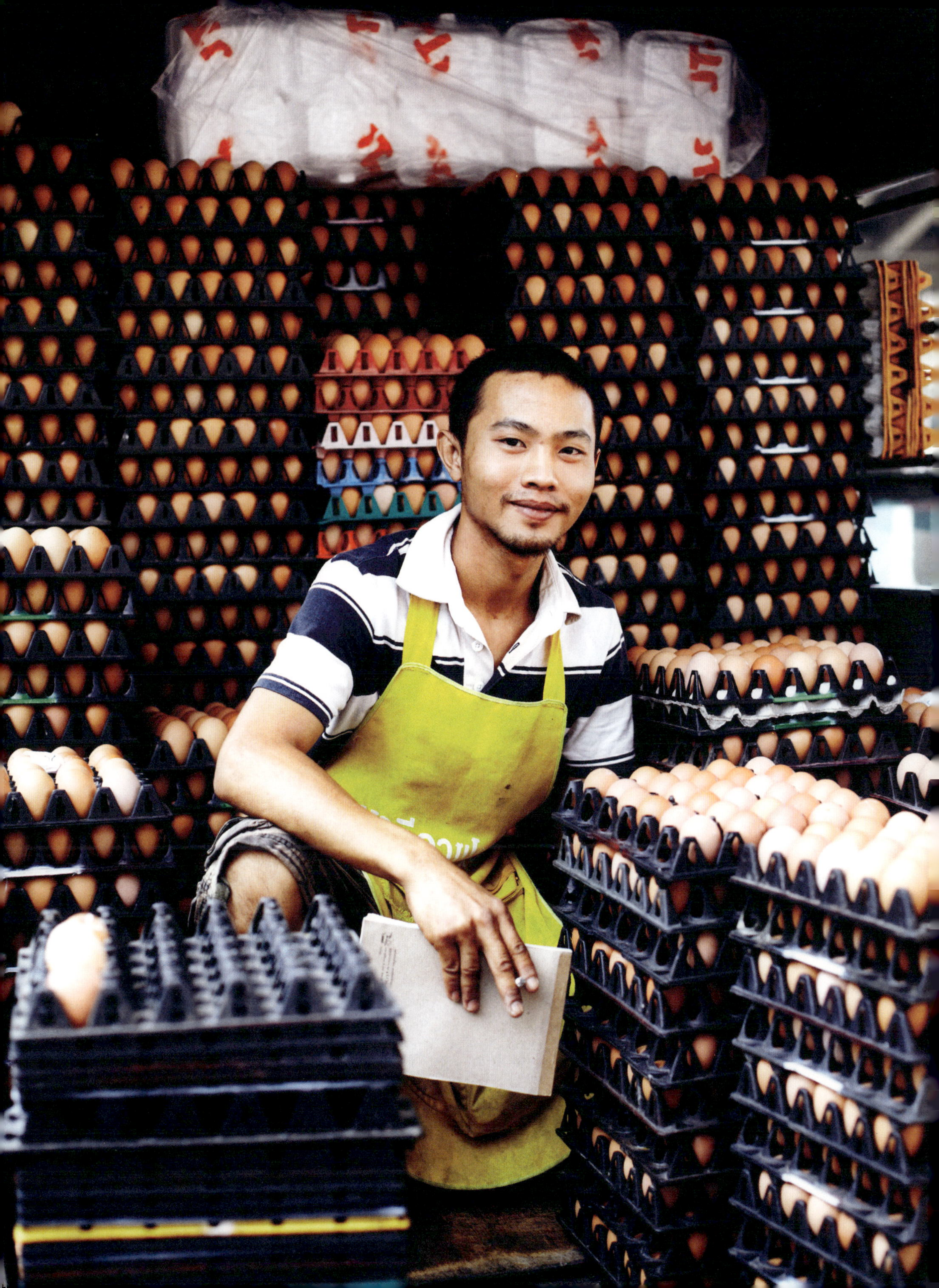

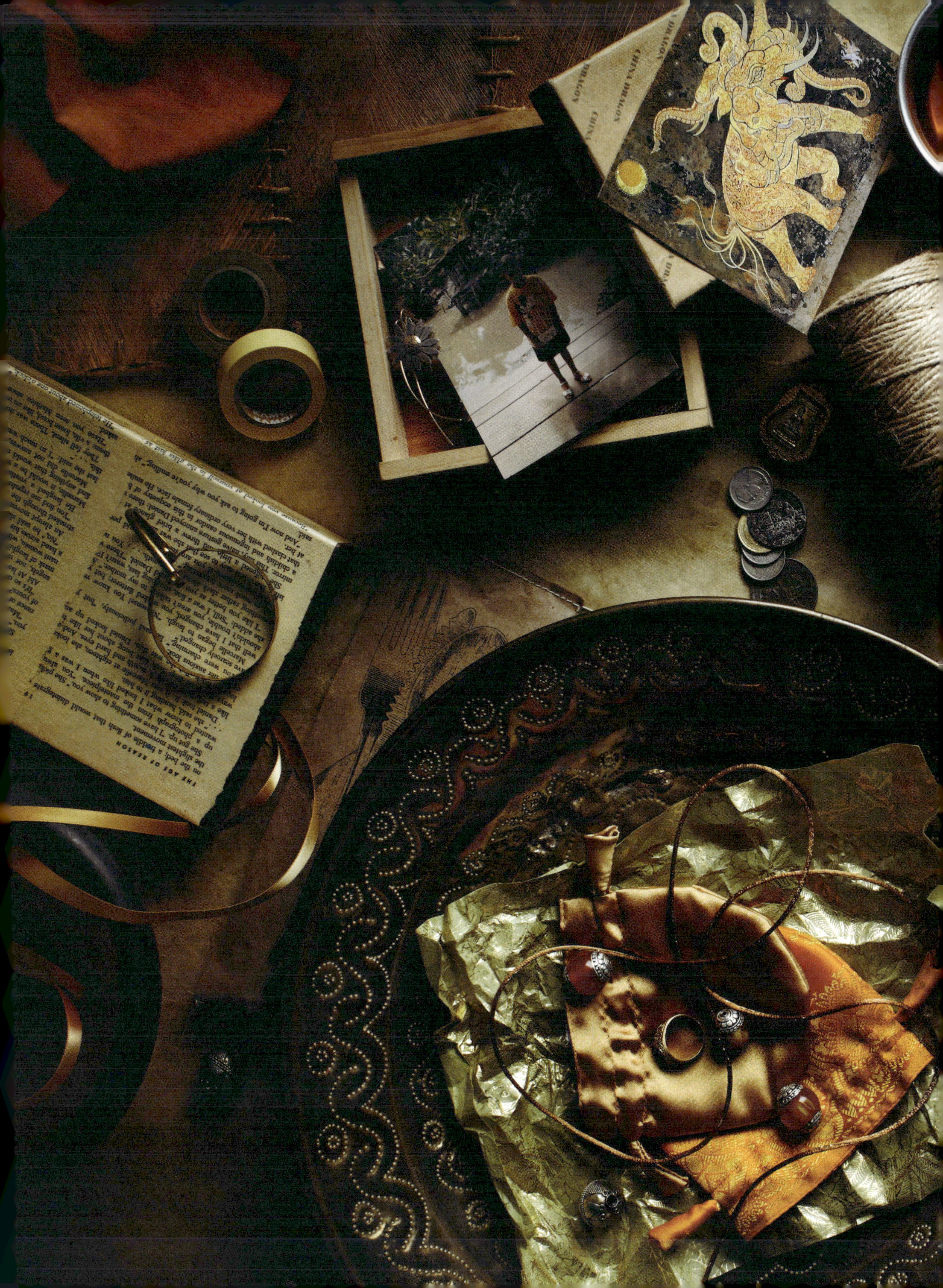

ON THE SIDE

INSPIRATION

I had an art teacher in high school who once said to me that you can't just sit around staring at a blank canvas and expect inspiration to come to you. You have to chase inspiration, get out into the world and find it yourself.

What will I cook today? The answer is laid out on a market stall table or in bright orange plastic tubs. It might be fennel season, which calls for a crisp fennel salad. There might be fat bunches of beetroot pleading to be roasted or the Asian grocer might have fresh bunches of kang kong imploring me to throw them into a wok with some garlic and oyster sauce.

Traipsing through a Bangkok street market I watch ladies spreading floury paste on to a hot plate and peeling it off to make packets of spring roll wrappers. Wandering through Darwin's Parap Market I watch the *som tum* (green pawpaw salad) vendors pounding and scooping their spicy wares. And at home I take my pick from at least eight different varieties of potato sitting in their large plastic tubs just waiting to be mashed, chipped or roasted. Inspiration comes from a farmers' market, an Asian market, a fish market or even a butcher's shop. Shopping for produce means getting out there into the world and chasing inspiration.

Years ago now, I sat at my desk writing stories for my next deadline and felt completely uninspired. I was a journalist staring at a blank canvas and waiting for inspiration to come to me. I was waiting to figure out how I could make a career for myself in food, the one thing I truly loved. I had to get out into the world of food even if I wasn't sure what it was I wanted to cook. I had to get out and watch and smell and taste my way into a new job. And so I did. I left without a plan and immersed myself in a new market. I stopped staring at the blank canvas, I chased inspiration and I found it!

The monks at the temple near my mother's village, Nakhon Chum, exuded such a powerful sense of peace and calm.

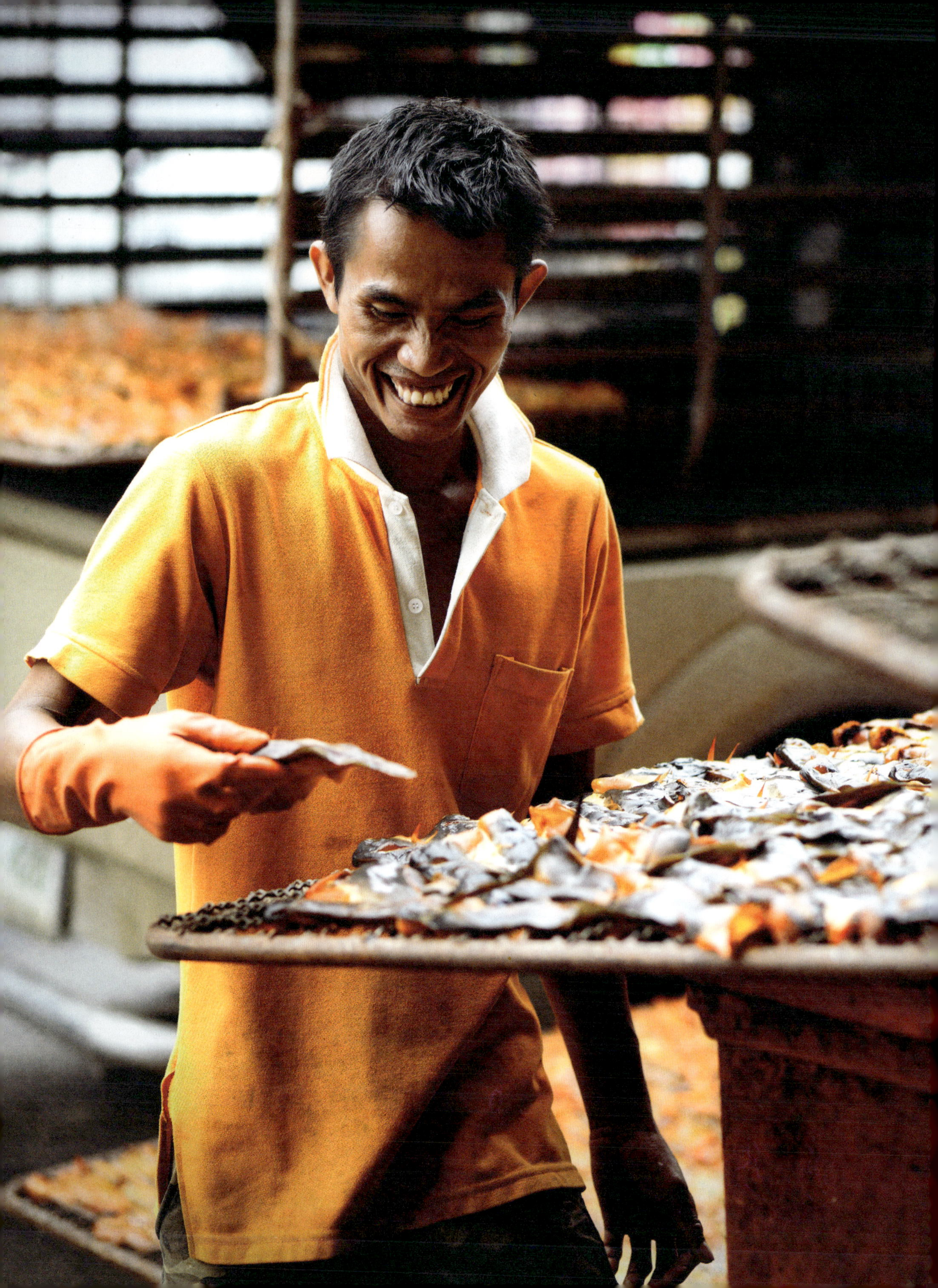

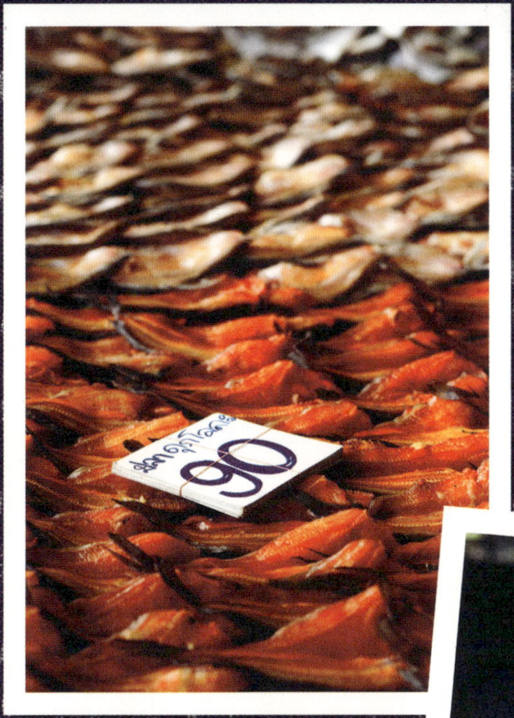
90
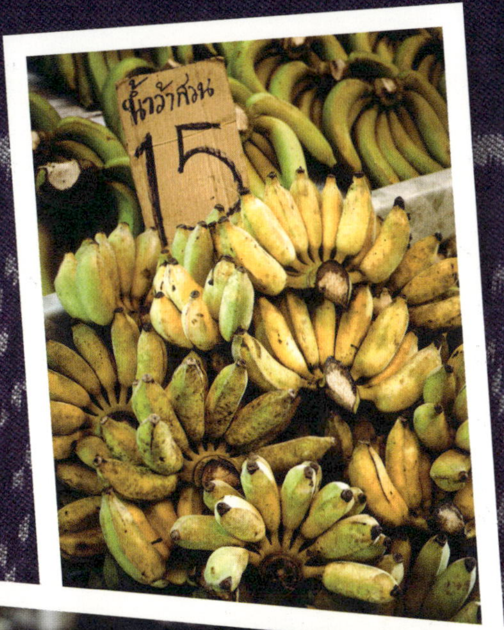
15
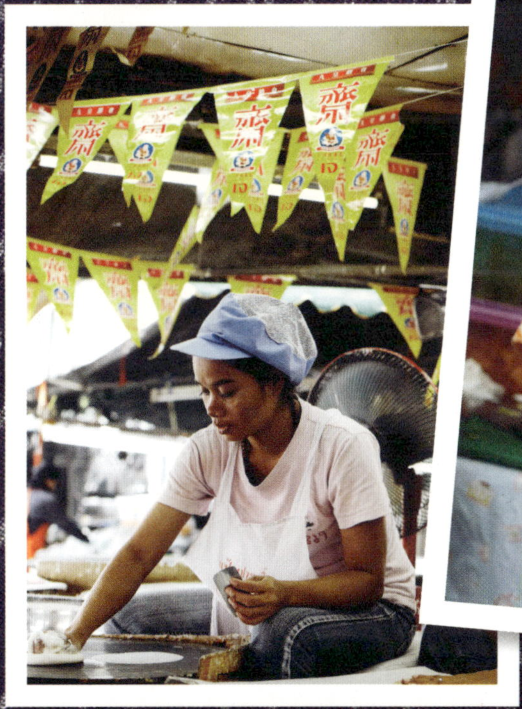
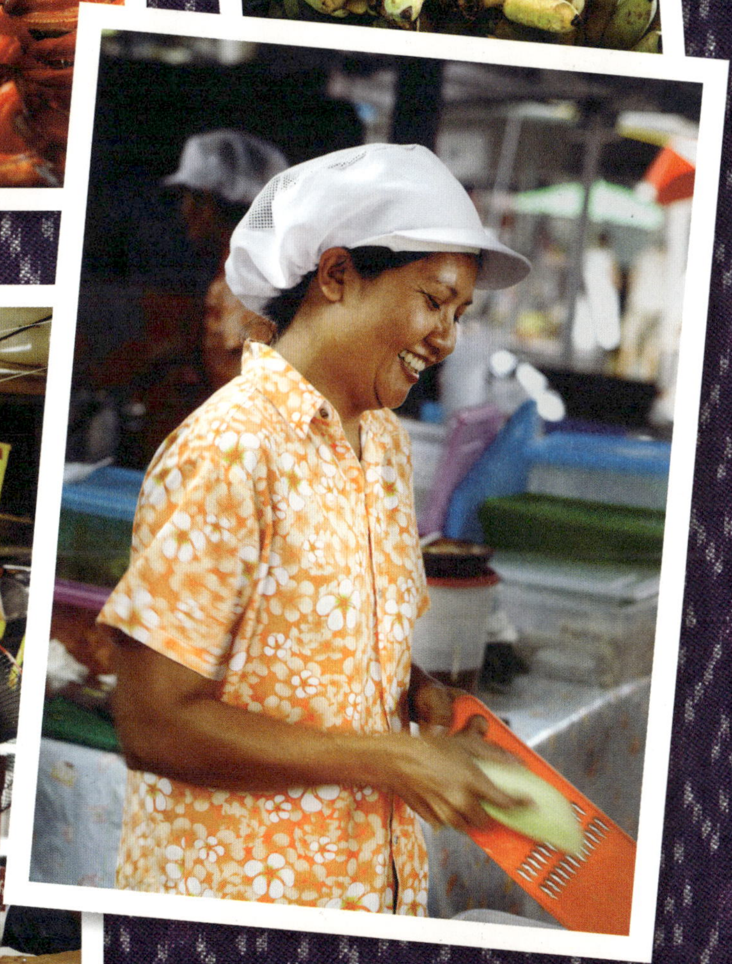

BANANA
PAW PAW
MANGO
TACK FRUIT

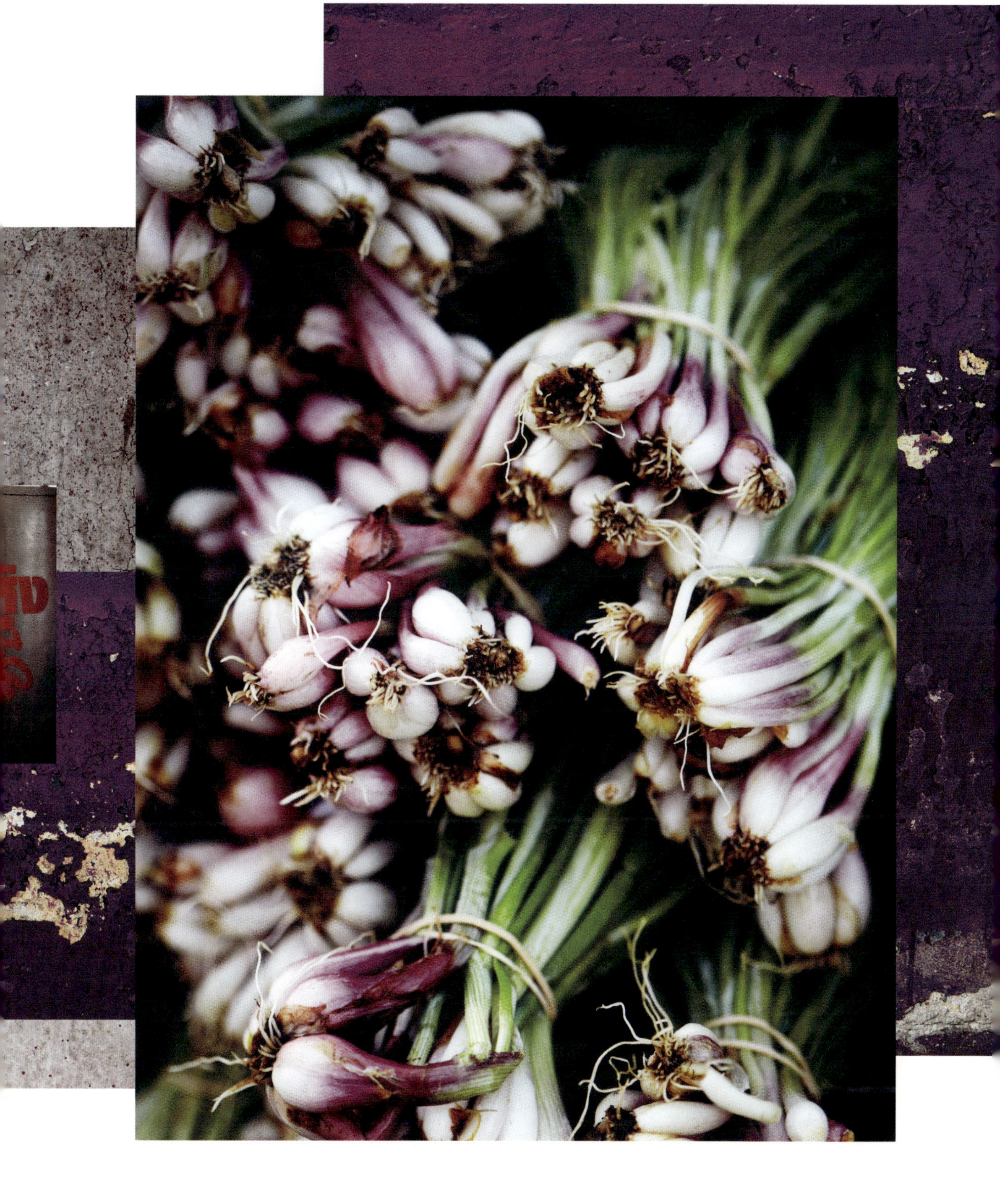

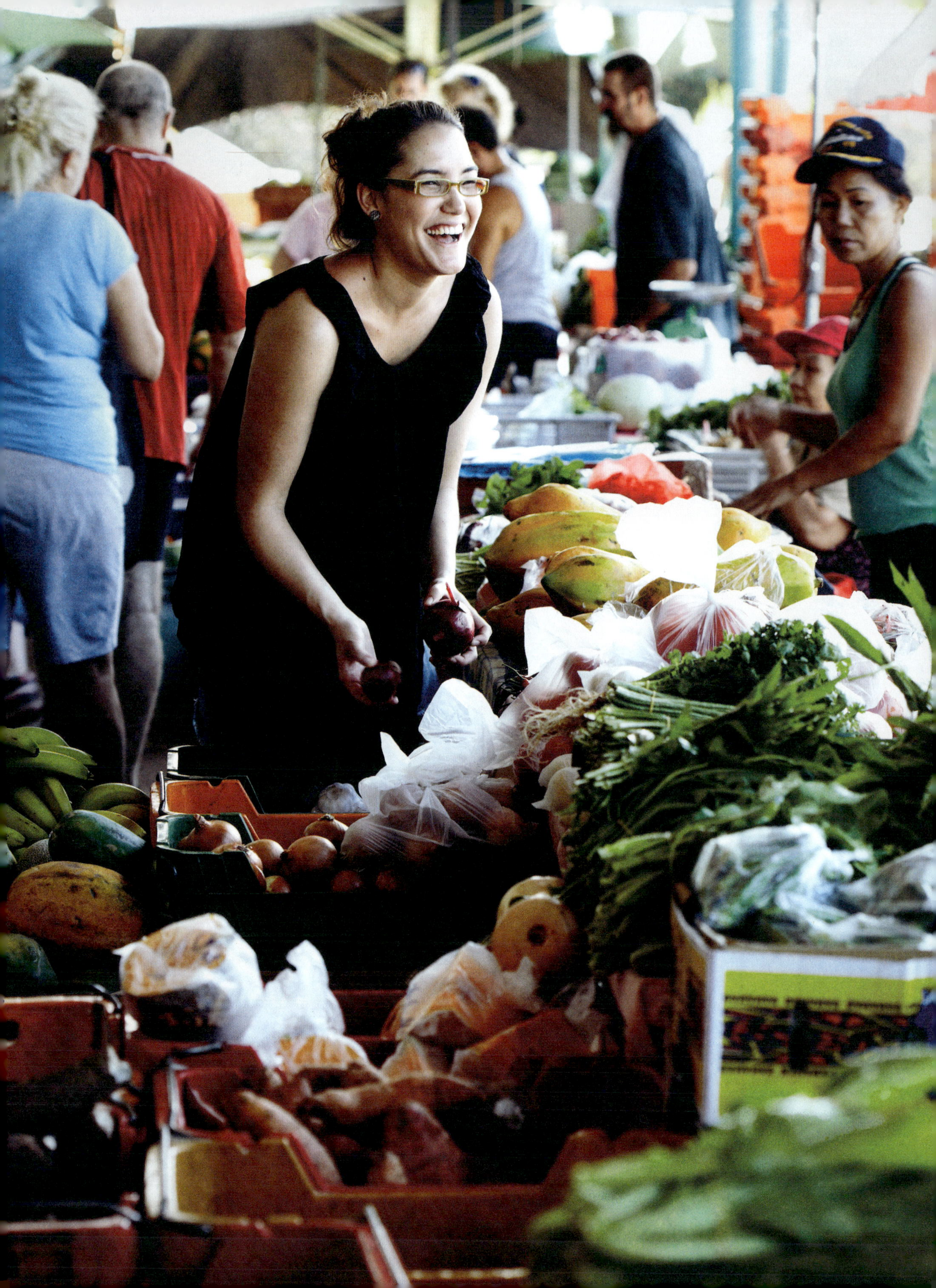

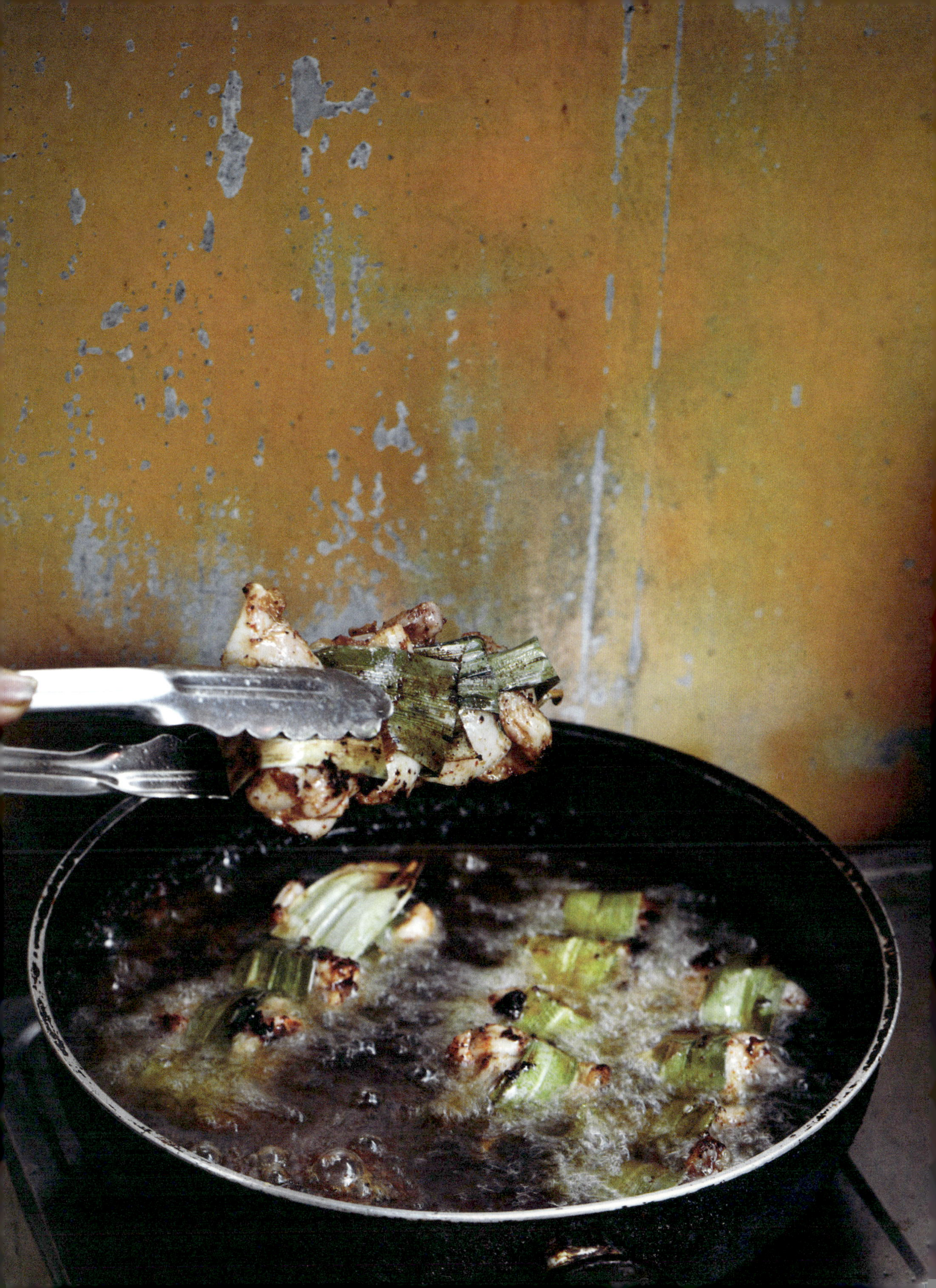

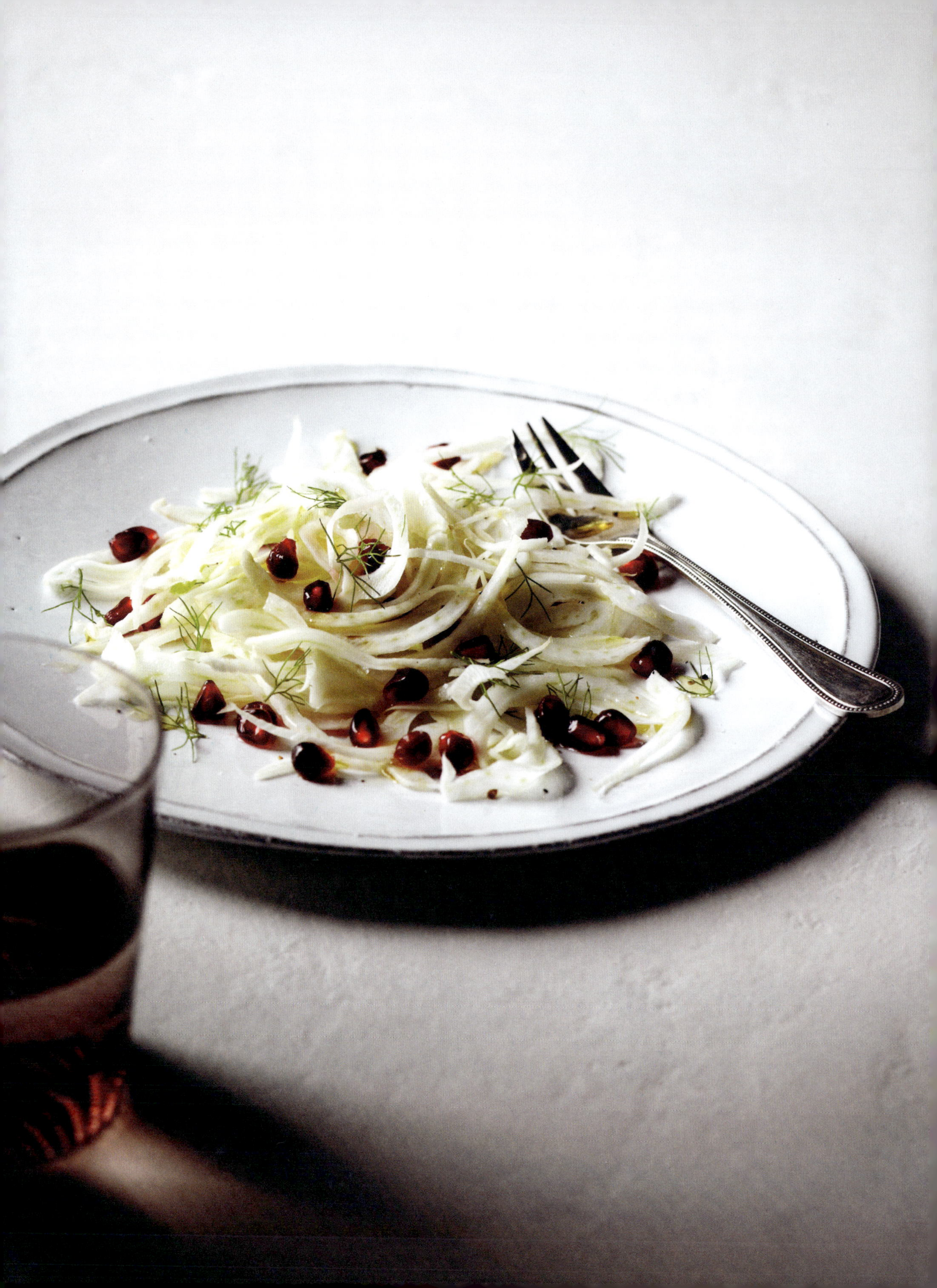

POMEGRANATE & FENNEL SALAD

This is a simple salad made from extraordinary ingredients: brilliant ruby red pomegranate seeds against a crisp white canvas of shaved fennel. Serve with roasted chicken, grilled fish, a juicy steak or even barbecued snags — she's not a fussy salad and will happily make friends with just about any dish you wish to pair her with.

1 pomegranate
1 large fennel bulb (about 600 g), trimmed and leafy fronds reserved
2 tablespoons extra-virgin olive oil
1 tablespoon lemon juice
¼ teaspoon sea salt
freshly ground black pepper

Cut the pomegranate in half, then use your hands to break each piece in half again. Hold a piece of pomegranate, cut-side down, over a bowl and give the back of it a bash with a wooden spoon. The seeds should fall out into the bowl. Use your fingers to scoop out any remaining seeds. Discard the skin and any white pith. Repeat with the remaining pomegranate pieces.

Thinly slice the fennel, using a mandoline for super fine slivers or a large knife, and add to the bowl. Add the olive oil, lemon juice, salt and pepper and give everything a gentle toss to combine. Scatter with reserved fennel fronds and serve.

SERVES 6

ON THE SIDE 155

CABBAGE & ALMOND COLESLAW

Everyone should have a good coleslaw recipe up their sleeve. I like to make my own mayonnaise base for the dressing but you could substitute a good-quality store-bought whole-egg mayonnaise.

1 cup slivered almonds
½ small Savoy cabbage, very thinly sliced (use a mandoline if you've got one)
1 cup torn mint leaves, plus extra leaves to serve
¼ cup grated parmesan, plus extra to serve
1 teaspoon sea salt
freshly ground black pepper

DRESSING
¼ cup rice bran oil or vegetable oil
¼ cup extra-virgin olive oil
2 egg yolks
2 teaspoons Dijon mustard
1 teaspoon white wine vinegar
2 tablespoons lemon juice
¼ cup milk

For the dressing, combine the oils in a pouring jug. Whisk the egg yolks, mustard and vinegar together in a bowl. While whisking continuously, add the combined oils, drop by drop. Once the mixture starts to look like a thick yellow cream, begin adding the oil in more of a steady stream, all the while, whisking and whisking. If you don't need the exercise, you could do this in a food processor or use an electric whisk. Once all the oil is added and you've got a lovely thick mayonnaise, mix in the lemon juice and milk. The dressing should have the consistency of pouring (single) cream. If it looks a little thick, just add a splash more milk.

Place the almonds in a dry frying pan over high heat and toast, tossing regularly, for about 2 minutes, or until golden. Transfer to a large bowl.

Add the cabbage, mint, parmesan, salt and a generous grinding of pepper to the almonds. Pour over the dressing and toss until well combined and each little shard of cabbage is coated. Top with a few extra mint leaves and a smattering of extra parmesan just before serving.

SERVES 8

WILD ROCKET SALAD

I had wild rocket spring up like weeds around the edges of my garden. Its leaves were much larger than the rocket I was used to buying from the supermarket and it had the most incredible peppery burst of flavour. If you don't have rocket growing like weeds in your garden, simply substitute regular rocket from the supermarket or farmers' markets.

300 g wild rocket
50 g parmesan, thinly shaved with a vegetable peeler
2 tablespoons extra-virgin olive oil
1 tablespoon balsamic vinegar
sea salt and freshly ground black pepper

Place the rocket, parmesan, olive oil and vinegar in a large bowl, season to taste with the salt and pepper and gently toss to combine.

SERVES 4

STEAMED RICE

One of the many habits I've inherited from my mother is that I must always have rice in my pantry. I use jasmine or long-grain rice when I'm serving Thai food.

2 cups rice, rinsed

Place the rice in a saucepan with 3 cups of water. Give it a little stir so that any floating grains of rice sink to the bottom. Place over high heat and bring to the boil, then reduce the heat to low, cover and cook for about 12 minutes. Give it a stir after about 6 minutes.

Remove from the heat and allow to sit, covered, for about 5 minutes. Use a fork to fluff up the rice just before serving.

SERVES 4

ROSY ISRAELI COUSCOUS

Israeli couscous or moghrabieh is more like a pasta than its regular couscous cousin. I just adore the rosy scent and jewelled appearance of this brilliant side dish, which I serve with moroccan tagine dishes or even on its own as a lunchtime salad.

2 cups Israeli couscous ← [see notes]
¼ cup dried sour cherries, roughly chopped
¼ cup roughly chopped coriander leaves
1 small red onion, finely chopped
1 garlic clove, finely grated or bashed to a paste using a mortar and pestle
finely grated zest of 1 lemon
2 tablespoons lemon juice
2 tablespoons extra-virgin olive oil
2 tablespoons dried rose petal leaves
¼ teaspoon sumac ← A middle Eastern spice with a lovely lemony sort of flavour and is available in select supermarkets or gourmet food stores
[see notes] → ¼ teaspoon rosewater
¼ teaspoon sea salt

You cook the Israeli couscous in a similar way to pasta. Bring a saucepan of salted water to a rolling boil, then add the couscous and cook for 10–15 minutes. Taste the couscous after about 10 minutes to check if it's ready. You want it to be soft on the outside with just a hint of a bite in the centre (similar to al dente pasta). Drain and transfer to large bowl.

Add the remaining ingredients and give it all a good toss. Serve warm or at room temperature or even cold.

SERVES 6

NOTES: You can find Israeli couscous and dried sour cherries at gourmet food stores, Middle Eastern grocers and health food stores. If you can't find dried sour cherries, use dried blueberries, currants or sultanas.

For the dried rose petals, I use the Herbie's Spices brand. If you grow your own roses that have not been sprayed with chemicals, then use these fresh instead of the dried petals.

BROCCOLINI WITH GARLIC & ANCHOVIES

This is one of my all-purpose side dishes, which makes an appearance with roasted meats, steak, grilled chicken and just about anything else I care to make for dinner. If you're not an anchovy lover, you could leave them out but where's the fun in that, I ask you?

2 bunches broccolini, bottom 1 cm trimmed and discarded
¼ cup extra-virgin olive oil
3 garlic cloves, thinly sliced
2 anchovy fillets
1 tablespoon balsamic vinegar
1 tablespoon grated parmesan
freshly ground black pepper

Blanch the broccolini in a saucepan of boiling water for about 2 minutes. Drain and refresh under cold running water. Drain again.

Heat the olive oil in a large frying pan over medium heat, add the garlic and anchovies and fry for about 1 minute, or until they start to smell yummy and the garlic is softened. Use a wooden spoon to break the anchovies up into the oil.

Add the broccolini and toss to coat and warm through. Splash over the vinegar and let it bubble for about half a minute.

Transfer to a serving plate, making sure to scoop all the oily saucy goodness over the broccolini. Scatter over the parmesan and grind over a generous amount of pepper.

SERVES 4

WOK-FRIED KANG KONG

The key to this dish is to get all of the ingredients ready in one bowl and to have the wok smoking hot. As the veg and sauce hit the wok, they'll immediately start to char, which gives you that wonderful smoky, wok-fried flavour. But work quickly, as there's a fine line between lovely charring and yucky burning.

1 bunch kang kong → *Also known as water spinach, and is available from Asian grocers and select greengrocers*
½ fresh long red chilli, thinly sliced
4 garlic cloves, roughly chopped
2 tablespoons oyster sauce
1 tablespoon soy sauce
1 teaspoon white sugar
1 tablespoon vegetable oil

Using your fingers, snap off and discard the bottom 5 cm of the stalks of the kang kong as they can be woody and tough. Now snap the rest of the stalks and leaves into 5-cm lengths and place in a large bowl. Add the chilli, garlic, oyster and soy sauces and sugar.

Heat the vegetable oil in a wok over high heat. When the oil is just smoking, throw in the entire contents of the bowl. Give everything a toss for about 1 minute. Pile onto a plate and serve.

SERVES 6

ROASTED KIPFLER POTATOES

Kipflers are one of my favourite potato varieties. They're usually quite small in size and have an elongated, tubular shape. I love their waxy nature and dense yellow character. If you can't get a hold of kipflers, use any other type of potato you like.

1 kg kipfler potatoes, washed and unpeeled
1 heaped tablespoon sea salt, plus extra for sprinkling
2 tablespoons extra-virgin olive oil, plus extra for drizzling
1 tablespoon finely chopped dill or flat-leaf parsley
freshly ground black pepper

Preheat the oven to 180°C.

Place the potatoes in a large saucepan, cover with cold water and add the heaped tablespoon of salt. Bring to the boil, then reduce the heat and simmer for 15 minutes. Drain and halve lengthways.

Throw the potatoes onto a baking tray and toss with the olive oil and extra salt. Roast for about 45 minutes, or until crisp and golden.

Remove the potatoes from the oven, drizzle with a good slug of olive oil and toss with the dill or parsley, a good pinch of salt and generous grindings of pepper.

SERVES 4

CRUSHED PURPLE CONGO POTATOES

No, we didn't use purple dye for the photo shoot. Yes, these potatoes really are purple and they don't lose their colour when cooked. Just thought I'd get that out of the way. Purple congo potatoes have a slightly nutty sort of flavour and quite a dry texture, so they need a good slug of olive oil. If you can't find purple congoes, you could use kipflers, dutch creams or any mashing potato.

Look out for purple congo potatoes at farmers' markets or select greengrocers during the colder months

500 g purple congo potatoes, washed and unpeeled

1 heaped tablespoon sea salt, plus 2 teaspoons extra

3 tablespoons extra-virgin olive oil, plus extra for drizzling

1 spring onion, thinly sliced

1 tablespoon finely chopped dill

1 tablespoon finely chopped flat-leaf parsley

freshly ground black pepper

Place the potatoes in a large saucepan, cover with cold water and add the heaped tablespoon of salt. Bring to the boil, then reduce the heat and simmer for 25 minutes, or until tender. Drain and peel off the skins. You need to do this while they're hot, so hold a potato in a tea towel in one hand and use a small knife to peel them with the other hand. Throw each peeled potato back into the warm pan (make sure it's drained of all water, first).

Return the pan to low heat, toss in the extra salt, the olive oil, spring onion and dill and use a wooden spoon to lightly crush the potatoes while mixing with the other ingredients.

Remove from the heat and spoon the gorgeous crushed potatoes onto a serving plate. Sprinkle with the parsley, grind over a generous amount of pepper and drizzle generously with the extra olive oil.

SERVES 4

DUTCH CREAM MASH

A potato called 'dutch cream' simply has to be good for mashing. And it certainly doesn't disappoint. It has an incredibly rich, yellowy, creamy flesh that whips into a rich, yellowy, creamy mash.

1 kg dutch cream potatoes, washed, peeled and cut into equal-sized chunks

1 heaped tablespoon sea salt, plus 1 teaspoon extra

100 g unsalted butter

¼ cup milk

Place the potatoes in a large saucepan, cover with cold water and add the heaped tablespoon of salt. Bring to the boil, then reduce the heat and simmer for 25 minutes, or until tender. Drain well, then pop them straight back into the same warm pan. Set the pan over medium heat for about 1 minute to let the potatoes dry out a bit.

Add the butter, milk and extra salt and mash together, then get out a wooden spoon and vigorously whip the potatoes until your arms can whip no more. Have a taste and add more butter or salt to your liking.

SERVES 4

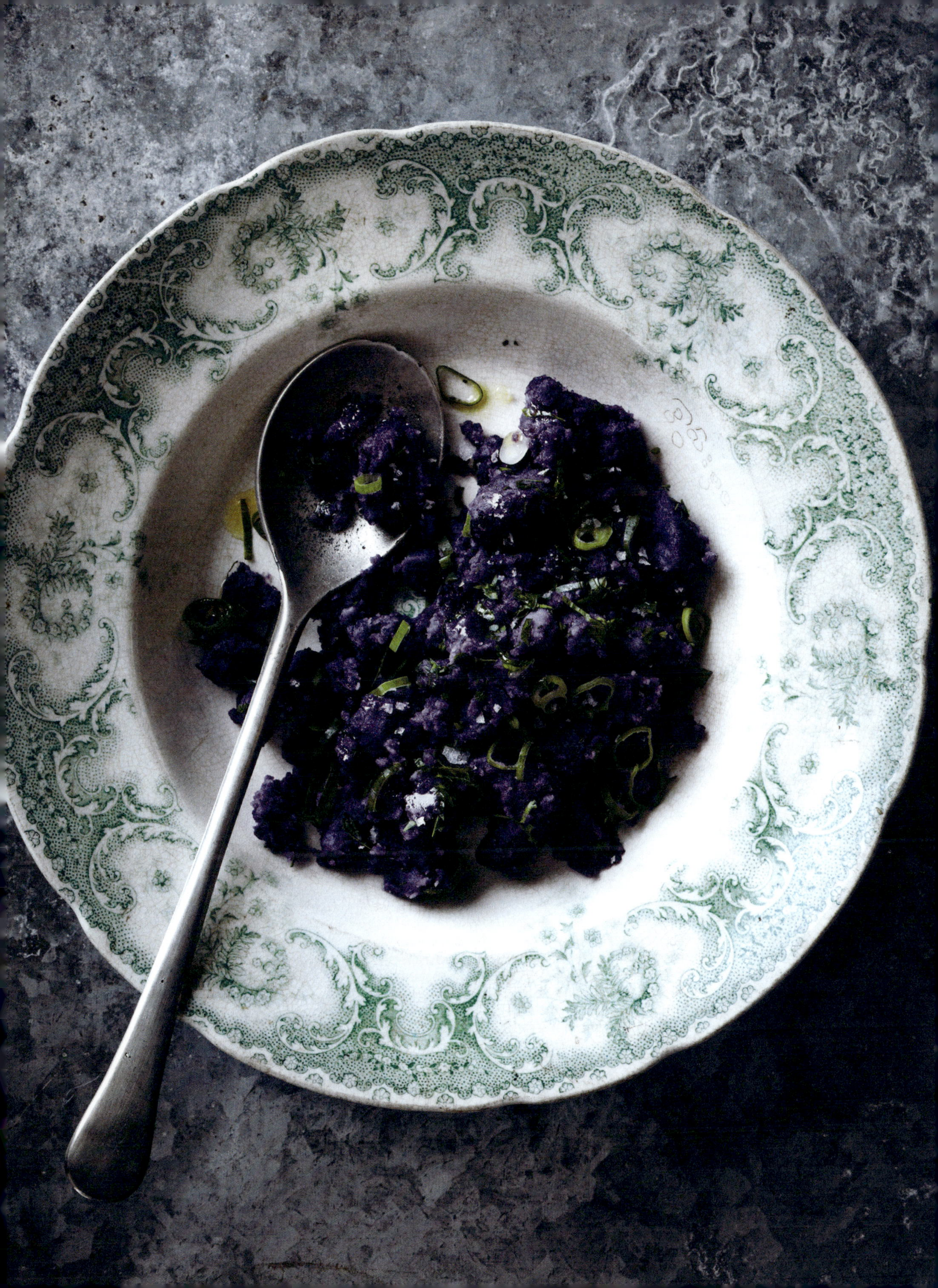

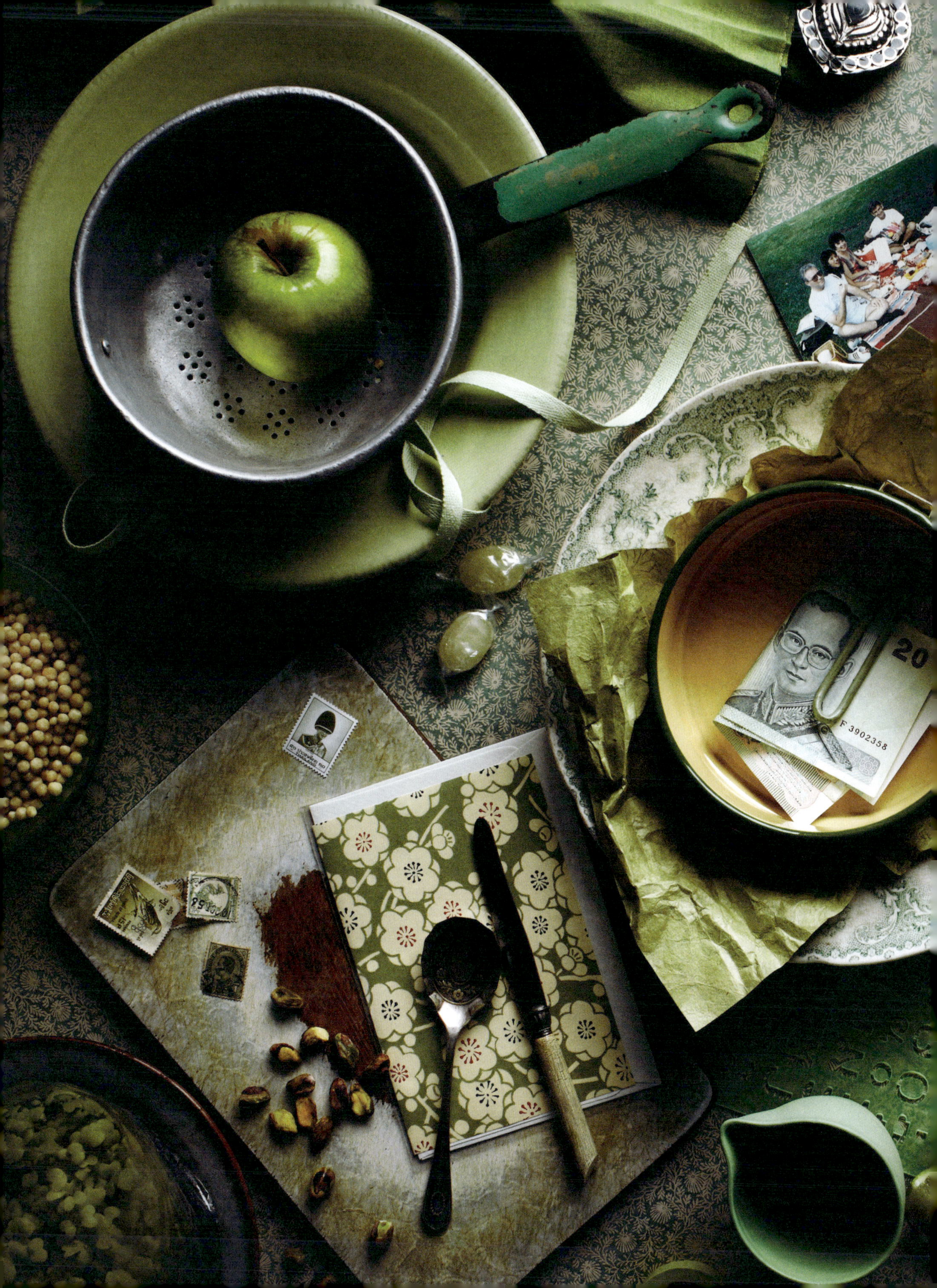
20
F 3902358

SWEETNESS

HAVE NO FEAR

There are far worse things going on in the world than a failed tart. For those of us who cook at home, the importance placed on what we make should be kept in perspective. So what if your soufflé is more like a deflated balloon than an epic tower of fluffiness. Never mind if your lamb resembles stringy bark. And it's best to laugh if your pavlova looks like blackened crispbread. Pour a glass of wine and order a pizza if you need to. You still have life and limb (hopefully, unless your kitchen disaster involves a sharp implement!), so things can't be all that bad.

We all have bad days in the kitchen. Days when something as simple as a satay sauce can trip us up. But we should never fear. Fear stifles creativity and most certainly creates a joyless cooking experience. Food should be fun and sometimes a little crazy. Don't be scared to break the rules. Fish sauce in a dessert? Give it a go. If it doesn't work out then you've taught yourself a lesson.

Herein lies the joy of cooking at home. We can create and cook in our kitchens without fear. Our livelihoods don't depend on a good review. We won't get our butts kicked by a heavy-handed head chef because the hollandaise has split. We are free to make mistakes and use our own taste as an indicator of merit.

Growing up in a developing country such as Papua New Guinea has given me a very grounded perspective on what should matter in life. In that country, there are far worse things going on than a failed tart; the problem for many families is how to get food on their table, not *how* it is cooked. So many of us are so lucky. It's for that reason that we should be very picky about the things we choose to worry about. A little disaster in the kitchen shouldn't be one of them.

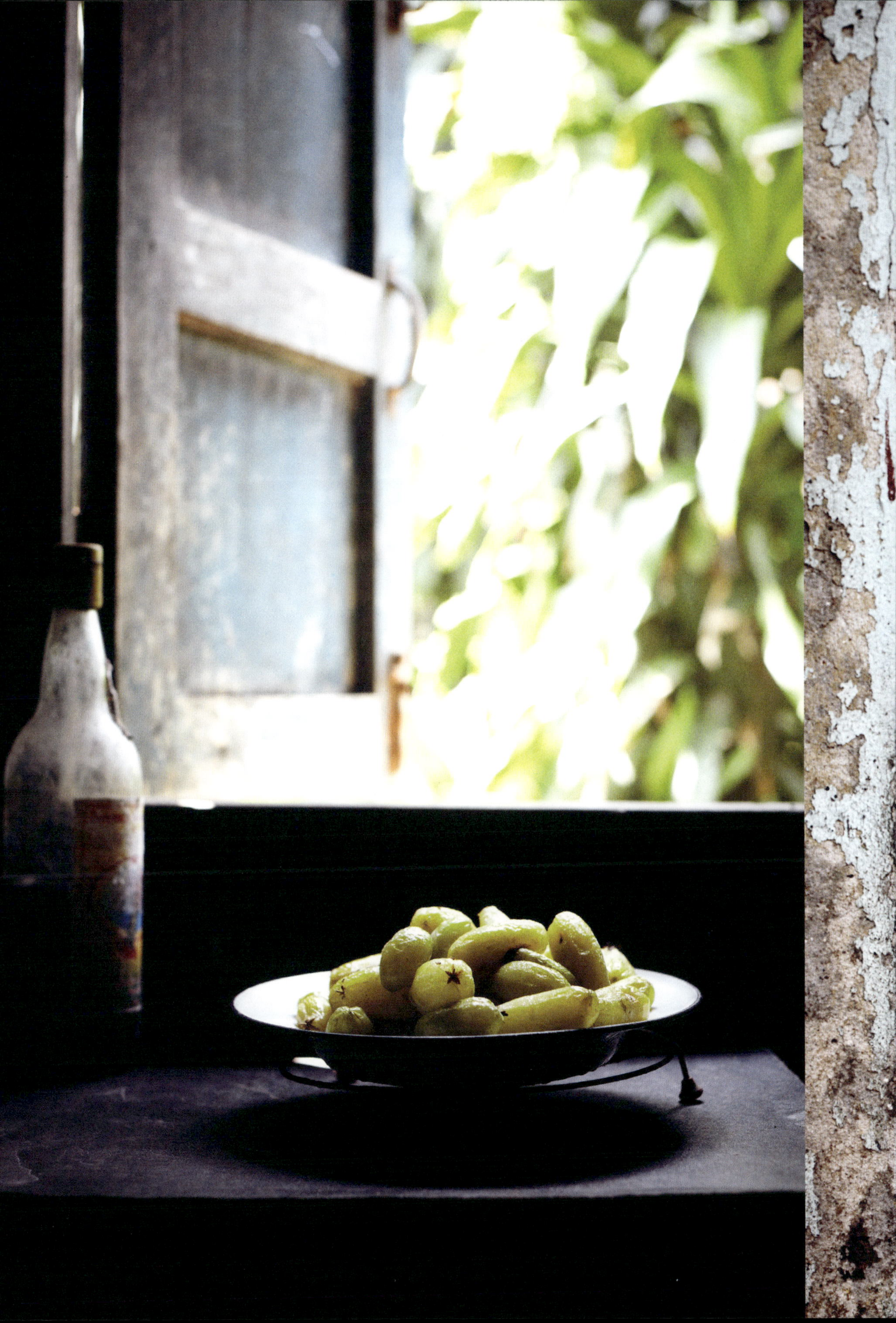

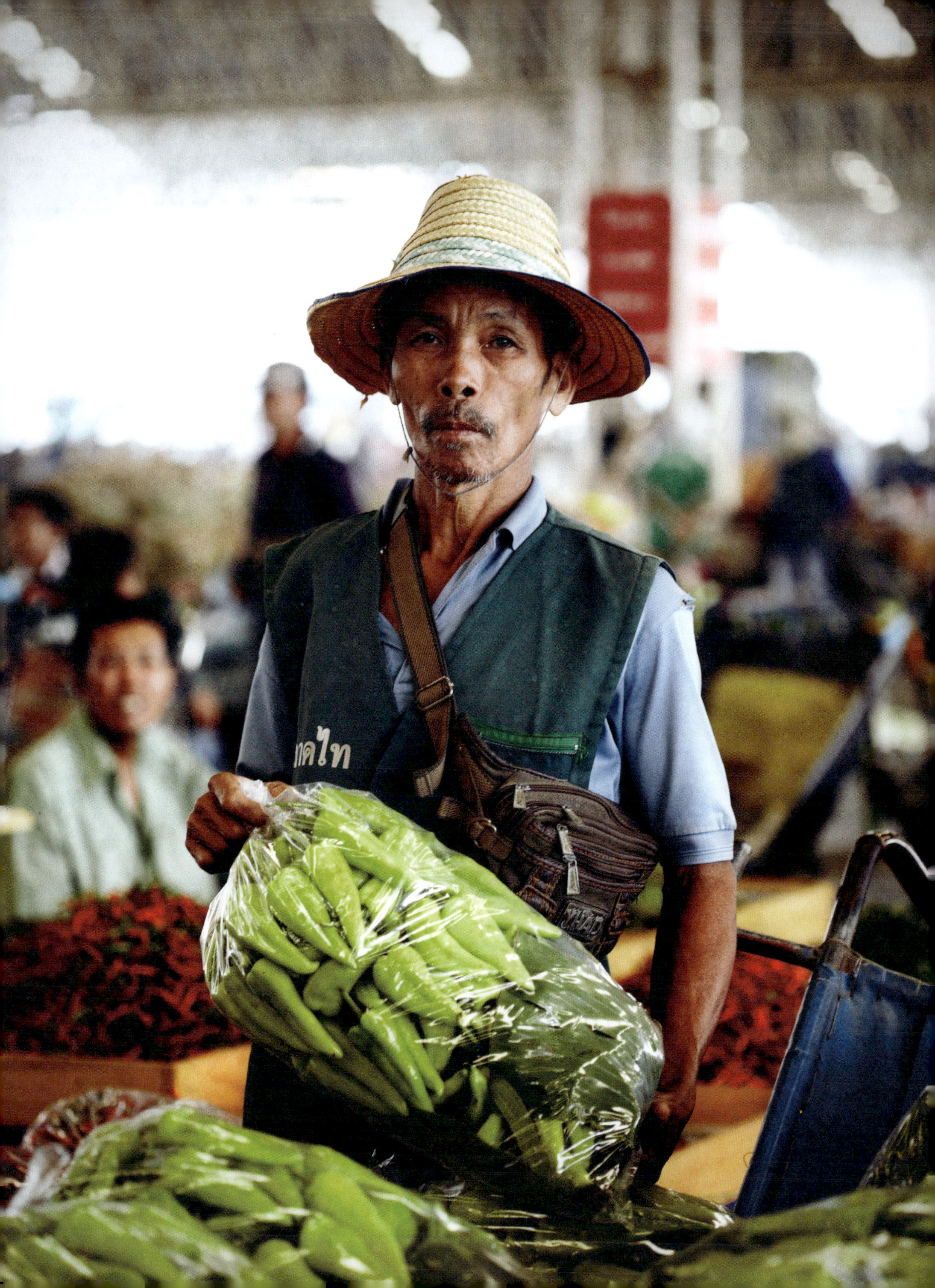

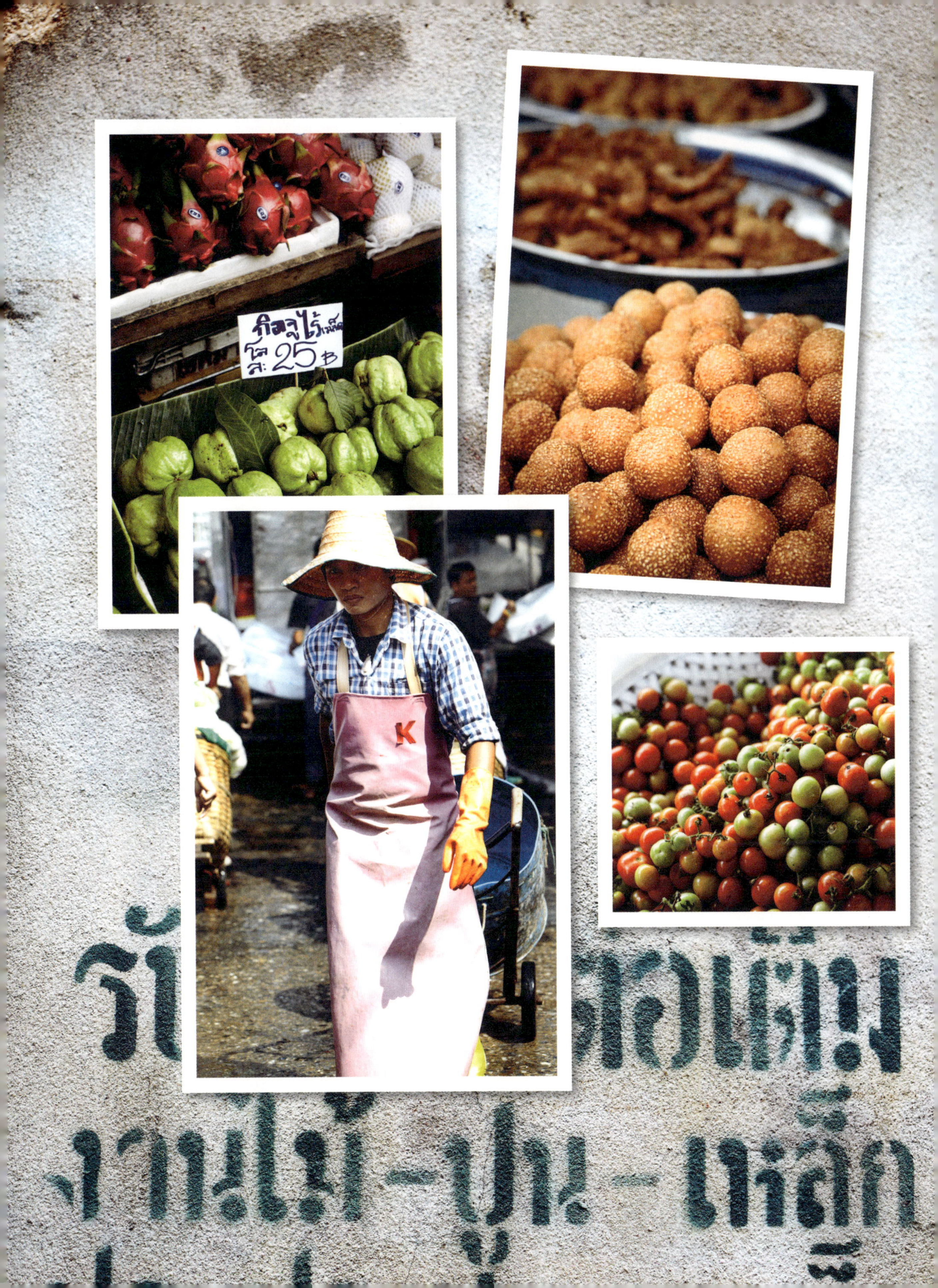
งานไม้-ปูน-เหล็ก

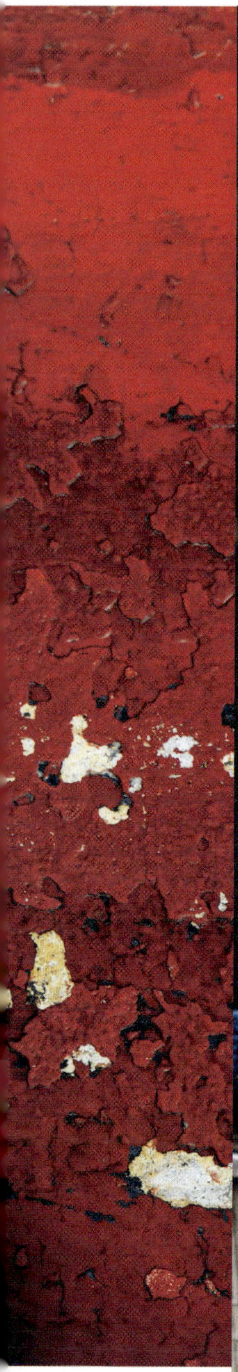

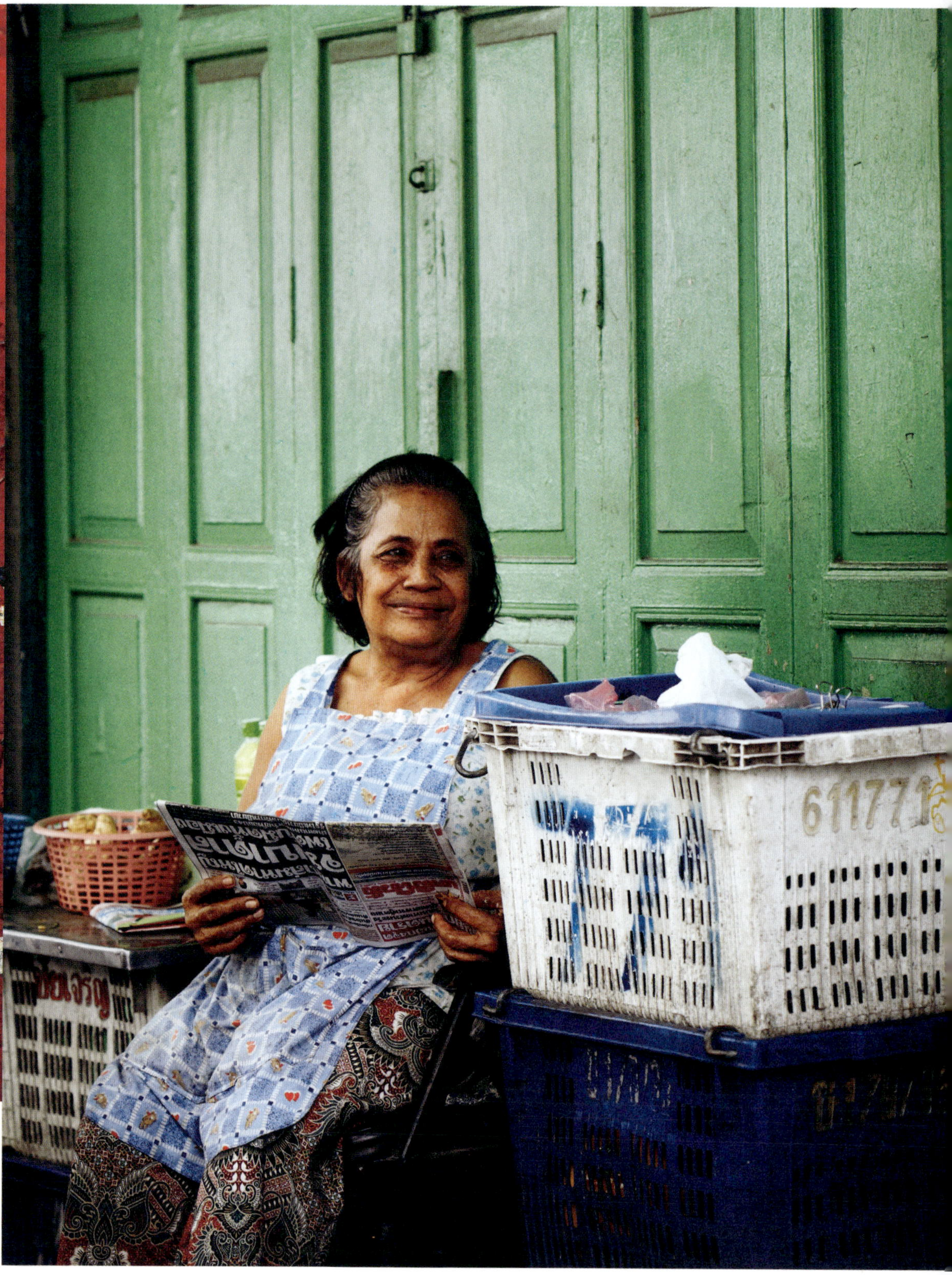
611771

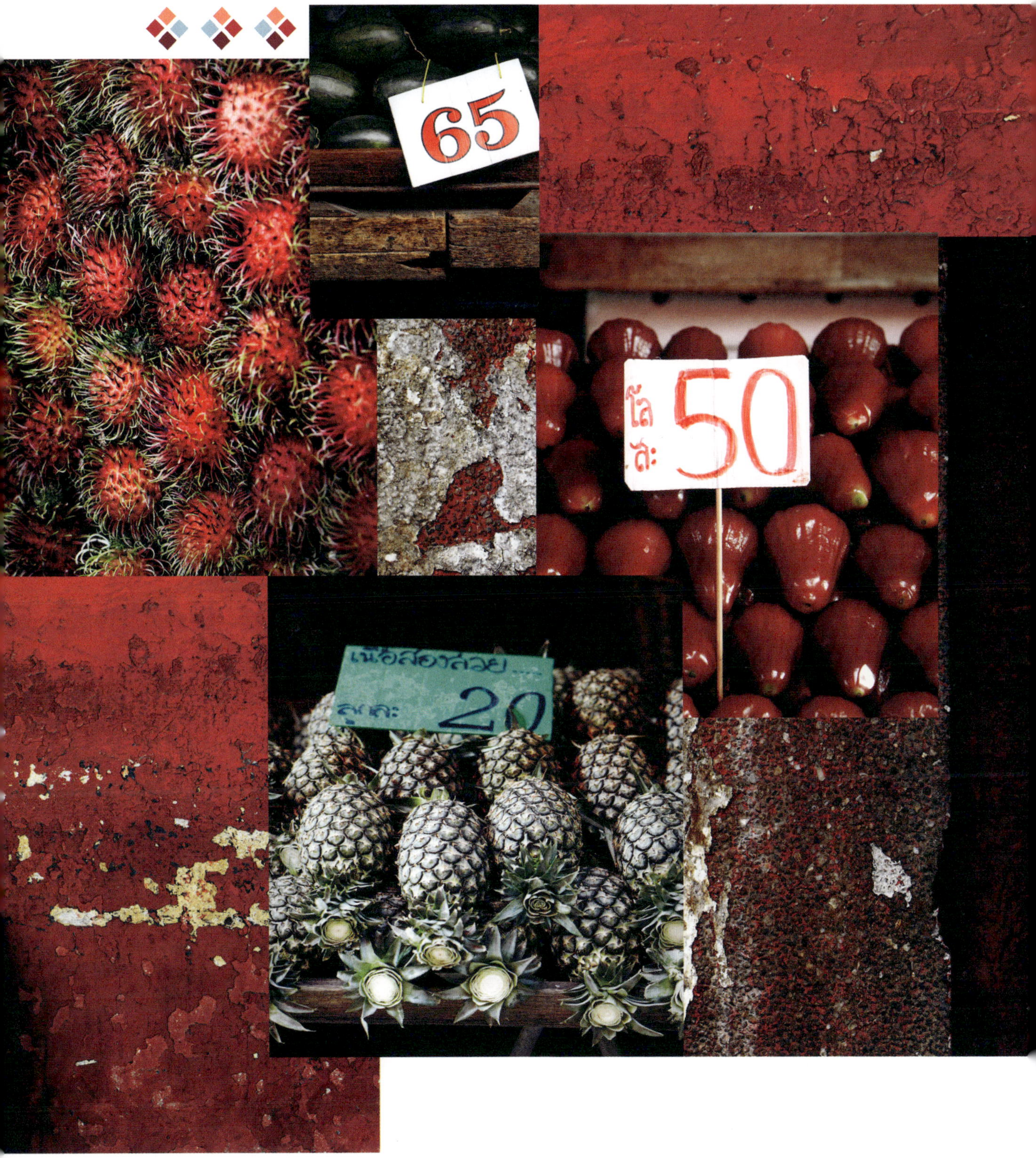
65
โล
ละ
50
20

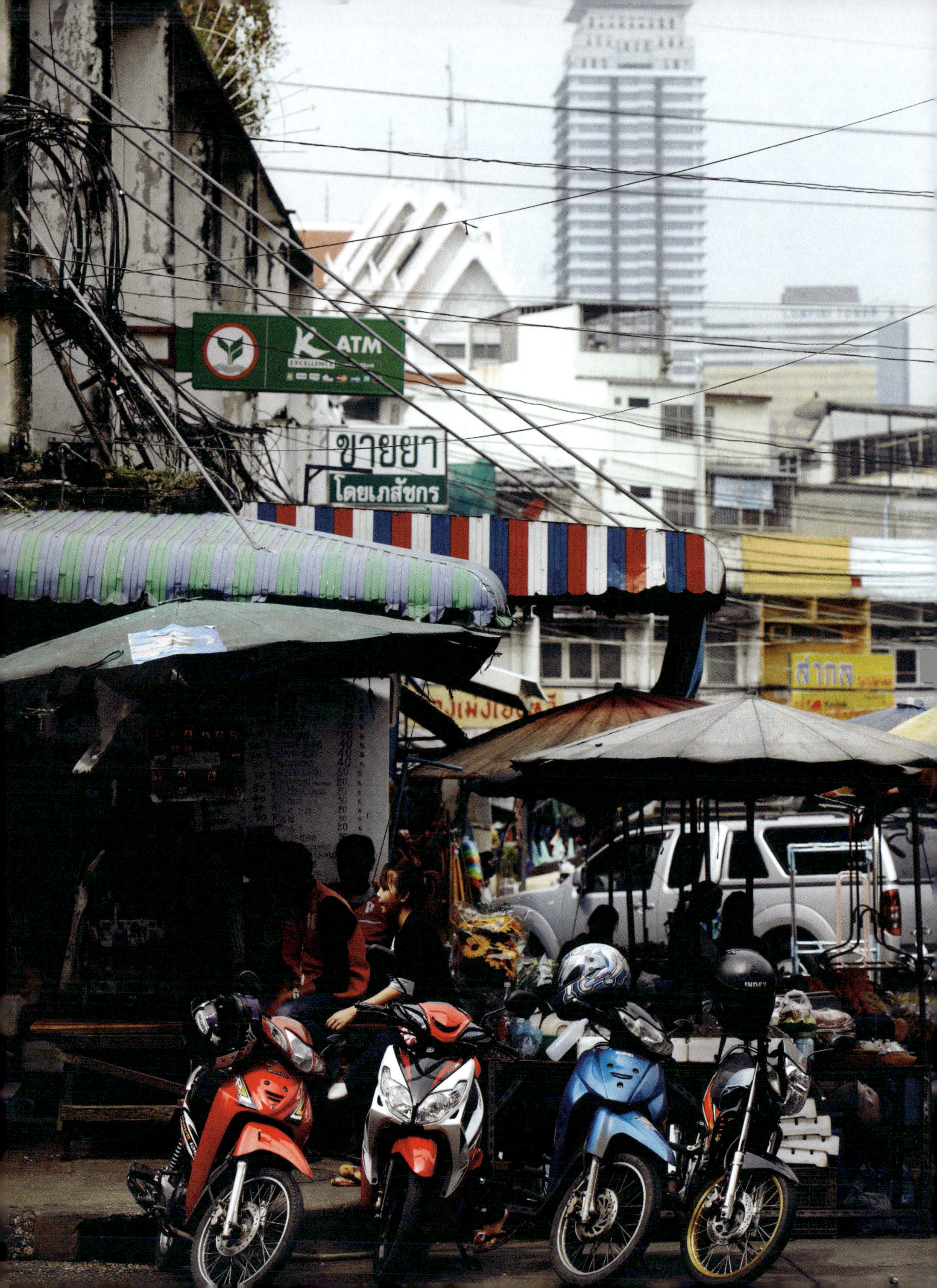
ATM
ขายยา
โดยเภสัชกร
สากล

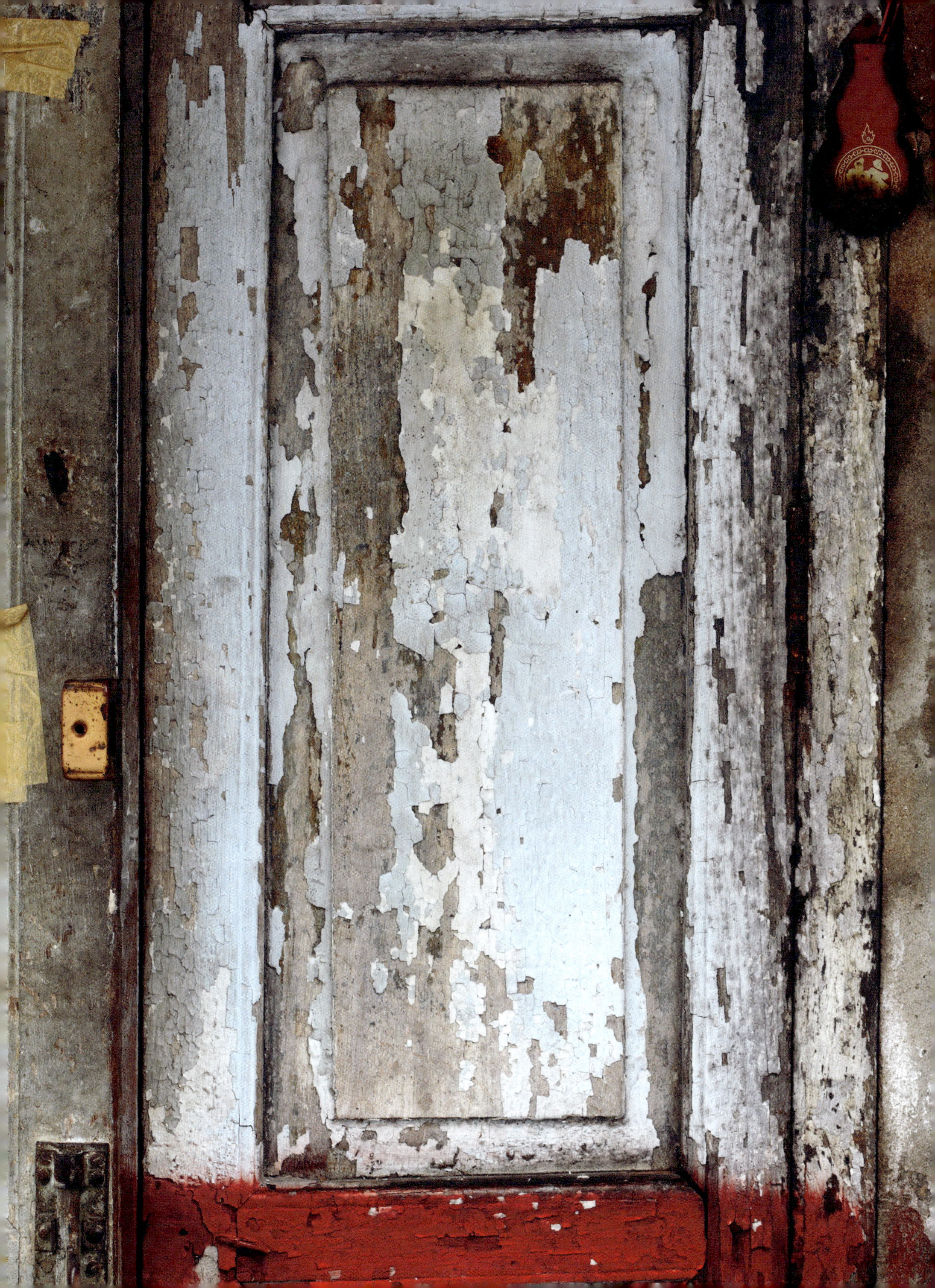

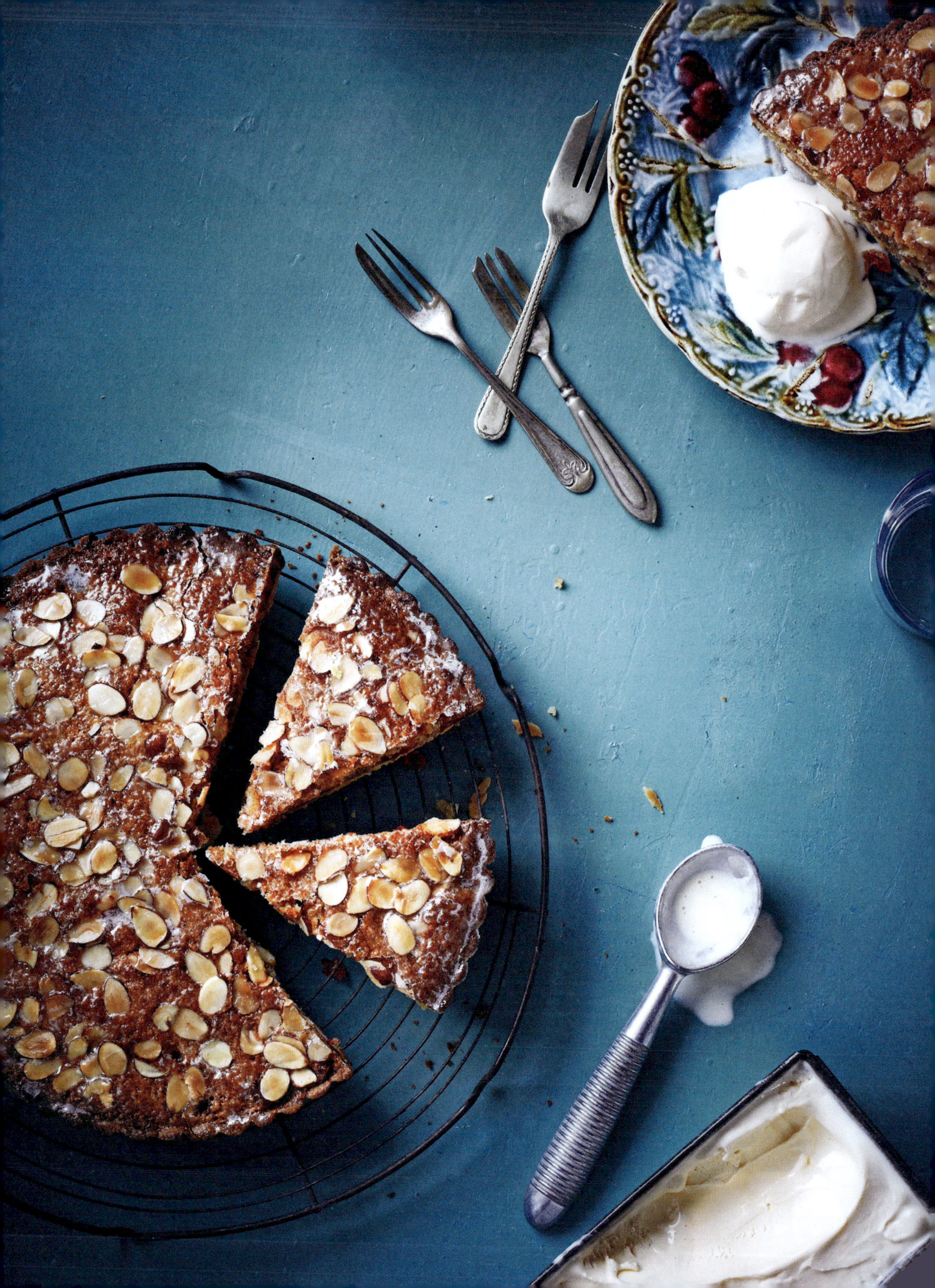

CONNIE'S ALMOND & CHERRY TART

Connie Rotolo is my Italian mum. Her daughter Rosalie took me in when I quit my job as a journalist because I was desperate to do something, anything, related to food. And so I became the phone girl and general office runabout at Bottega Rotolo in Adelaide — an absolute mecca for food nerds, chefs, wine geeks and cheese lovers. For two years I worked alongside a team of passionate food people, including Rosalie, her mother Connie and her father Alfonso or Fonz as he is affectionately known. The Rotolos gave me vegetable cuttings for my garden, truffles from Italy, cheese from France, jamón from Spain and, most importantly, they gave me their knowledge, their recipes and their love.

Connie and I like to use whole, unblanched almonds because we like the slight bitterness and colour of the skins in the filling

1 cup almonds ←
170 g butter, softened
¾ cup caster sugar
3 eggs
¼ cup plain flour
finely grated zest of 1 lemon
1 teaspoon natural vanilla extract
200 g maraschino cherries or glacé cherries, halved
25 g flaked almonds
½ cup pure icing sugar, sifted
2 tablespoons lemon juice
ice cream, mascarpone or double (thick) cream, to serve

SHORTCRUST PASTRY
85 g chilled unsalted butter, cut into cubes
1¼ cups plain flour, plus extra for dusting
½ cup caster sugar
3 egg yolks
1 teaspoon natural vanilla extract

To make the shortcrust pastry, place the butter, flour and sugar in a food processor and process until you get a fine breadcrumb-like texture. Add the egg yolks and vanilla and pulse until the pastry just starts to clump into a big yellow blob. If the dough doesn't come together, add 1 teaspoon of water and pulse again. Tip the mixture onto a lightly floured bench and smoosh the pastry together. Don't play around with it too much or you'll end up with a buttery mess. Just clump it together and cover it in plastic wrap. Refrigerate for 30 minutes to firm up.

Dust the bench with flour and place the pastry on the bench. Lightly dust the top of the pastry and rub flour all over a rolling pin. The trick to rolling pastry is to keep the pastry moving so it doesn't stick to the bench. Roll the rolling pin across the pastry a couple of times, then turn the pastry 90 degrees. Roll a couple of times, then turn 90 degrees again. Keep rolling and turning, dusting with flour as you go to stop the pastry sticking, until it is about 5 mm thick. Now the tricky part is getting this pastry into the tin because it is very delicate and will break (but that's okay because it means our cooked pastry will be beautifully buttery and biscuity). So what I do is attempt to transfer the sheet of pastry to a 24-cm fluted tart tin. Then I grab any bits of pastry that didn't make it into the tin and just fill in the holes and gaps. Give everything a gentle smoosh with your fingers and you'll never know the difference. Trim any excess pastry, then pop into the fridge for another rest, about 20 minutes.

Meanwhile, preheat the oven to 180°C.

[continued overleaf] →

SWEETNESS 175

CONTINUED...

Place the almonds in a food processor and process until they look like fine breadcrumbs.

Use an electric beater to cream the butter and caster sugar together in a large bowl until light, creamy and fluffy. While beating, add the eggs, one at a time, beating well after each addition, then fold in the ground almonds, flour, lemon zest and vanilla.

Get the pastry case out of the fridge and scatter the maraschino or glacé cherries over the base. Cover with the almond mixture and use a spatula to smooth the top. Scatter over the flaked almonds and bake for about 40 minutes, or until golden brown on top and cooked through. To test if it's ready, insert a skewer into the centre; if it comes out clean, the tart is cooked.

Whisk together the icing sugar and lemon juice. When the tart's ready to come out of the oven and, while it's still hot, spread the icing sugar mixture over the top of the tart. Leave to cool in the tin for about 15 minutes, then transfer to a wire cake rack.

Serve warm or at room temperature. Cut into wedges and serve with a big spoonful of ice cream, mascarpone or cream on the side.

SERVES 8–10

GOOEY CHOC BAR & WHISKY PUDDINGS

It's the ooze that makes these puddings so irresistible. As you break through the cracked, cakey surface, all the chocolatey goodness starts to ooze out. And as if gooey chocolate and a splash of whisky weren't enough indulgence for one little pudding, I like to mix in big chunks of peanutty chocolate bars to add some caramel and crunch.

125 g unsalted butter, cut into cubes, plus extra for greasing ramekins
100 g good-quality dark chocolate, broken into pieces
3 eggs
½ cup white sugar
2 tablespoons plain flour
1 tablespoon Scotch whisky (optional)
2 x 50 g caramelly or nutty chocolate bars, such as Snickers, Mars or Picnics
pouring (single) cream or ice cream, to serve

Preheat the oven to 200°C. Grease 4 x 1-cup capacity ramekins with a good amount of butter.

Place the butter and chocolate in a heatproof bowl set over a saucepan of simmering water and stir every so often until melted into a pool of rich, glossy liquid.

Whisk the eggs, sugar, flour and whisky together in a large bowl until just combined. Gradually whisk in the chocolate mixture.

Break the chocolate bars into pieces and divide among the prepared ramekins. Pour over the pudding mixture and give each a quick stir to evenly distribute those crunchy pieces of chocolate bar.

Transfer the ramekins to a baking tray and bake for about 20–25 minutes. You want the tops to be firm – they will crack a little – while the centres should be lava-like chocolate with little streams of caramel. Serve hot with a big bowl of cold cream or place a scoop of ice cream in the centre of each pudding and watch it melt and sink into the rich pool of chocolate in the centre.

SERVES 4

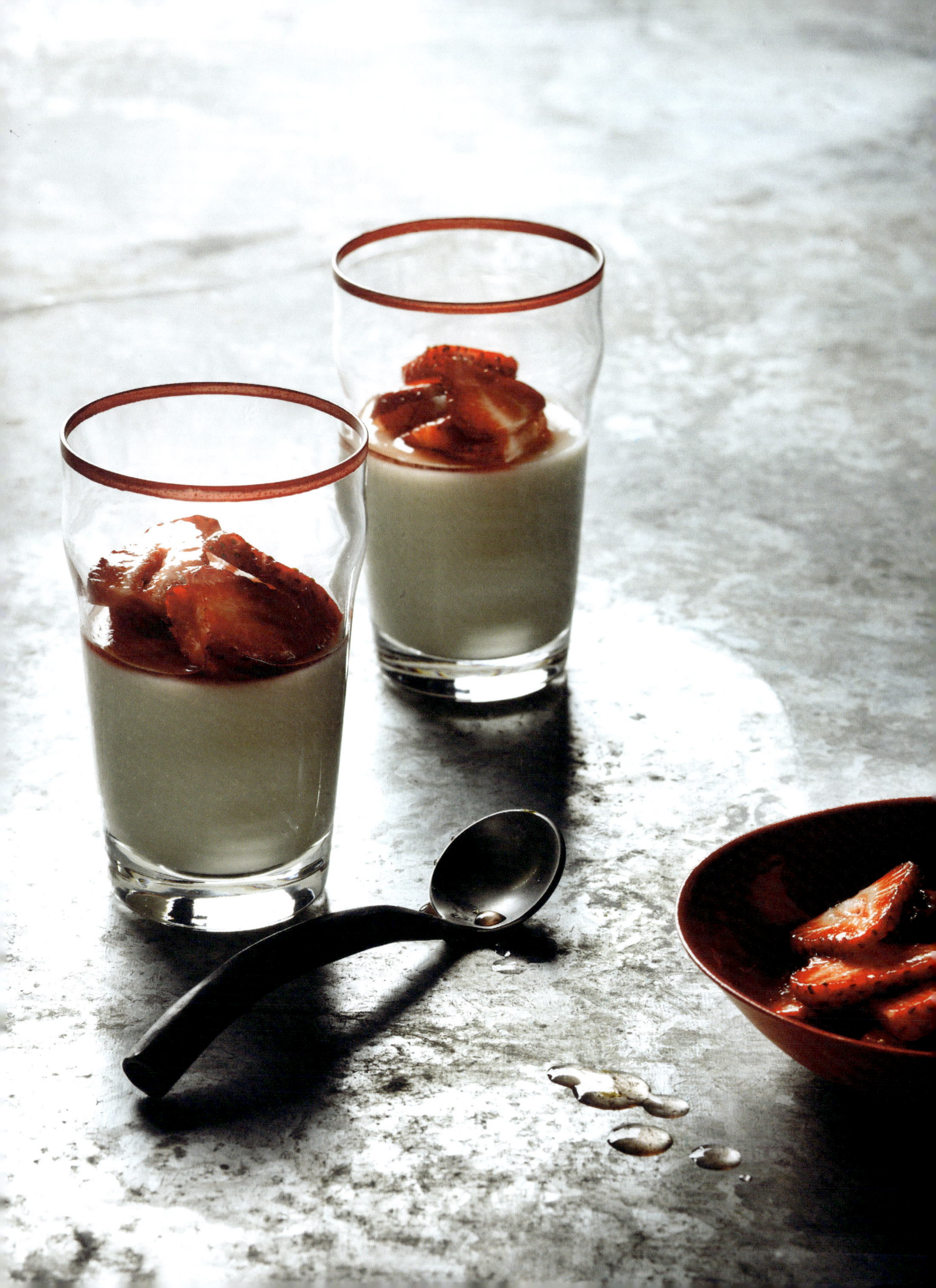

COCONUT & KAFFIR LIME PANNA COTTAS WITH STRAWBERRIES & LIME SYRUP

I'm so in love with this dessert. The sweet, coconutty panna cotta has just a hint of something unexpected, something you can't quite put your finger on — unless you're in the know. You could substitute the strawberries for diced mango, which also works a treat. For this dessert you'll need to find a good-quality coconut cream that looks smooth and creamy. When you open up your can of coconut cream — if it looks grainy and lumpy, then your panna cottas will turn out grainy and lumpy.

2 cups coconut cream
1½ cups pouring (single) cream
¼ cup white sugar
8 kaffir lime leaves, thinly sliced
3 sheets gold-strength (6 g) gelatine leaves → *I like gelatine sheets much better than the powdered version. Pick them up at a good deli or providore.*
250 g strawberries, hulled and sliced

LIME SYRUP
½ cup white sugar
finely grated zest of 1 lime
2 tablespoons lime juice

Place the coconut cream, cream, sugar and kaffir lime leaves in a saucepan over low heat, bring to a gentle simmer and cook for 5 minutes. Remove from the heat and set aside for 30 minutes for the lovely kaffir lime fragrance to infuse.

Return the pan to low heat and bring to a gentle simmer. Soak the gelatine in a bowl of cold water until softened. Gather up the gelatine in the palm of your hand and squeeze out the excess water. Whisk the gelatine into the coconut cream mixture until dissolved. Strain into a pouring jug and discard the lime leaves. Pour into your choice of glass tumblers, martini glasses or even plastic cups for a more laid-back affair. If you use about ½ cup per serve, then you'll have enough for six. Refrigerate for at least 4 hours, or until set.

For the lime syrup, heat the sugar and ½ cup of water in a small saucepan over medium heat, stirring until the sugar has dissolved. Remove from the heat and stir through the lime zest and juice. Set aside until ready to serve.

Just before serving, toss the strawberries in the lime syrup. Top each panna cotta with a spoonful of the strawberries and a drizzle of limey syrup.

MAKES 6

BANANA FRITTERS WITH FISH SAUCE BUTTERSCOTCH

It may seem just a little bit odd, but the addition of traditionally savoury condiments such as soy and fish sauce make for incredibly interesting desserts. Fish sauce, in particular, adds a deep yet subtle salty accent to a sweet dish. I think it works wonders in a butterscotch sauce. If you've got leftover butterscotch sauce, you can keep it in the fridge for up to a week. Just take it out and bring it to room temperature again before you serve it.

vegetable oil, for deep-frying
1 cup self-raising flour, sifted
½ cup rice flour, sifted
½ teaspoon sea salt
1 tablespoon white sugar
6 bananas, cut into 3-cm lengths
vanilla ice cream, to serve

FISH SAUCE BUTTERSCOTCH
150 g palm sugar, shaved with a knife
50 g unsalted butter
½ cup pouring (single) cream
2 teaspoons fish sauce

For the fish sauce butterscotch, place all of the ingredients in a saucepan over medium heat, bring to a gentle simmer, reduce the heat to low and stir for about 5 minutes, or until it's the consistency of double (thick) cream. Remove from the heat and set aside while you make the banana fritters.

Heat 10 cm of oil in a wok or large saucepan to 180°C. You can tell if the oil is hot enough by dipping a wooden spoon into it – if furious little bubbles form around the spoon, then the oil's ready to go.

While you're waiting for the oil to heat up, place both the flours, salt and sugar in a large bowl. Add 1½ cups of water and whisk until a smooth batter forms. Throw in the chunks of banana and gently mix to coat each piece.

Gently drop the banana pieces into the hot oil, frying no more than about 6 at a time. Deep-fry for 1–2 minutes, or until golden, making sure you flip the bananas every so often so they get an even tan. Drain on paper towel.

Serve the banana fritters hot with a huge scoop of ice cream and drizzle the whole lot with fish sauce butterscotch.

SERVES 6

MANGO & STICKY RICE

My childhood was full of mangoes. In Darwin they came from the giant tree in our backyard. In Papua New Guinea they came from the outdoor markets where my mum would buy them by the boxful. And in Thailand they came in my favourite dessert in the whole wide world — mango and sticky rice. The key ingredient here, apart from the mangoes, is salt. It's the subtle salty flavour in the coconut sauce and rice that gives the sweet, sweet mango a delicious intensity. You'll need to soak the sticky rice overnight before you make this dish.

2 cups sticky rice → Also called glutinous rice.
1 cup coconut milk   You'll find it at Asian grocers.
¾ cup white sugar
¼ teaspoon sea salt
3 mangoes, thickly sliced

COCONUT SAUCE
1 cup coconut milk
1 teaspoon cornflour
¼ teaspoon sea salt

Place the sticky rice in a bowl, cover with 1 litre of water and set aside to soak for at least 6 hours, or overnight.

To cook the sticky rice, fill a wok about one-quarter full with water and bring to a simmer. Line the base of a large bamboo steamer basket with a clean tea towel. Drain the sticky rice and pile it onto the tea towel in the steamer basket. Cover with the steamer lid, place in the wok and steam for about 15 minutes. ← [see note]

Heat the coconut milk, sugar and salt in a saucepan over medium heat for about 5 minutes, or until the sugar has dissolved. Scoop the sticky rice into the coconut milk mixture and stir until just combined. Remove from the heat, cover and set aside for about 20 minutes to let the rice soak up the sweet coconut milk.

For the coconut sauce, place all of the ingredients in a saucepan and whisk until just combined. Place over medium heat and cook, stirring for 2 minutes, or until glossy and thickened to a pouring (single) cream consistency.

To serve, mound a pile of rice on a plate and spoon over a generous amount of coconut sauce. Top with the mango slices.

SERVES 6

NOTE: Your steamer needs to be large enough to sit above the water in the wok. If not, use a smaller saucepan to heat the water.

GINGERBREAD HOUSES ARE COOL

4½ cups plain flour, plus extra for dusting
2 tablespoons ground ginger
1 teaspoon ground cinnamon
½ teaspoon ground nutmeg
¼ teaspoon ground cloves
1½ teaspoons bicarbonate of soda
250 g unsalted butter, softened
¾ cup firmly packed brown sugar
⅓ cup golden syrup
2 eggs
200 g dark chocolate buttons
copious amounts of lollies:
jubes, chocolates, candy canes, marshmallows, sprinkles, jelly beans, musk sticks and Smarties

or whatever else you fancy

ICING
4 eggwhites
1 tablespoon lemon juice
2 cups pure icing sugar, sifted

EQUIPMENT
cardboard, ruler and scissors, to make stencils
1 large chopping board
aluminium foil
piping bags and nozzles

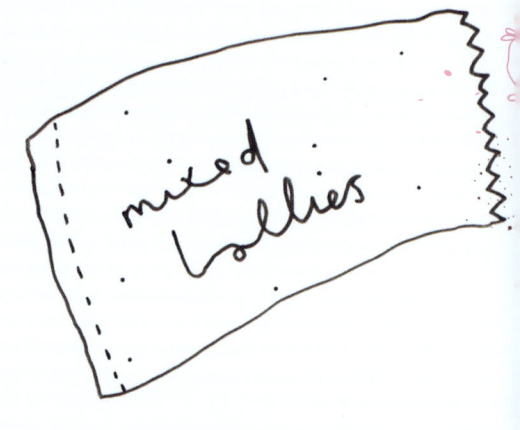

mixed lollies

① Get out some cardboard and a ruler, make stencils using the illustrated stencils on this page as a guide. Cut out a stencil for 1 side wall, 1 front/back wall, 1 roof and a door. But when you go to cut out your gingerbread pastry pieces you'll need to use some of those stencils twice so that you have 2 side walls, 2 front/back walls, 2 roof pieces and 1 door.

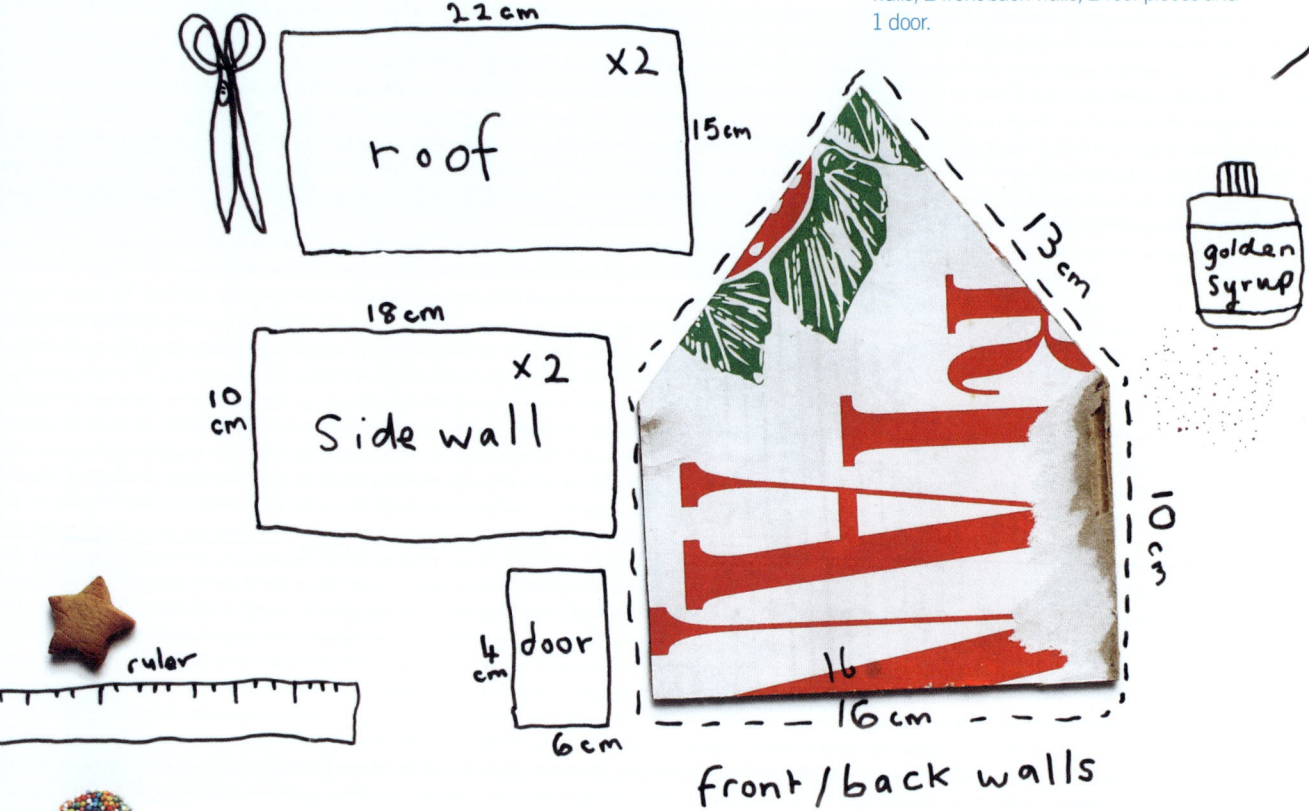

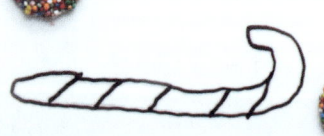

roof — 22 cm × 15 cm, ×2

side wall — 18 cm × 10 cm, ×2

door — 4 cm × 6 cm

front/back walls — 13 cm, 10 cm, 16 cm ×2

Gingerbread houses may be as naff and uncool as green jelly and ice-cream (which I also adore, by the way), but I just can't help but get excited about filling my shopping trolley with all things naughty — musk sticks, sugary jubes, mini-marshmallows, jelly beans, licorice allsorts, chocolate buttons, and giant freckles. I can't help but giggle at the sight of my dining-room table covered in an undulating sea of technicolored sugary bliss.

My mum, dad and I have always made our Christmas gingerbread house together. Some years we'd make two or three to give away as presents. It's our family tradition.

② Sift the flour, spices and bicarbonate of soda into a large bowl. Using an electric beater, beat the butter, sugar and golden syrup together in a large separate bowl for about 3 minutes, or until pale and fluffy. While beating, add the eggs, one at a time, beating well after each addition. Gradually fold in the flour mixture. Tip the dough out onto a lightly floured bench and knead for a couple of minutes, or until smooth and Plasticine-like. Shape into a thick disc, wrap in plastic wrap and pop in the fridge for 30 minutes.

③ Preheat the oven to 180°C. Roll out the dough to 5 mm thick. Use a knife and the stencils to trace out the house pieces. Place the pieces on baking trays lined with baking paper and bake for about 12 minutes, or until pale and only just starting to turn golden at the edges. Transfer to a wire cake rack to cool.

④ Once the gingerbread pieces are well and truly cooled, you can get started on the nerve-racking process of building a house. To make a base for the house, cover a chopping board tightly with aluminium foil, making sure the surface is quite smooth. [CONTINUED OVERLEAF] →

CONTINUED...

Now for the chocolate concrete

5 Place the chocolate buttons in a heatproof bowl set over a saucepan of simmering water and stir every so often until melted and smooth. Scoop the chocolate into a piping bag fitted with a small plain nozzle.

6 Stick a front wall piece and a side wall to each other, then to the chopping board base, piping the melted chocolate along the edges to attach each piece. Hold in place for a couple of minutes, using tumblers or ramekins to help prop up the walls.

7 Attach the remaining walls using the same process. Let the walls firm up for about 10 minutes. Use the melted chocolate to attach the roof, then the door. Congratulations on your new house! Don't worry if it tumbles down. We usually have at least one collapse every year. Just have a giggle and start again.

Now for the icing

8 Using an electric beater, beat the eggwhite for 2 minutes, or until foamy. Add the lemon juice and beat for 2 minutes. Beat the icing sugar into the mixture, one dessertspoonful at a time. Once you've added all the icing sugar, beat the mixture for a further 10 minutes, or until the icing is thick and silky. Transfer to a piping bag fitted with a medium plain nozzle.

icing sugar

Now comes the fun bit: house decorating

(9) I like to pipe icing over all of the joins of the house, so that when the icing sets rock hard, I know my house isn't going to fall down under the weight of a million lollies. Use the icing to attach the lollies, chocolates and any other kind of goodies to the house. Pipe the icing over the chopping board base to create a snow-covered yard. Now stand back and marvel at your beautiful house. Yay!

make a marshmellow man

MAKES 1 COSY HOUSE

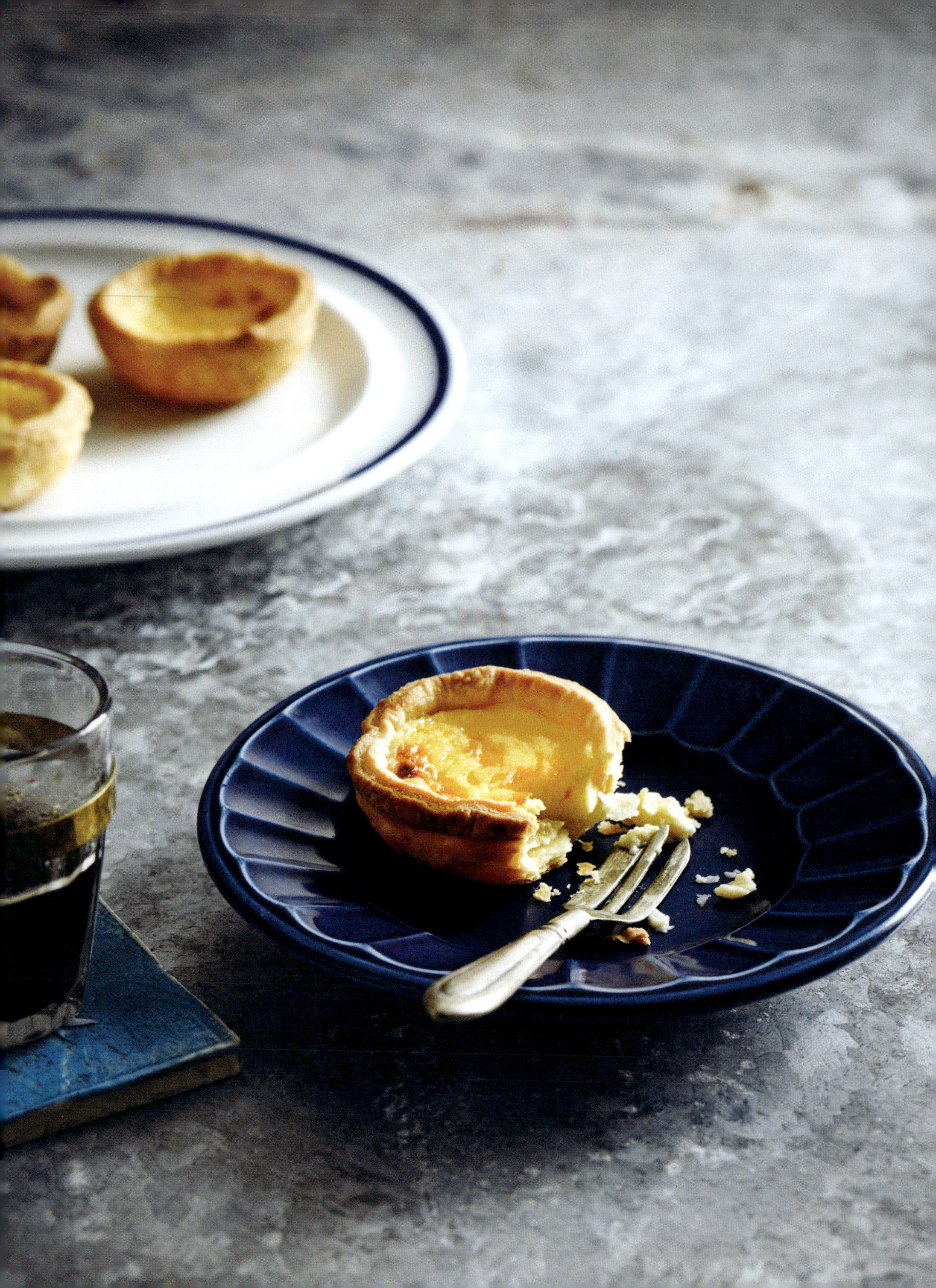

YUM CHA CUSTARD TARTS

Yum cha has been a regular ritual in my family for as long as I can remember. Mum, Dad and I sit in hungry anticipation for the first steaming trolley to roll by. Mum has a little whinge about how long it's taking for her bowl of steamed rice to arrive at the table. Dad pours the tea. And I keep my eyes peeled for custard tarts. Now, custard tarts can mean many things to different people. But at yum cha, no matter which restaurant you're dining at, the custard tarts are, almost always, exactly the same. The pastry is so incredibly soft that the whole thing threatens to crumble before you even take a bite, and the filling is a yellowy, barely set eggy custard. This is the exacting standard to which I hold my yum cha custard tarts. One of the great things about this recipe is that there's no need to blind-bake the tart shells before filling them, which means you can get to the eating part quicker.

1 quantity Maggie Beer's Sour Cream Pastry (see page 129)
plain flour, for dusting
1 cup milk
1 cup pouring (single) cream
3 eggs
3 egg yolks
½ cup caster sugar
1 tablespoon natural vanilla extract

Follow the instructions on page 129 to make Maggie Beer's sour cream pastry, but divide the pastry into 2 equal-sized discs before wrapping in plastic wrap and refrigerating for 20 minutes to rest. Roll a disc out to 5 mm thick. For 7-cm round (measured at the top) muffin or cupcake moulds, I cut out 11-cm rounds from the pastry. Cut out a round and gently press into a muffin tin mould. Leave the excess pastry sticking up above the muffin tin to make the pastry case taller (which will give you some shrinkage allowance). Keep cutting out rounds and lining the moulds until you've exhausted the pastry sheet. When you've cut as many rounds out as you can, smoosh the pastry cuttings back together, dust with the flour and roll it out again to cut out more rounds. Keep doing this until you've exhausted the first disc of pastry, then take out the second disc and do it all over again. You should have 18 lined muffin moulds. Pop the muffin tin in the fridge for 30 minutes to rest. Do not skimp on the resting, as this is crucial to the pastry not shrinking too much and becoming one big eggy mess in the oven.

Preheat the oven to 200°C.

Place the milk, cream, eggs, egg yolks, sugar and vanilla in a large bowl and whisk until just combined. Transfer to a jug, and pour into the pastry cases, filling just over halfway – don't be tempted to fill them any more because the eggy filling will expand. Carefully place the tin in the oven and bake for 10 minutes, then reduce the temperature to 180°C and bake for a further 10 minutes.

Remove from the oven and allow the tarts to cool in the tin for about 5 minutes, then ease them out with a butter knife. Serve straight away or store in an airtight container for a day or so – although I find they never last long in my house.

MAKES 18

DRUNKEN FRUIT SALAD

I've recently come to a very harsh realisation: I am rampantly obsessive-compulsive when it comes to mixing fruit. Just the thought (or even a whiff) of one of those mixed fruit smoothie concoctions, all brown and flecky with bits of mushy banana and bitsy orange, is enough to give me the heebie-jeebies. Similarly, even the slightest hint of mush in a fruit salad will completely unnerve me. And so, a normal recipe for fruit salad (written by someone without this debilitating disorder) would say very simply, 'choose a selection of your favourite fruits', whereas I've been very specific instead. This is the way I do it, complete with naff balls of rockmelon and watermelon (I reckon the melon baller is such an under-utilised kitchen tool). But if you're not obsessive-compulsive about mixing your fruits and you don't have a melon baller, then feel free to freestyle your own drunken fruit salad.

½ cup white sugar
2 tablespoons lemon juice
250 g strawberries, hulled and quartered
300 g seedless red grapes
½ small rockmelon, scooped into balls
(or cut into bite-sized chunks)
1 small wedge of watermelon, scooped into balls
(or cut into bite-sized chunks)
Grand Marnier, to taste
vanilla ice cream, slightly softened, to serve

First we need to make a lemony sugar syrup. Heat the sugar with ⅓ cup of water in a small saucepan over high heat for about 3 minutes, stirring until the sugar has dissolved. Leave the sugar syrup to cool completely, stir in the lemon juice.

Place all of the lovely fruits in a large bowl. Pour over the lemony sugar syrup and a generous splosh of Grand Marnier (at least ¼ cup). Use salad servers to very gently and carefully persuade the fruit to make friends with the sugar syrup. Don't be rough about it or you'll end up with a bruised mess. Spoon the fruit and some of the lush syrup into serving bowls. I like to serve mine with soft vanilla ice cream that melts and puddles around the fruit.

SERVES 6

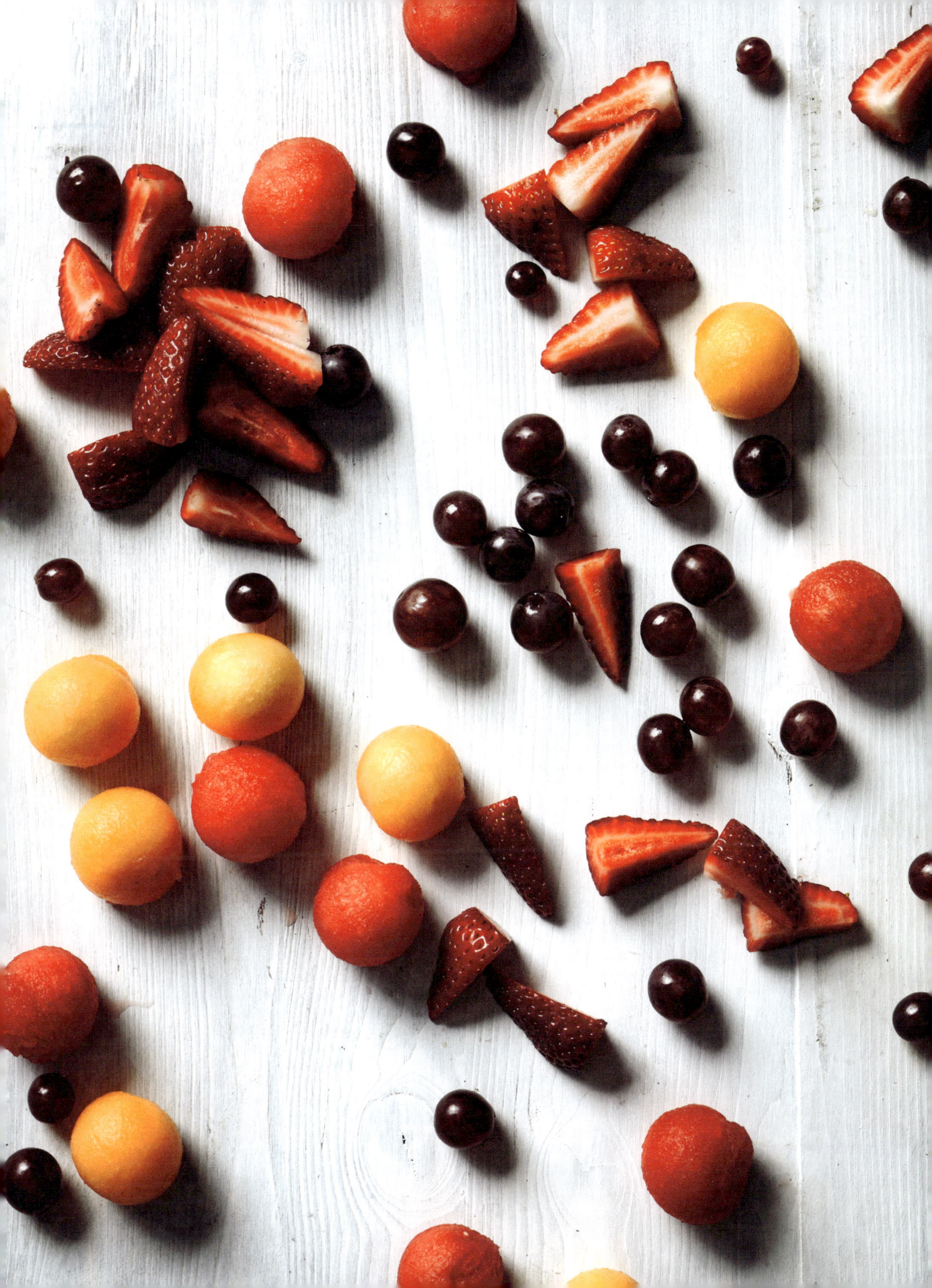

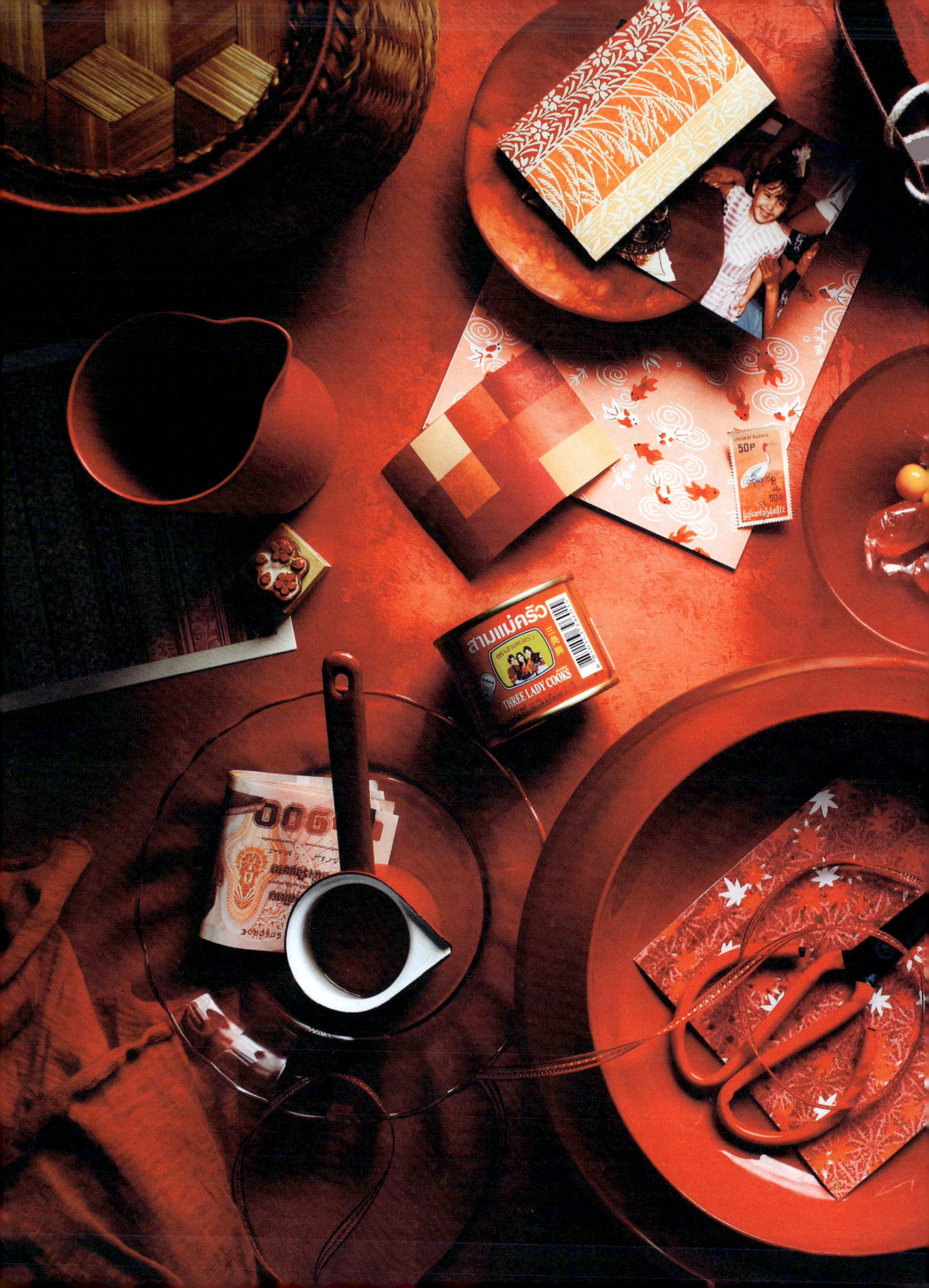
สามแม่ครัว
THREE LADY COOKS
50P

THINGS IN JARS

HOME-GROWN LOVE

My little backyard garden in McLaren Vale may not have been pretty, but it sure was filled with delicious goodies. Large rosemary shrubs towered over buds of radicchio and clusters of thyme. Tomato plants, interspersed with flowering chilli bushes, dotted the garden surrounding the back patio. My partner Tim and I had never had our own backyard before, let alone a veggie patch, so we just planted as much as possible in a very ad hoc sort of way. (Well, Tim did the planting and composting... I did the picking.) Then we simply crossed our fingers and waited to see what would grow.

It was our lack of planning and our excitement about planting that saw an absolute glut of spinach, silverbeet and rainbow chard sprout up all over the garden one winter. I would head out into the garden and come back with huge laundry baskets overflowing with stalks of hardy greens. There was far too much for even an avid greens lover to consume, so I started taking rainbow chard and silverbeet 'bouquets' to my friends instead of flowers.

And then came the tomato onslaught. We had cherry tomatoes by the bucketload. What a delicious problem to have. So come summer my friends were gifted jars of spicy tomato relish instead of their bouquets of edible greenery.

The love always came full circle. My friend Caroline, otherwise known as 'Chef', would come for dinner bearing jars of preserved lemons, freshly picked mushrooms or a loaf of wood-oven-baked bread. Paul and Maria would pop over with a three kilogram snapper caught the day before. And bottles of wine would pile up on the kitchen bench as our dinner guests arrived. I guess you would expect nothing less when a good proportion of your friends are in some way connected to a McLaren Vale winery.

I cherish the culture of home-grown love. It's such a privilege to have lived in a community where gifts from the ground are not only dinner-party treats but, more importantly, are also a way of life and, for many of our friends, a source of livelihood.

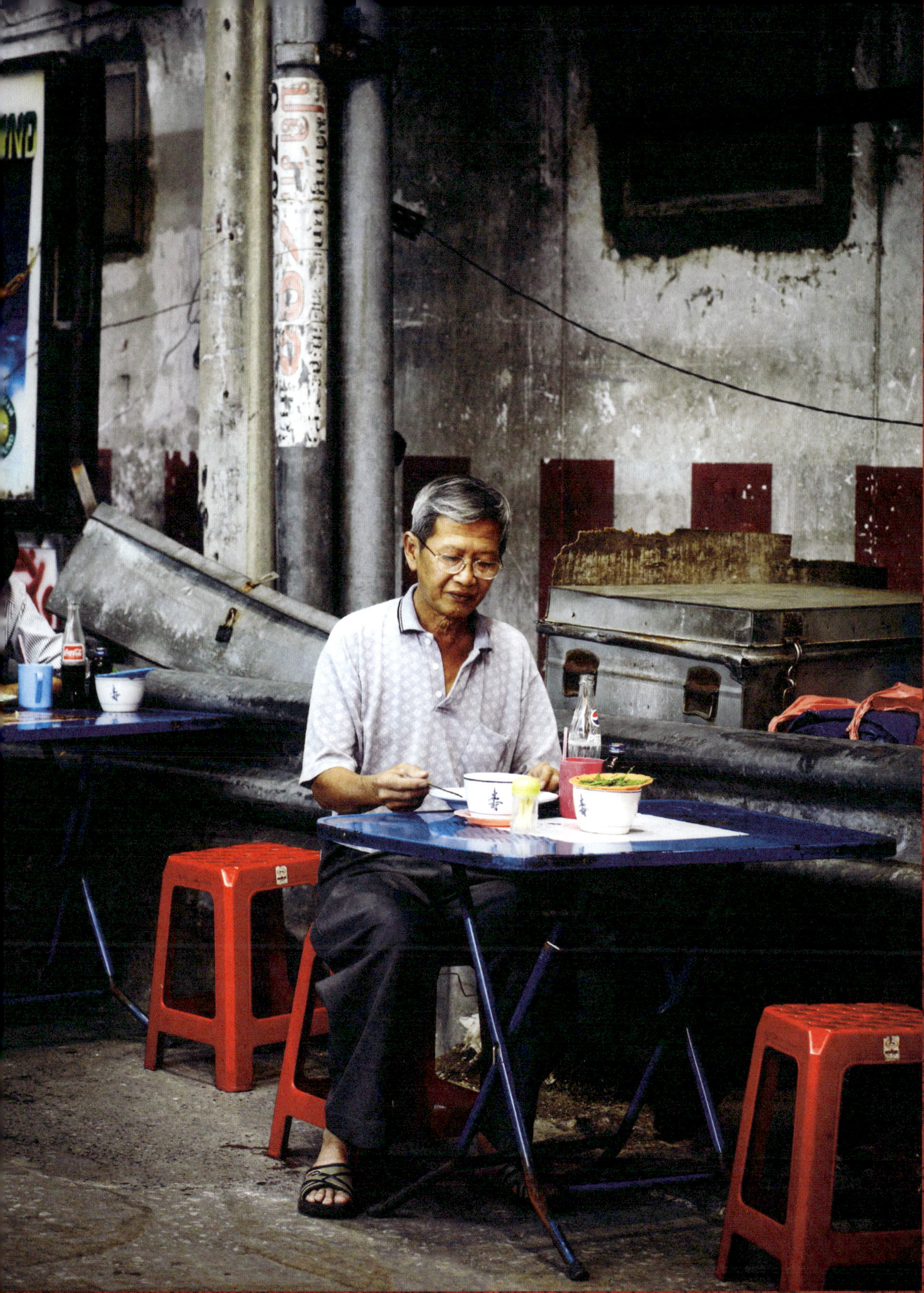

เต้าหู้
TOFU
CHINESE RADISH
เผือก
TARO
SPRING ROLL
ข้าวโพด
CORN
เจ

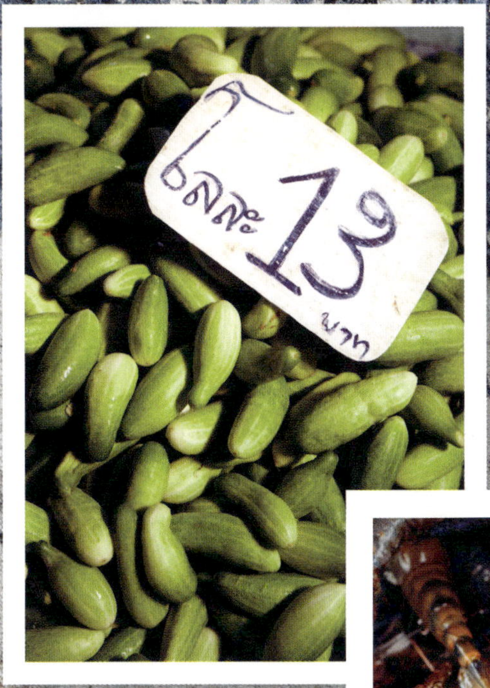
โลละ 13
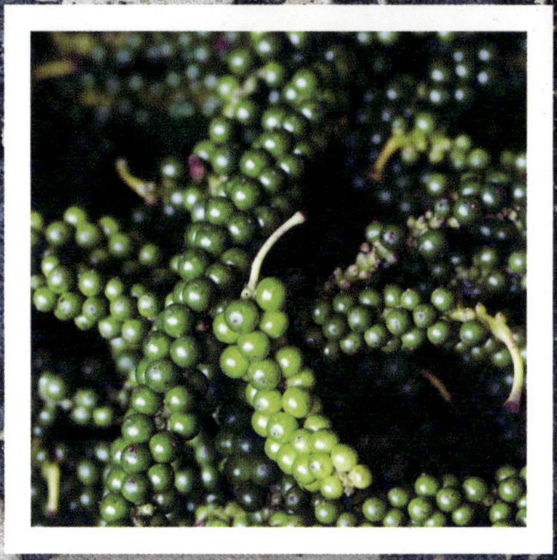
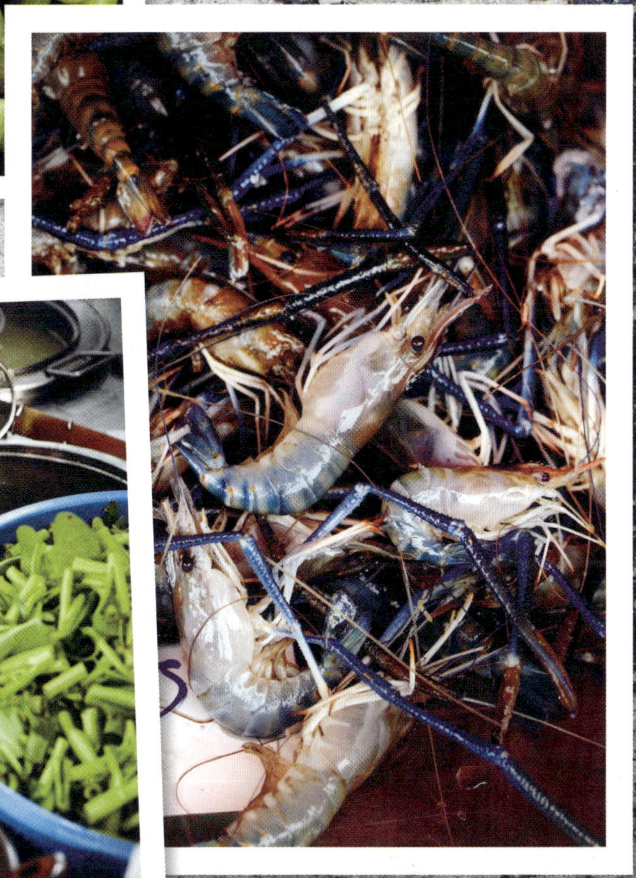
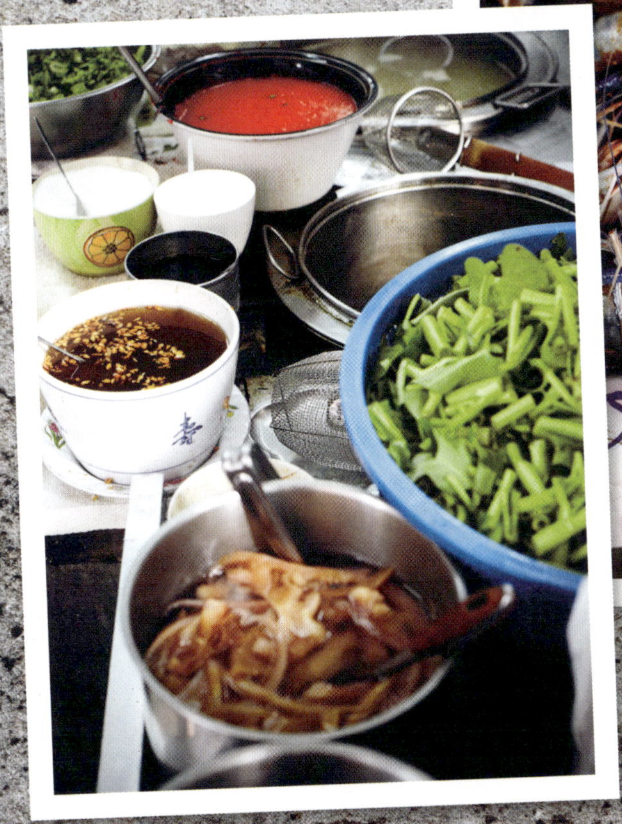

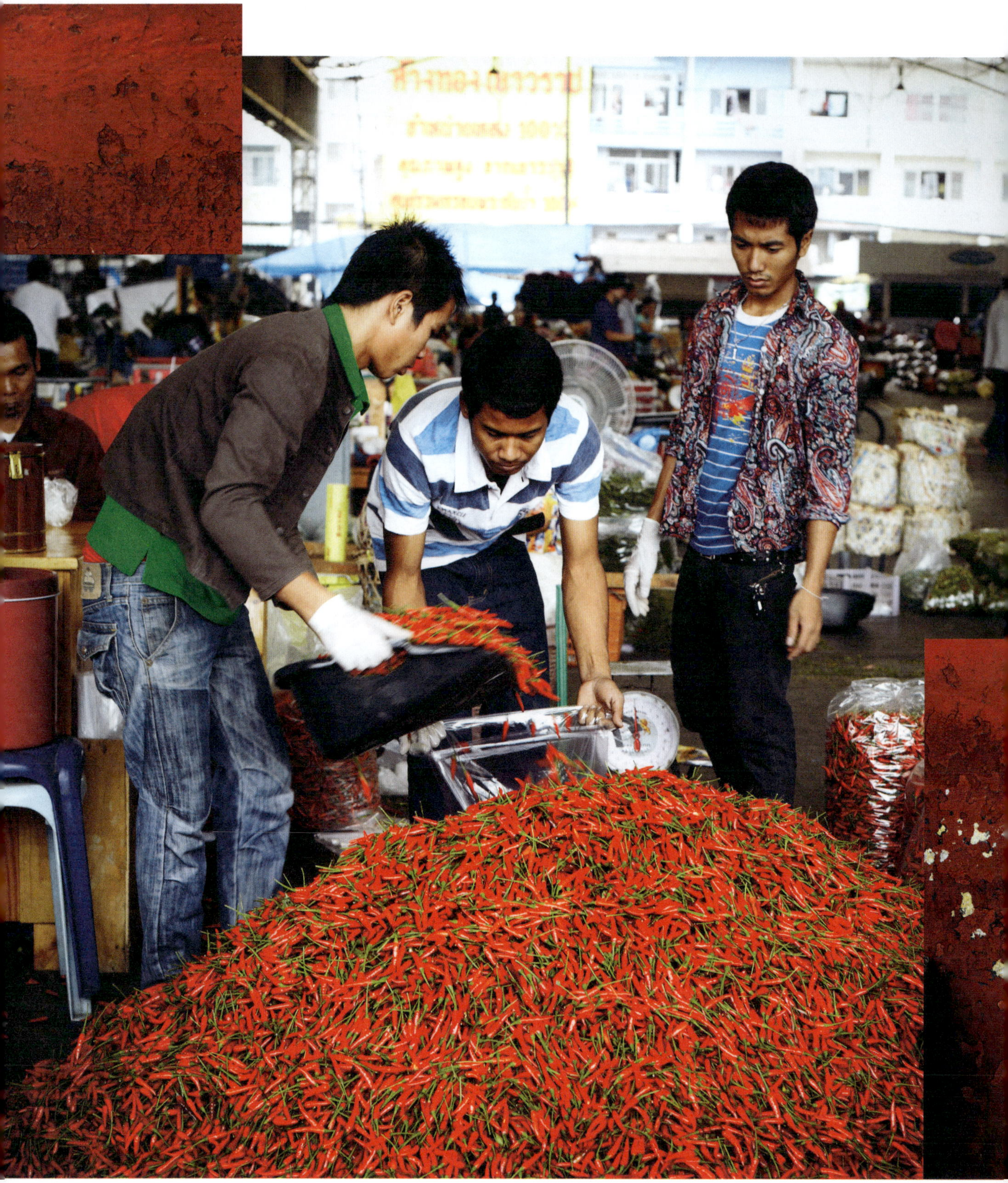

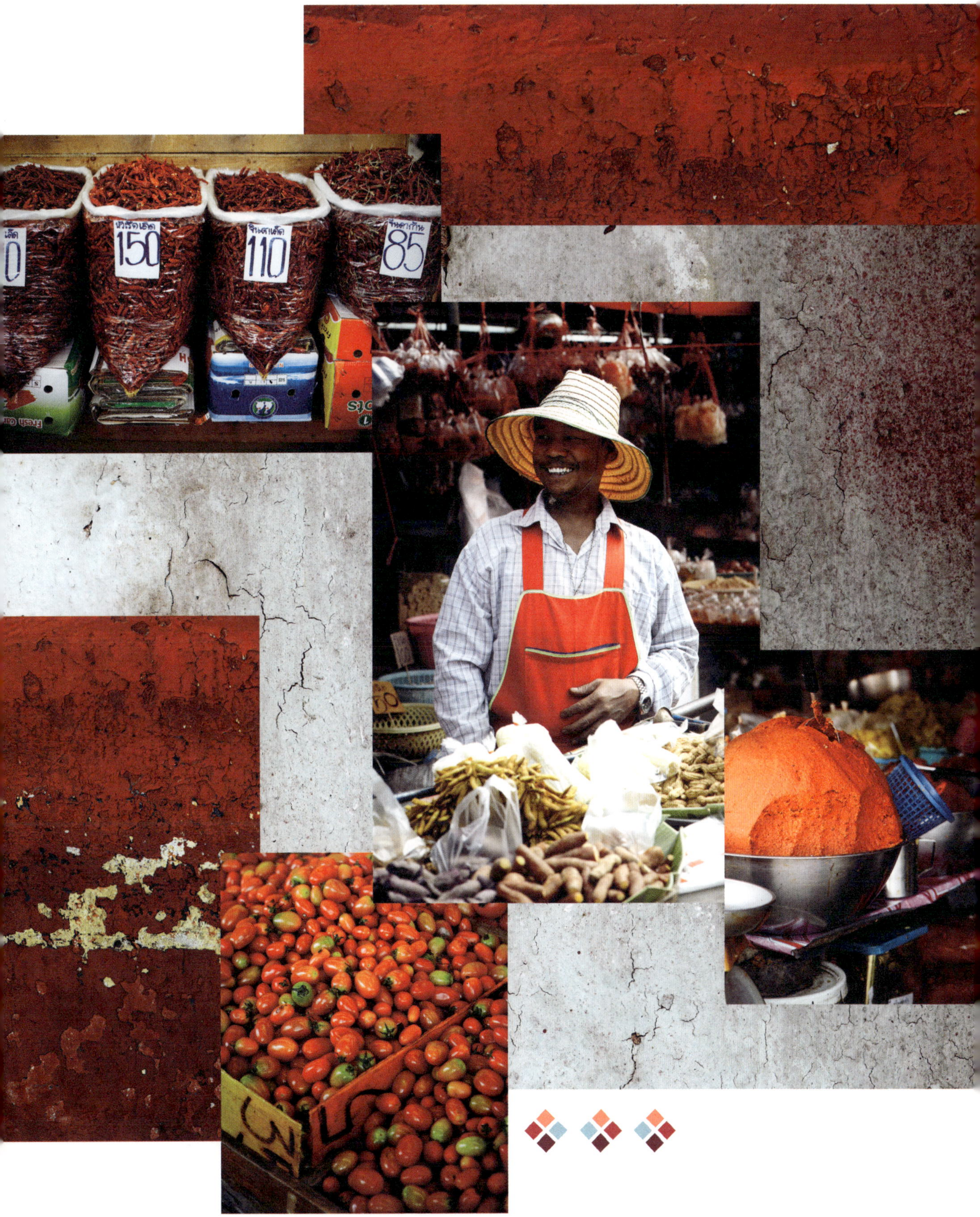
150
110
85

I'm always mesmerised by smells, the spectacle and the chaos of a Bangkok market.

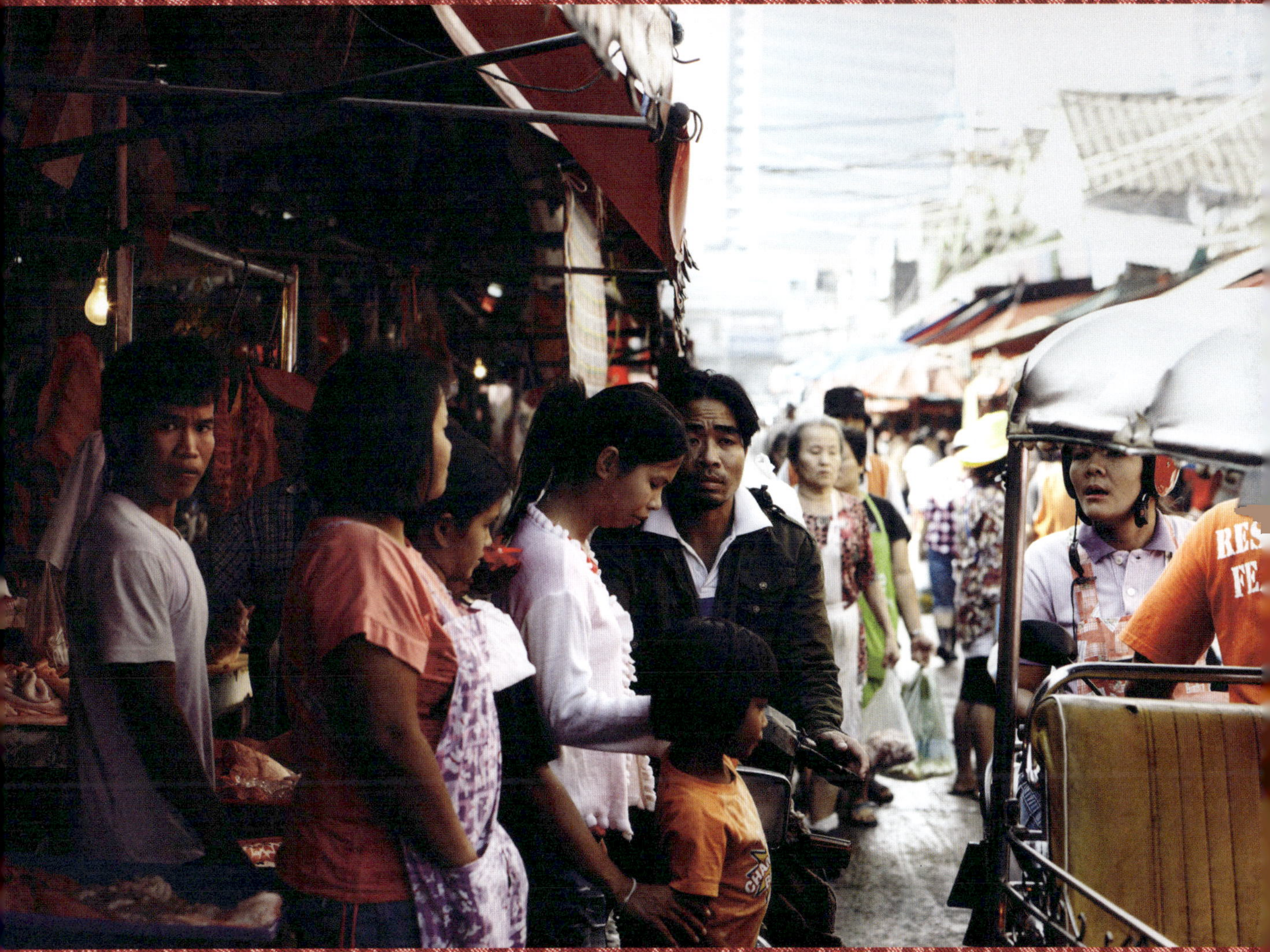

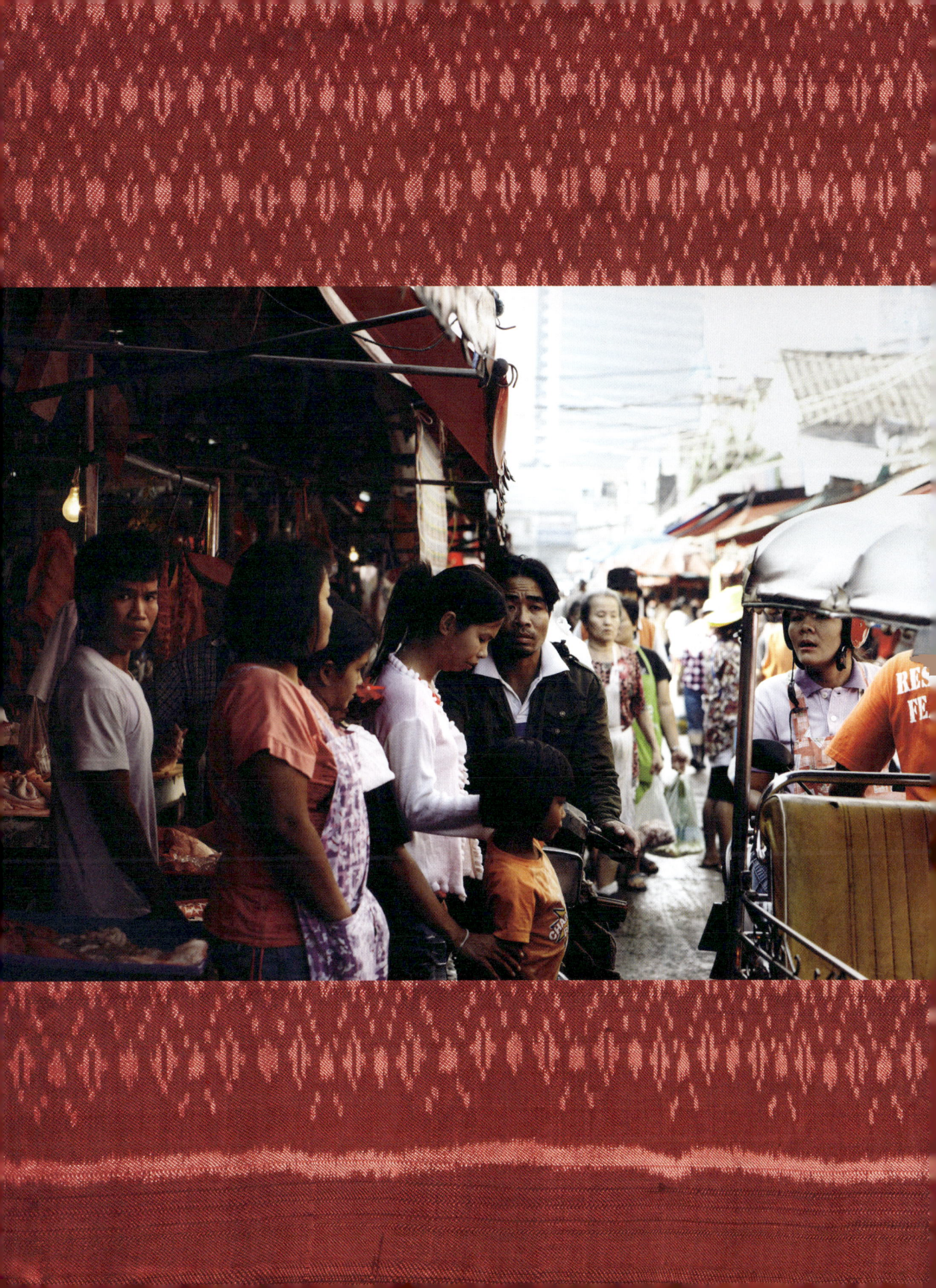

MUM'S RED GINGER JAM

A little spicy, a little sweet, a little sour and a lot gingery. My mum calls it a jam but it's more like an all-purpose sweet and sour sauce (but not the gloopy Chinese takeaway sort). I use this like most people use tomato sauce. What to do with your red ginger jam? Use as a dipping sauce for cooked prawns; serve with poached or grilled chicken breast and rice; slather it on buttered toast and top with thick chunks of leg ham; stir it through warm spaghetti and top with loads of basil and grated parmesan; or spoon it onto a sausage sandwich instead of tomato sauce.

1 cup white sugar
⅓ cup white vinegar
2 teaspoons sea salt
¼ cup vegetable oil
3 red onions, roughly chopped
1 head of garlic, cloves separated and roughly chopped
1 big hunk of fresh ginger, peeled and roughly chopped (about ½ cup)
2 fresh long red chillies, roughly chopped
2 large red capsicum, seeds removed and cut into chunks
500 g tomatoes, roughly chopped

First we need to make a vinegary sugar syrup. Place the sugar, vinegar, salt and ½ cup of water in a saucepan over medium heat, bring to a simmer and cook for about 5 minutes, or until the sugar has dissolved. Remove from the heat.

Meanwhile, heat the vegetable oil in a large saucepan over medium heat, add the onion, garlic, ginger and chilli and cook, stirring occasionally, for about 5 minutes, or until you can smell all the lovely ingredients but don't let the onion or garlic brown.

Add the capsicum, tomato and the sugar syrup you made earlier to the pan and gently simmer for about 20 minutes, or until the capsicum has softened and the tomato has released all of its juices.

Use a stick blender or food processor to whiz the mixture to a thick sauce consistency. Pour into sterilised jars (see note), seal with the lids and store in the fridge for up to 2 weeks.

MAKES ABOUT 1.25 LITRES

NOTE: To sterilise, place the jars and their lids separately in a saucepan and cover with boiling water. Drain and place in a preheated 160°C oven to dry. Fill while both the jars and the jam are warm.

SPICED PICKLED BEETROOT

It can be easy for us to forget that food doesn't grow in cans or in cartons. It comes from the ground, from a tree or from a real live cow. I love pickling my own beetroot — as the raw and ragged dirt-covered bulbs transform into precious, glistening beetroot bits, I'm reminded that food isn't something that just magically appears in the aisle of a supermarket. The magic is in the cooking.

There are many ways with these pickled beauties: take a fork and eat your beetroot straight from the jar (shhhhh...); pile them up on a plate next to grilled fish and a wedge of lemon; or mix with cooked brown lentils, goat's cheese, lemon zest and a drizzle of olive oil for an easy lunchbox salad.

1 kg fresh beetroot (about 5 medium or 10 baby bulbs)
2 cups red wine vinegar
1 cup white sugar
4 star anise
1 teaspoon whole allspice
1 teaspoon black peppercorns
1 teaspoon coriander seeds
1 teaspoon table salt

Using kitchen scissors, cut the tops off the beetroot, leaving a couple of centimetres of stalk. Discard the tops. Wash off any dirt from the beetroot and leave them unpeeled. Place in a large saucepan and cover with cold water. Cover with a lid, place over high heat and simmer until the beetroot are tender. To test for their readiness, pierce them with a knife or a skewer; they should be soft with just a little bit of resistance (you don't want mushy beets). I find the smaller bulbs take about 30–45 minutes, but if you've got big tough old beetroot, then you might find it will take 1 hour or more.

Once the beetroot are cooked, scoop out 2 cups of the inky purple cooking liquid and strain through a sieve lined with muslin or a Chux into a saucepan. We'll use this to add flavour to and to colour the pickling liquid.

Drain the beetroot into a colander and set aside to cool for a couple of minutes. When I peel beetroot, I always rub my hands with olive oil to help keep them from staining purple, but you could also wear rubber gloves. Break off the tops of the beetroot and use your fingers to peel off the skins – they should slip off quite easily.

Cut each beetroot into your preferred shape – wedges, thick slices or even leave them whole, if they're small. Pack them into sterilised jars (see note on previous page) or plastic containers.

Add the remaining ingredients to the reserved beetroot cooking liquid, place over medium heat, bring to a simmer for about 30 minutes, stirring until the sugar has dissolved. Remove from the heat and set aside to cool until warm to the touch. Pour the liquid and spices into the jars, making sure the beetroot are completely covered. Seal with the lids and pop them in the fridge. You can eat them straight away or keep them in the fridge for up to 1 month.

MAKES ABOUT 700 G

READY-TO-GO ROASTED CAPSICUM

A jar of homemade roasted capsicum is fast food at its best. Don't be too fussy when peeling the skins off the blistered capsicum — a few flecks of the blackened burnished skin add a slightly smoky flavour.

Those lovely charred slivers of roasted capsicum make a brilliant bruschetta topping: grill slices of baguette or ciabatta bread, rub with a cut garlic clove and smoosh the capsicum over the bread.

Or for a quick pasta, warm the capsicum in a pan with some of the olive oil, toss with pasta and fresh basil and top with heaps of grated parmesan.

They'll add sweetness to a frittata: whisk 8 eggs with 1/2 cup pouring (single) cream, heat capsicum and olive oil in a non-stick frying pan, add the egg mixture, drop in dollops of goat's cheese, grate over some parmesan and finish under a hot grill. Or simply serve alongside barbecued snags and lamb chops.

2 red capsicum
2 green capsicum
2 yellow capsicum
2 cups white wine vinegar
6 garlic cloves, thinly sliced
2 cups extra-virgin olive oil

Preheat the oven grill to high. Slice off the sides of the capsicum and discard the seeds and core. Place the capsicum, skin-side up, on a large baking tray lined with aluminium foil. Grill for about 15 minutes, or until the skins are blackened and blistered. You may need to grill the capsicum in batches. Transfer to a bowl and cover with plastic wrap and leave to steam for a minute or so to loosen the charred skins. Peel off the skins and discard. Slice the flesh into slivers and place in a bowl.

Heat the vinegar in a small saucepan until just boiling. Pour over the capsicum and leave to soak for about 5 minutes, then drain and discard vinegar.

Toss the garlic through the capsicum and divide the mixture between sterilised jars (see note on page 200). Pour the oil over the capsicum to completely cover, seal with the lids and pop in the fridge ready to use at a moment's notice. Use them up within 2 weeks.

MAKES ABOUT 3 CUPS

SPICED TOMATO RELISH

I first made this relish after what I call our 'summer of tomatoes'. We had planted a vegetable garden and went a little bit crazy with the cherry tomatoes. I had bucketloads of them, so I made this sweet, sour and packed-with-spice relish. You can use any tomatoes you like — cherry, roma, beefsteak or whatever you can get your hands on. I often throw a few green tomatoes into the mix for a bit of colour.

Ways with your tomato relish: slather it on bread, top with Gruyère cheese and grill; serve as a condiment with Indian curries; or use it instead of tomato sauce.

1 cup vegetable oil
1 tablespoon yellow mustard seeds
1 tablespoon grated fresh ginger
5 garlic cloves, finely chopped
2 tablespoons ground cumin
1 tablespoon ground ginger
2 teaspoons ground turmeric
2 kg mixed tomatoes, larger ones quartered, smaller ones halved
2–3 fresh long red chillies, finely chopped
1½ cups malt vinegar
1½ cups white sugar
1 tablespoon sea salt

Heat the oil in a large saucepan over medium heat and gently fry the mustard seeds until you hear them start to crackle and pop. Add the ginger, garlic, cumin, ground ginger and turmeric and fry, stirring continuously, for about 2 minutes. It should smell delicious at this stage. Stir in the remaining ingredients. Bring to a gentle simmer and let it bubble away for about 45 minutes. By this stage the tomato should have broken down into a thick, chunky and incredibly spiced sauce. Spoon into sterilised jars (see note on page 200), seal with the lids and pop in the fridge. Keep for up to 1 month.

MAKES 4–5 CUPS

STRAWBERRY, BALSAMIC VINEGAR & VANILLA JAM

I like my jam to be studded with plump bits of soft yielding fruit, which is why I always use whole strawberries for this recipe. I love seeing that chunky smear of deep, dark strawberry as I spread the jam across a piece of buttery toast (for breakfast, a snack or even dinner). Oh, the joys of jam. You could even use it as a saucy topping for creamy vanilla ice cream or swirl it through your breakfast yoghurt.

2 kg strawberries, hulled
2 kg white sugar
¼ cup balsamic vinegar
2 tablespoons lemon juice
strips of peel from 1 lemon, tied in muslin
1 vanilla bean, halved lengthways

Place all of the ingredients and ¼ cup of water in a large heavy-based saucepan. Give everything a bit of a mix and place over high heat. Bring to a simmer, then reduce the heat to low and cook for about 45 minutes. You'll get some foamy stuff rising to the surface, so skim it off every so often. Place a couple of small plates in the freezer to chill.

After 45 minutes, test to see if the jam has reached 'setting' stage. Place a spoonful of the jam onto a chilled plate and run your finger through it. If the jam doesn't run back into the line you've made with your finger, then it's done. If not, cook the jam for another 10 minutes and test again.

Once you've succeeded in getting the jam to 'setting' point, remove it from the heat and pull out the bag of lemon peel and the vanilla bean with tongs. Pour your lovely gloopy jam into sterilised jars (see note on page 200) and seal with the lids. Store in a cool, dark place for up to 12 months. Refrigerate any jars that have been opened and use within 1 month.

MAKES 2 LITRES

MENUS THAT MAKE ME HAPPY

TAKE ME TO THAILAND FOR DINNER

I am loathe to call this a 'Thai banquet' because, unfortunately, that title conjures up images of grubby, plastic-sleeved 15-dollar-a-head set menus at dingy restaurants. But a banquet it is. I love the culture of sharing that encompasses a Thai dinner – the passing of plates, the ritual of rice. My mum has some strict rules about rice: you should never serve yourself rice without offering it to everyone else at the table, and it's bad luck to be greedy with your rice or to throw any of it away.

I find this sort of cooking and eating an easy way to feed my friends. I soak my sticky rice and make my spring rolls and curry the day before. The afternoon of my dinner, I prepare all the ingredients for the snapper, omelette and kang kong and I cook the sticky rice and leave it to rest in the sweet coconut milk. All that's left to do when my friends arrive is a bit of deep-frying, a little stir-frying and some reheating. You can use the same oil for the spring rolls and the snapper to make life easier.

MENU

Pork Spring Rolls
with Sweet Carrot Dipping Sauce [page 32]

Roast Duck & Pineapple Curry [page 110]

Deep-fried Whole Snapper
with Three-flavoured Sauce [page 89]

Lap Chong Omelette [page 124]

Wok-fried Kang Kong [page 46]

Steamed Rice [page 157]

Mango & Sticky Rice [page 191]

MENUS THAT MAKE ME HAPPY

SUMMER LUNCHING, HAVING A BLAST

Set the table, put out the wine glasses and pop a steely Clare Valley Riesling into the fridge. It's summer time! What is it about the summer sun and eating outdoors that makes me so happy? It could be anything... my glass of chilled white wine sparkling in the sun, the sweet juiciness of a perfectly ripe tomato or the simple satisfaction of a ruby red strawberry.

You can make your dip, schnitters and panna cottas the day before your summer lunching. Prepare your cabbage and almond coleslaw in the morning, but toss through the dressing just before you serve it. I like to delay the constructing of my buffalo mozzarella and tomato salad for when there's an audience. I like to think the breaking open of a creamy sphere of fresh buffalo mozzarella is entertainment in itself.

MENU

Smoked Trout & Goat's Cheese Dip [page 63]

Buffalo Mozzarella & Tomato Salad [page 73]

Herb & Parmesan Chicken Schnitzels [page 101]

Cabbage & Almond Coleslaw [page 156]

Coconut & Kaffir Lime Panna Cottas with Strawberries & Lime Syrup [page 179]

MENUS THAT MAKE ME HAPPY

SURF, TURF & TART

Geez I love a good steak dinner. I crave steak like some people crave chocolate. Although, I do crave chocolate as well . . . and toasted cheese sandwiches and flaky pastry. Okay, so I crave a lot of things. Never mind, there are worse things in this world to be addicted to. Back to the menu. My surf starter of ocean trout with jalapeño dressing is such a joyous and tantalising dish to begin a meal with. The brilliant colour, the tang of the dressing and that slightly numbing jalapeño spice is quite simply beautiful in my mind. The turf speaks for itself and is perfectly backed by my two favourite support acts. And who doesn't like a good tart at the end of a long day?

You could prepare your chimichurri sauce and bake your tart the day before your dinner. Buy your ocean trout the day you wish to serve it. Slice it just before your guests arrive and have it chilling in the fridge. You can cook and refresh your broccolini in the afternoon so you just need to warm them through the garlicky oil. Start your potatoes boiling as you serve your surf starter and finish them off while your steak is cooking.

MENU

Ocean Trout with Jalapeño Dressing [page 67]

Sumac-crusted Scotch Fillet with Chimichurri [page 119]

Broccolini with Garlic & Anchovies [page 159]

Crushed Purple Congo Potatoes [page 162]

Connie's Almond & Cherry Tart [pages 175–6]

MENUS THAT MAKE ME HAPPY 211

WHEN IT'S COLD OUTSIDE

It's not just the eating that warms the soul. A house filled with the smell of simmering, bacony soup and roasting chicken is the perfect antidote to a shivering winter's day even before you sit down to eat. My warming winter menu is just as feasible for a weeknight after-work huddle as it is for a special Saturday night dinner. I often make up a big batch of the Cavalo Nero, Potato & Bacon Soup so that I can slowly devour it over a couple of days.

The garlicky, herby roast chicken is so easy to make and I'll often interchange the lentils with roasted kipflers or dutch cream mash as my mood sees fit. And the only problem I have with finishing off a cold winter's evening with a rich, oozing pudding is that I'm so warm and so happily content that I have a tendency to fall asleep on the couch post-dinner.

MENU

Cavolo Nero, Potato & Bacon Soup
[page 40]

Rosemary & Garlic Roasted Chicken with Braised Lentils
[page 106]

Gooey Choc Bar & Whisky Puddings
[page 177]

MENUS THAT MAKE ME HAPPY 213

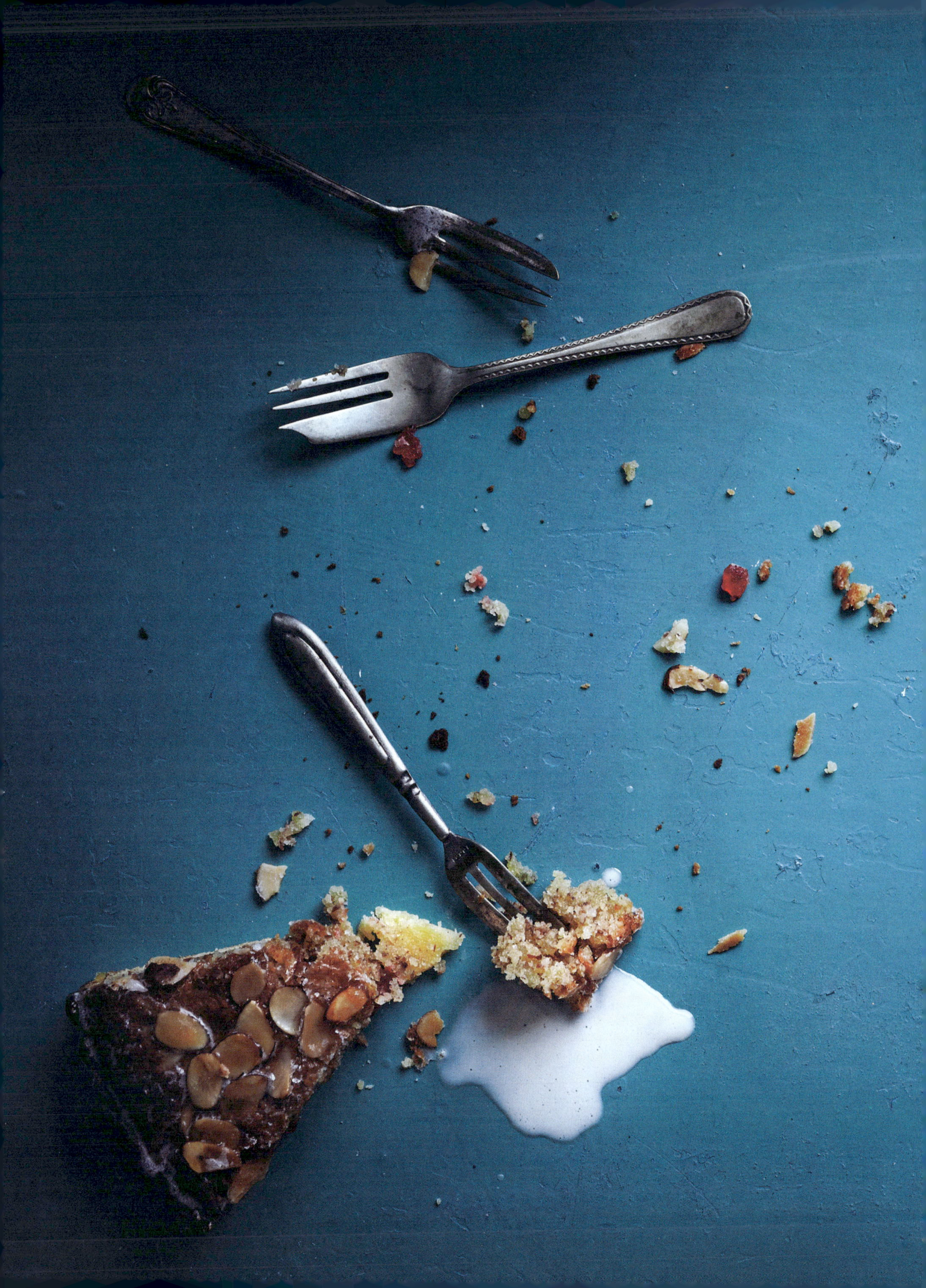

THANKS

I feel so incredibly lucky and so unbelievably grateful. There are a great many people who made this book what it is and a great many more who made my life what it is. I can't thank you all enough.

Thanks Mum and Dad for your unconditional support for all the crazy things I decide to do in my life. You make even the biggest dreams seem possible.

Thank you Tim for your tireless work behind the scenes. Thank you for being my best friend and my inspiration. You make every day lovely.

Thank you to my family in Thailand for welcoming me and for sharing stories, recipes and love.

Big love to the people who made this book. To Pan Macmillan for welcoming me with lots of smiles, hugs and a song. To Mary Small for taking the book I imagined in my head and making something even more lovely and even more 'me' than I thought possible. And thank you for my giant rolling pin. To Ellie Smith for your imagination, artistic flair and extraordinary attention to detail. You make everything beautiful.

To Sharyn Cairns for sleeping on wooden floors and taking brilliant shots in-between meals. And to Tess Kelly for your studio assistance. Thanks to Simon Bajada for your wonderfully eclectic style and for putting up with six girls for six days. To Deborah Kaloper for your commitment to great produce and for your beautifully skillful cooking. And to Toula Ploumidis for your endless smiles and skill in the kitchen. To Trisha Garner for your impeccable good taste in design. To Belinda So for your meticulous editing. And thank you Jane Reiseger for your unique illustrations.

I'd also like to thank all those involved in making a little show called *MasterChef*. Thanks for taking a punt on me. Thanks to the producers, babysitters, chefs, camera guys, audio people, runners, the judges and my lovely fellow contestants for the kind of extraordinary experience you get only once in a lifetime.

Love from Marion xx

INDEX

A
almonds
  Cabbage and almond coleslaw 156
  Connie's almond and cherry tart 175
apples
  Apple salad 64
  Apple sauce 126
anchovies
  Broccolini with garlic and anchovies 159
  Chilli, garlic and anchovy spaghetti 133

B
bacon
  Cavolo nero, potato and bacon soup 40
  see also pancetta; prosciutto
Banana fritters with fish sauce butterscotch 180
beef
  Beef carpaccio 68
  Beefy beef burgers 117
  Sticky beef ribs with sweet coriander sauce 115
  Sumac-crusted scotch fillet with chimichurri 119
beetroot
  Colour-me-Autumn salad 137
  Spiced pickled beetroot 201
Beggar's chicken 100
braises
  Beggar's chicken 100
  Braised lentils 106
  Cinnamon chicken tagine 102
  Five-spice pork and egg stew (Kai palo) 125
  Oxtail ragù with fresh pappardelle 112
  Sticky beef ribs with sweet coriander sauce 115
bread
  Tomato and bread soup (Pappa al pomodoro) 39
breakfast
  Goat's cheese and chorizo scramble 17
  Mushroom and taleggio toasties 16
  Poached eggs with smoked trout and herbs 15
  Ricotta pancakes with figs and honey butter 13
  Sugar-glazed peaches with rosewater and honey yoghurt 10
  Thai breakfast soup (Khao tom) 18
  Toasted brioche with ginger ricotta, strawberries and honey 12
broccoli and broccolini
  Broccolini with garlic and anchovies 159
  Wok-fried noodles with chilli vinegar (Pad siew) 99
Buffalo mozzarella and tomato salad 73
butters
  Honey butter 13
  Truffle butter 134

C
cabbage
  Cabbage and almond coleslaw 156
  Pork spring rolls with sweet carrot dipping sauce 53
capers
  Skate with caper and lemony burnt butter sauce 93
capsicum
  Mum's red ginger jam 200
  Ready-to-go roasted capsicum 202
carrot
  Pork spring rolls with sweet carrot dipping sauce 53
  Sweet carrot dipping sauce 53
Cavolo nero, potato and bacon soup 40
cheese
  Buffalo mozzarella and tomato salad 73
  Colour-me-Autumn salad 137
  Fennel risotto with taleggio and rosemary pangrattato 140
  Figs, gorgonzola and prosciutto 70
  Goat's cheese and chorizo scramble 17
  Herb and parmesan chicken schnitzels 101
  Mushroom and taleggio toasties 16
  Ricotta pancakes with figs and honey butter 13
  Smoked trout and goat's cheese dip 63
  Toasted brioche with ginger ricotta, strawberries and honey 12
cherry
  Cherry sauce 107
  Connie's almond and cherry tart 175
  Rosy Israeli couscous 158
Chiang Mai noodle soup (Khao soi) 32
chicken
  Beggar's chicken 100
  Cinnamon chicken tagine 102
  Herb and parmesan chicken schnitzels 101
  Rosemary and garlic roasted chicken with braised lentils 106

Saturday afternoon chicken stock 30
Sweet pepper chicken 105
Wok-fried noodles with chilli vinegar (Pad siew) 99

chillies
Chilli and coriander sauce 57
Chilli mud crab 95
Chilli vinegar 18, 99
Chilli, cucumber and coriander sauce 62
Chilli, garlic and anchovy spaghetti 133
Green nahm jim dressing 58
Jalapeño dressing 67
Mum's red ginger jam 200
Red curry paste 110
Soy and chilli sauce 34
Three-flavoured sauce 87
Chimichurri sauce

chocolate
Gooey choc bar and whisky puddings 177

chorizo
Goat's cheese and chorizo scramble 17
Simple seafood and chorizo soup 36
Cinnamon chicken tagine 102

coconut
Chiang Mai noodle soup (Khao soi) 32
Coconut and kaffir lime panna cottas with strawberries and lime 179
Coconut sauce 181
Mango and sticky rice 181
Roast duck and pineapple curry 110
Colour-me-Autumn salad 137
Confit duck with star anise and cherry sauce 107
Connie's almond and cherry tart 175

coriander
Chilli and coriander sauce 57
Chilli, cucumber and coriander sauce 62
Coriander, garlic and peppercorn paste 57
Green nahm jim dressing 58
Oysters with coriander and green nahm jim dressing 58
Sweet and sour coriander sauce 131
Sweet coriander sauce 115

couscous
Rosy Israeli couscous 158
Crushed purple congo potatoes 162

cucumber
Chilli, cucumber and coriander sauce 62
curries
Roast duck and pineapple curry 110
curry pastes
Red curry paste 110

D
Deep-fried eggs with smoked eel mash 60
Deep-fried peppery pork belly 131
Deep-fried whole snapper with three-flavoured sauce 87
desserts
Banana fritters with fish sauce butterscotch 180
Coconut and kaffir lime panna cottas with strawberries and lime 179
Connie's almond and cherry tart 175
Drunken fruit salad 188
Gooey choc bar and whisky puddings 177
Mango and sticky rice 181
Sugar-glazed peaches with rosewater and honey yoghurt 10
Yum cha custard tarts 187
Dill mayonnaise 117
dips
Smoked trout and goat's cheese dip 63
dressings
Dressing for beef carpaccio 68
Dressing for cabbage and almond coleslaw 156
Green nahm jim dressing 58
Jalapeño dressing 67
see also mayonnaise; sauces, savoury
Drunken fruit salad 188
duck
Confit duck with star anise and cherry sauce 107
Roast duck and pineapple curry 110
Dutch cream mash 162

E
eel
Deep-fried eggs with smoked eel mash 60
eggs
Deep-fried eggs with smoked eel mash 60
Egg and chive soup 31
Five-spice pork and egg stew (Kai palo) 125

INDEX 217

eggs *(cont.)*
  Goat's cheese and chorizo scramble 17
  Greens and eggs 142
  Lap chong omelette 124
  Poached eggs with smoked trout and herbs 15
  Prawn fried rice (Khao pad goong) 97
Eight-hour lamb roast with tomato and herb gravy 120

F

fennel
  Fennel risotto with taleggio and rosemary pangrattato 140
  Fish parcels with fennel and cherry tomatoes 86
  Pomegranate and fennel salad 155
figs
  Figs, gorgonzola and prosciutto 70
  Ricotta pancakes with figs and honey butter 13
fish
  Deep-fried whole snapper with three-flavoured sauce 87
  Fish parcels with fennel and cherry tomatoes 86
  Ocean trout with jalapeño dressing 67
  Poached eggs with smoked trout and herbs 15
  Quick-grill trout 92
  Skate with caper and lemony burnt butter sauce 93
  Smoked trout and goat's cheese dip 63
  Steamed fish in banana leaves (Haw mok plaa) 90
  Thai fishcakes 62
  see also seafood
Fish sauce butterscotch 180
Five-spice pork and egg stew (Kai palo) 125
Fresh pappardelle 112
fruit
  Cinnamon chicken tagine 102
  Drunken fruit salad 188
  see also specific fruit

G

garlic
  Broccolini with garlic and anchovies 159
  Chilli, garlic and anchovy spaghetti 133
  Coriander, garlic and peppercorn paste 57
  Garlic oil 18, 31
  Rosemary and garlic roasted chicken with braised lentils 106
  Three-flavoured sauce 87
ginger
  Gingerbread houses are cool 182
  Mum's red ginger jam 200

  Sweet pepper chicken 105
  Toasted brioche with ginger ricotta, strawberries and honey 12
Gooey choc bar and whisky puddings 177
Gravy 126
Green nahm jim dressing 58
Green pawpaw salad (Som tum) 138
greens
  Cavolo nero, potato and bacon soup 40
  Greens and eggs 142
  Wok-fried kang kong 160
Grilled prawns with chilli and coriander sauce 57
Grilled quails 69

H

Haw mok plaa (Steamed fish in banana leaves) 90
Herb and parmesan chicken schnitzels 101
herbs
  Herb and parmesan chicken schnitzels 101
  Herb butter sauce 123
  Poached eggs with smoked trout and herbs 15
  Tomato and herb gravy 120
  see also specific herbs
honey
  Honey butter 13
  Rosewater and honey yoghurt 10
  Toasted brioche with ginger ricotta, strawberries and honey 12

J

Jalapeño dressing 67
jams
  Mum's red ginger jam 200
  Strawberry, balsamic vinegar and vanilla jam 204

K

kaffir lime
  Coconut and kaffir lime panna cottas with strawberries and lime 179
Kai palo (Five-spice pork and egg stew) 125
Khao pad goong (Prawn fried rice) 97
Khao soi (Chiang Mai noodle soup) 32
Khao tom (Thai breakfast soup) 18

L

lamb
  Eight-hour lamb roast with tomato and herb gravy 120
  Smoked lamb cutlets with herb butter sauce 123

Lap chong omelette 124
lemons
   Lemony burnt butter sauce 93
lentils
   Braised lentils 106
lime
   Coconut and kaffir lime panna cottas with strawberries and lime 179
   Lime syrup 179

M

Maggie Beer's sour cream pastry 129
Mango and sticky rice 181
mayonnaise
   Dill mayonnaise 117
   Wasabi mayonnaise 59, 64
Mum's red ginger jam 200
Mushroom and taleggio toasties 16
Mustard sauce 129
My first mussels 85

N

noodles
   Chiang Mai noodle soup (Khao soi) 32
   Pork ball noodle soup 34
   Wok-fried noodles with chilli vinegar (Pad siew) 99

O

Ocean trout with jalapeño dressing 67
oils
   Garlic oil 18, 31
Oxtail ragù with fresh pappardelle 112
Oysters with coriander and green nahm jim dressing 58

P

Pad siew (Wok-fried noodles with chilli vinegar) 99
pancetta
   Pea soup with crisp pancetta 35
Pappa al pomodoro (Tomato and bread soup) 39
pasta
   Chilli, garlic and anchovy spaghetti 133
   Fresh pappardelle 112
   Tuesday-night truffle tagliatelle 134
pastry
   Maggie Beer's sour cream pastry 129
   Shortcrust pastry 175

patties
   Beefy beef burgers 117
   Piggy patties with wasabi mayonnaise and apple salad 64
pawpaw
   Green pawpaw salad (Som tum) 138
peaches
   Sugar-glazed peaches with rosewater and honey yoghurt 10
Pea soup with crisp pancetta 35
pepper
   Coriander, garlic and peppercorn paste 57
   Deep-fried peppery pork belly 131
   Salt and three-pepper prawns 59
   Sweet pepper chicken 105
pickles and preserves
   Spiced pickled beetroot 201
   Ready-to-go roasted capsicum 202
   Spiced tomato relish 203
   see also jams
pie
   Rabbit pie with mustard sauce 129
Piggy patties with wasabi mayonnaise and apple salad 64
pineapple
   Roast duck and pineapple curry 110
Poached eggs with smoked trout and herbs 15
pomegranate
   Pomegranate and fennel salad 155
pork
   Deep-fried peppery pork belly 131
   Five-spice pork and egg stew (Kai palo) 125
   Piggy patties with wasabi mayonnaise and apple salad 64
   Pork ball noodle soup 34
   Pork spring rolls with sweet carrot dipping sauce 53
   Roasted pork with apple sauce 126
potato
   Cavolo nero, potato and bacon soup 40
   Colour-me-Autumn salad 137
   Crushed purple congo potatoes 162
   Dutch cream mash 162
   Roasted kipfler potatoes 161
   Smoked eel mash 60
Prawn fried rice (Khao pad goong) 97
prosciutto
   Figs, gorgonzola and prosciutto 70

quail
  Grilled quails 69
Quick-grill trout 92
Quick prawn stock 36

Rabbit pie with mustard sauce 129
Ready-to-go roasted capsicum 202
Red curry paste 110
rice
  Fennel risotto with taleggio and rosemary pangrattato 140
  Mango and sticky rice 181
  Prawn fried rice (Khao pad goong) 97
  Steamed rice 157
Ricotta pancakes with figs and honey butter 13
Roast duck and pineapple curry 110
Roasted kipfler potatoes 161
Roasted pork with apple sauce 126
rocket
  Wild rocket salad 157
rosemary
  Fennel risotto with taleggio and rosemary pangrattato 140
  Rosemary and garlic roasted chicken with braised lentils 106
  Rosemary pangrattato 140
Rosewater and honey yoghurt 10
Rosy Israeli couscous 158

salads
  Apple salad 64
  Buffalo mozzarella and tomato salad 73
  Cabbage and almond coleslaw 156
  Colour-me-Autumn salad 137
  Green pawpaw salad (Som tum) 138
  Pomegranate and fennel salad 155
  Wild rocket salad 157
Salt and three-pepper prawns 59
Saturday afternoon chicken stock 30
sauces, savoury
  Chilli and coriander sauce 57
  Chilli vinegar 18, 99
  Chilli, cucumber and coriander sauce 62
  Chimichurri sauce 119
  Gravy 126
  Herb butter sauce 123
  Lemony burnt butter sauce 93
  Mustard sauce 129
  Soy and chilli sauce 34
  Sweet and sour coriander sauce 131
  Three-flavoured sauce 87
  Tomato and herb gravy 120
  see also dressings
sauces, sweet
  Apple sauce 126
  Cherry sauce 107
  Coconut sauce 181
  Fish sauce butterscotch 180
  Lime syrup 179
seafood
  Chilli mud crab 95
  Grilled prawns with chilli and coriander sauce 57
  My first mussels 85
  Prawn fried rice (Khao pad goong) 97
  Quick prawn stock 36
  Salt and three-pepper prawns 59
  Simple seafood and chorizo soup 36
  Thai breakfast soup (Khao tom) 18
  see also fish
Shortcrust pastry 175
Simple seafood and chorizo soup 36
Skate with caper and lemony burnt butter sauce 93
Smoked eel mash 60
Smoked lamb cutlets with herb butter sauce 123
Smoked trout and goat's cheese dip 63
Som tum (Green pawpaw salad) 138
soups
  Cavolo nero, potato and bacon soup 40
  Chiang Mai noodle soup (Khao soi) 32
  Egg and chive soup 31
  Pea soup with crisp pancetta 35
  Pork ball noodle soup 34
  Simple seafood and chorizo soup 36
  Thai breakfast soup (Khao tom) 18
  Tomato and bread soup (Pappa al pomodoro) 39
Soy and chilli sauce 34
Spiced pickled beetroot 201
Spiced tomato relish 203
Spring roll wrappers 53
Steamed fish in banana leaves (Haw mok plaa) 90
Steamed rice 157
Sticky beef ribs with sweet coriander sauce 115

stocks
   Quick prawn stock 36
   Saturday afternoon chicken stock 30

strawberries
   Coconut and kaffir lime panna cottas with strawberries and lime 179
   Strawberry, balsamic vinegar and vanilla jam 204
   Toasted brioche with ginger ricotta, strawberries and honey 12

Sugar-glazed peaches with rosewater and honey yoghurt 10
Sumac-crusted scotch fillet with chimichurri 119
Sweet and sour coriander sauce 131
Sweet carrot dipping sauce 53
Sweet coriander sauce 115
Sweet pepper chicken 105

T

tarts
   Connie's almond and cherry tart 175
   Yum cha custard tarts 187

Thai breakfast soup (Khao tomato) 18
Thai fishcakes with chilli, cucumber and coriander sauce 62
Three-flavoured sauce 87
Toasted brioche with ginger ricotta, strawberries and honey 12

tomatoes
   Buffalo mozzarella and tomato salad 73
   Fish parcels with fennel and cherry tomatoes 86
   Mum's red ginger jam 200
   Spiced tomato relish 203
   Tomato and bread soup (Pappa al pomodoro) 39
   Tomato and herb gravy 120

Truffle butter 134
Tuesday-night truffle tagliatelle 134

V

vanilla
   Strawberry, balsamic vinegar and vanilla jam 204

vegetables *see* specific vegetables

vinegar
   Chilli and coriander sauce 57
   Chilli vinegar 18, 99
   Chilli, cucumber and coriander sauce 62
   Strawberry, balsamic vinegar and vanilla jam 204
   Sweet and sour coriander sauce 131
   Sweet coriander sauce 115

W

Wasabi mayonnaise 59, 64
Wild rocket salad 157
Wok-fried kang kong 160
Wok-fried noodles with chilli vinegar (Pad siew) 99

Y

yoghurt
   Rosewater and honey yoghurt 10

Yum cha custard tarts 187

A Plum book
First published in 2011 by
Pan Macmillan Australia Pty Limited
Level 25, 1 Market Street,
Sydney, NSW 2000, Australia

Level 1, 15–19 Claremont Street,
South Yarra, Victoria 3141, Australia

Text copyright © Marion Grasby 2011
Photographs copyright © Sharyn Cairns 2011
Illustrations copyright © Jane Reiseger 2011

The moral right of the author has been asserted.

All rights reserved. No part of this book may be reproduced or transmitted by any person or entity (including Google, Amazon or similar organisations), in any form or by any means, electronic or mechanical, including photocopying, recording, scanning or by any information storage and retrieval system, without prior permission in writing from the publisher.

A CIP catalogue record for this book is available from the National Library of Australia.

Design and art direction by Trisha Garner
Typeset by Pauline Haas
Edited by Belinda So
Index by Lucy Malouf
Illustrations by Jane Reiseger
Photography by Sharyn Cairns (excluding childhood photographs in the introduction and on the opening pages. These images courtesy of the author.)
Prop styling by Simon Bajada
Food styling by Deborah Kaloper
Food preparation by Deborah Kaloper & Toula Ploumidis
Hair and make up by Paddy Puttock
Fashion styling by Connel Chiang

Colour reproduction by Splitting Image, Clayton, Victoria
Printed and bound in China by 1010 Printing International Limited

The publisher would like to thank the following for their generosity in providing props and locations for the book: The Abbotsford Convent, Bridget Amor and De Clieu, Abi Crompton and Third Drawer Down, Dinosaur Designs, Essential Ingredient, Izzi & Popo, Milton and The Humble Vintage.

10 9 8 7 6 5 4 3 2 1

white wine

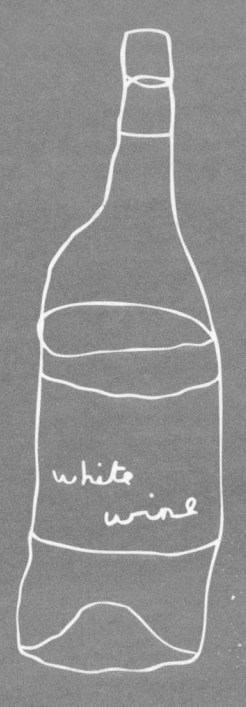